The Confederate Military Forces in the

Trans-Mississippi West, 1861-1865:

A Study in Command

The Confederate Military Forces in the Trans-Mississippi West, 1861-1865:

A Study in Command

William Royston Geise

Michael J. Forsyth, editor

Savas Beatie

California

Library of Congress Cataloging-in-Publication Data

Names: Geise, William Royston, author. | Forsyth, Michael J., 1966- editor.

Title: The Confederate Military Forces in the Trans-Mississippi West,
    1861-1865: A Study in Command / by William Royston Geise;
    edited by Michael J. Forsyth.
Description: El Dorado Hills, CA: Savas Beatie, [2022] | Includes
    bibliographical references and index. | Summary: "This intriguing study
    traces the evolution of Confederate command and how it affected the
    shifting strategic situation and general course of the war. The emphasis
    is on the functioning of headquarters and staff—the central nervous
    system of any military command. This was especially so for the
    Trans-Mississippi, which assumed a unique and vital role among
    Confederate military departments and provided a focus for continued
    Confederate resistance west of the Mississippi River" —Provided by publisher.
Identifiers: LCCN 2022021619 | ISBN 9781611216219 (hardcover) |
    ISBN 9781954547438 (ebook)
Subjects: LCSH: West (U.S.)--History--Civil War, 1861-1865. | Southwest,
    Old–History–Civil War, 1861-1865. | United States–History–Civil War,
    1861-1865–Campaigns. | Confederate States of America. Army. |
    Military art and science–Confederate States of America.
Classification: LCC E470.9.G45 2022 | DDC 973.7/3–dc23/eng/20220503
LC record available at https://lccn.loc.gov/2022021619

First Edition, First Printing

SB

Savas Beatie
989 Governor Drive, Suite 102
El Dorado Hills, CA 95762
916-941-6896 / sales@savasbeatie.com

Savas Beatie titles are available at special discounts for bulk purchases in the United States. Contact us for more details.

Proudly published, printed, and warehoused in the United States of America.

We felt our father's dedication would have been to our mother
Mary Ogden Geise (Mimi), his greatest supporter and the love of his life.

Anne, Bill and Carla

Contents

Contents (continued)

List of Maps

Photographs

Foreword

Dr. William R. Geise wrote this book in 1974. *The Confederate Military Forces in the Trans-Mississippi West, 1861-1865: A Study in Command* was his PhD dissertation at the University of Texas at Austin, and it required painstaking research more than two decades before the availability of the Internet. He never sought to publish his work. Fortunately, Civil War researcher Bryce Suderow stumbled upon this remarkable study and referred it to Theodore P. Savas, who in turn reached out to Dr. Geise's surviving family members for permission to make it available to a wider audience. Thankfully, they agreed and it is now available to the general reading public.

Modern readers may reasonably ask the question, "Why should I read this work?" A plethora of works are published on the Civil War every year with topics ranging from biographies of leaders and studies of battles and campaigns to the social aspects of the war. Unfortunately, very few contributions in this mountain of scholarship address any element of the Civil War that raged west of the Mississippi River. The war in the Trans-Mississippi Department remains a largely unknown and little-studied arena of the conflict; only a few scholars specialize in the region, and limited numbers of readers have any in-depth knowledge of the events that transpired there or the personalities who operated in that vast region. Thus, as during the war itself, the Trans-Mississippi as a field of study receives scant attention and offers fertile ground for much more research. Dr. Geise was one of but a handful of scholars who dedicated much of his professional life to the study of events there. His works offer unique contributions to the body of our Civil War knowledge. As a result, this study is timely, original, and needed.

William Royston Geise arrived at his academic career by an unconventional route. In 1974, when he received his PhD, he was already fifty-five years old. He was born in 1919 in St. Louis, Missouri, and was of military service age at the start of World War II. As a graduate of the Missouri Military Academy with an additional two years of education from the University of Texas, he was a valuable commodity to military recruiters when the war began to heat up in Europe in 1940. As a result, he received a commission as a second lieutenant of infantry in late 1940 before transferring to the Army Air Corps (which would become the U. S. Air Force in 1947). He had no way of knowing that he was embarking upon a military career that would last twenty-two years and include service in World War II and various locations worldwide.

Dr. Geise would finally earn his B.A. from the University of Arizona in 1957 while still serving his country. Following his retirement from the United States Air Force as a lieutenant colonel, he earned an M.A. in English from the University of Texas in 1963. Shortly thereafter, he began his second career as an assistant professor of history at San Antonio College. It was during his studies for his M.A that he developed a deep interest in the Civil war in the Trans-Mississippi that would become a life-long pursuit. Over the course of many years he wrote several articles on the war west of the Mississippi as well as the present work, which remained unpublished for five decades.

The thesis of this book, which Dr. Geise mentions in his brief Preface, is worth repeating (and discussing at greater length) here:

> [T]race in some detail the evolution of unity of command and the development of improved organization and administration in the Confederate forces west of the Mississippi River and to relate these changes to the shifting strategic situation and the general course of the war. Consequently, I have not emphasized military field operations but rather, headquarters and staff functions.

In Civil War historiography, this is an unusual tack for research. However, understanding how a military organization functions is critical to developing an appreciation for how that organization employs its forces in combat. The force structure and administration of military commands is underappreciated because of history's emphasis on leadership in battles and campaigns. A military unit, however, "could not function" without "the critical nervous system of any unit"—that is, the headquarters and the staff.[1] In other words, this study focuses on the elements of military operations that enable the forces to remain in the field to perform their tasks in defense of the nation it serves. To sustain any military force requires the ability to administer, feed, and move the force so that

---

1 William Royston Geise, "The Confederate Military Forces in the Trans-Mississippi West, 1861-1865: A Study in Command," doctoral dissertation (Austin, 1974), iv.

commanders can fight that organization in battle. This requires meticulous staff work to support a commander. It is not glamorous work, but it does constitute the bulk of the responsibility that every commander carries, and it takes up the preponderance of time available. Although fighting is the exciting aspect of military history, it is also episodic and less frequent than the daily requirement for a commander to look after every need of his troops. Dr. Geise reviews all this in detail, and in so doing, engrosses the reader with the difficulties Rebel commanders faced on a daily basis.

As noted, *The Confederate Military Forces in the Trans-Mississippi West, 1861-1865* was an original contribution to Civil War scholarship when it was written in 1974, and it remains so today. What makes it a groundbreaking study is that it traces the evolution of the command structure of the Confederate Trans-Mississippi Department from start to finish. Dr. Geise also details how the department carried out its defense mission after 1863 by providing administration for the War Department in the region, as well as all the civilian departments, in order to ensure the national authority of the Confederate government west of the Mississippi.

This wide authority over civilian interests by the military came about when Federal forces split the Confederacy in two by capturing Vicksburg and Port Hudson. The military Department of the Trans-Mississippi was the only agency capable of demonstrating central authority. There was wide dissatisfaction with the Confederate government among the states west of the Mississippi because their governors believed that the Jefferson Davis administration did not pay appropriate attention to their needs. They felt abandoned by Richmond. A belief in the Rebel capital that the Trans-Mississippi states might break away from the Confederacy prompted the Davis administration to give wide latitude to the western military command to govern the region, as Dr. Geise notes in great detail in Chapter 10 ("Isolation: July to December 1863") and Chapter 11 ("Kirby Smith's War Department, 1864").

The range of authority the Confederate government in Richmond bestowed upon the department had no precedent in the war. For a country so sensitive to states' rights, the authority vested in the department is truly remarkable. What is even more astounding is that the Southern governors west of the Mississippi accepted this authority. At an in August 1863 conference at Marshall, Texas, the governors of Texas, Arkansas, Louisiana, and Missouri endorsed the military's assumption of administrative powers to ensure continuity of Confederate authority west of the river. Because of this compact accepting military leadership, the Department of the Trans-Mississippi assumed responsibility for virtually every function of the central government, including regulation of foreign trade and the issuance of sovereign debt. Dr. Geise had already written about this extensively in an article published in *Southwestern Historical Quarterly* in 1962.[2] His detailed writing demonstrates the depth of his research and knowledge of the subject, and establishes his place as an authority on the military command west of the Mississippi. Yet, this is only part of the content of this work.

One of the several topics covered herein includes the revolving door of poor leaders posted by the Confederacy to the Trans-Mississippi. Though there were notable exceptions to this rule, most officers sent west were proven incompetents upon arrival, a circumstance Dr. Geise demonstrates as he unfolds the evolution of the command. The poor leadership is indicative of another theme noted in the book: the strategic incoherence of Confederate national security policy as it concerned the Trans-Mississippi region. This strategic incompetence was one of the several reasons for the undertone of discontent among the Western governors and the public. The lack of a coherent policy led rapidly to the loss of territory to the Union and the use of the Mississippi River as a highway of invasion for enemy forces.

Another subject Dr. Geise traces with precision throughout this study is the ad hoc manner by which the Confederacy finally established the Department of the Trans-Mississippi. As a result, the Confederate high command generally reacted to Federal initiatives. The Union forces established a sound command structure much sooner, which enabled its forces to take advantage of its fragmented Southern adversary. The command structure issues are connected to the constant clashes of personality created by the lack of a unified command. These almost constant conflicts during the department's four years of existence highlight a major obstacle to Confederate efforts in defending the Trans-Mississippi.

Finally, Dr. Geise discusses how the lack of infrastructure inhibited Southern efforts and the lengths to which the Confederates went to overcome this challenge. By 1864, the department under command of General Edmund Kirby Smith had performed admirably in overcoming this difficult obstacle. The thread that pulls these themes together is the thesis of this book—the evolutionary process by which the Confederacy created a unified command structure to deal with its intractable problems. This unique aspect of study will keep readers both engaged and amazed at how the Confederacy dealt with these challenges.

The initial contributions to our knowledge about the war west of the Mississippi came from the participants themselves in primary source accounts. The veterans contributed articles to *Confederate Veteran* and other periodicals, including *The Century Magazine*, whose

---

2 William R. Geise, "Missouri's Confederate Capital in Marshall, Texas," *Southwestern Historical Quarterly*, Vol. 66, No. 2 (October 1962), 193-207, details the Marshall Conference and the agreement among the governors of the states west of the river to cooperate with the military department as the representative of Confederate central authority.

editors Robert Underwood Johnson and Clarence Clough Buel repackaged the popular articles into the influential 4-volume *Battles and Leaders of the Civil War* (1884-1887). The former soldiers also provided monograph-length narrative accounts of their experiences, such as John P. Blessington's *The Campaigns of Walker's Texas Division by a Private Soldier* (1875) and William W. Heartsill's *Fourteen Hundred and Ninety One Days in the Confederate Army* (1874-76).

A second wave of contributions came much later, starting in the 1950s and continuing into the early 1970s. These works included Jay Monaghan's *The Civil War on the Western Border* (1955), *The Red River Campaign: Politics and Cotton in the Civil War* (1955), a seminal study by Ludwell Johnson, and Robert L. Kerby's *Kirby Smith's Confederacy: Kirby Smith's Confederacy* (1972). These scholars established the baseline for understanding events that took place west of the Mississippi.

Another wave of scholarship in the 1990s gave attention to the war in the west with the publication of studies that included William L. Shea and Earl J. Hess's *Pea Ridge: Civil War Campaign in the West* (1992), Gary D. Joiner's *One Damn Blunder From Beginning to End: The Red River Campaign of 1864* (2002), Jeffrey S. Prushankin's *A Crisis in Command: Edmund Kirby Smith, Richard Taylor, and the Army of the Trans-Mississippi* (2005), and Kyle S. Sinisi's *The Last Hurrah: Sterling Price's Missouri Expedition of 1864* (2015). These monographs relied upon recently discovered material and thus revised and updated our knowledge of the war beyond the river. It is important to note that none of these provide in-depth analysis of the development of the Confederate Trans-Mississippi Department or the difficulty of administering the vast region while defending it from a determined foe. This is what makes Dr. Geise's book needed, relevant, and although belatedly published, a timely contribution to understanding why events happened as they did there. His study also opens the door for further investigation by future scholars. *The Confederate Military Forces in the Trans-Mississippi West, 1861-1865: A Study in Command* enjoys a distinct niche in the existing literature.

The task of editing this text was both easy and enjoyable, yet it did require some effort to provide clarification and additional notations. Therefore, a comment is required on the process used to edit the original manuscript.

First, I made no changes in context to any element of this work. The book was well-written in its original form, and since Dr. Geise used a typist and held a master's degree in English, there were few errors. Nevertheless, when a misspelling or some other minor blemish was discovered, I made the correction to ensure smooth reading. As was common in writings of the Civil War period, many of the persons in the text are referred to by only their last name and initials—a couple of instances used only a last name—and Dr. Geise followed this practice. Finding and adding the first names of these individuals would have required a monumental research effort in the early 1970s before the existence of Internet. The task is much easier now using the National Park Service's Civil War Soldier and Sailor database and other sources. I located many of the first names and inserted them without noting the update. There are still many instances in which the initials remain because no first name appeared in the database. I also smoothed out instances of awkward wording, short single-sentence paragraphs, and so forth, rearranging words or clauses here or there only for clarity and style. Additionally, there were three instances in which he used relatively unknown antiquated words. In each case I added a footnote providing the definition to assist the reader so the pace of reading can continue unabated.

Dr. Geise was an excellent researcher, and his original dissertation contained scores of citations and additional information presented through endnotes. These were changed to footnotes to match the publisher's normal method of presentation. His original notes remain intact within the text. However, I added several additions to his original notes. These provide more information on alternative interpretations, recommended reading on scholarship published since this study was written, and other clarifying information. A double backslash (//) is used to denote every instance where there is an addition to an existing footnote, or a completely new footnote with supplemental information. In other words, everything that appears before the // is Dr. Geise's original notation, and everything thereafter is updated information added by me in the process of editing.

The Confederate Military Forces in the Trans-Mississippi West, 1861-1865: A Study in Command is a treasure for Civil War scholars and buffs alike. Dr. Geise's presentation of the administrative headaches of command and the vital necessity that the commander must manage these requirements with competence adds an entirely new dimension to the scholarship of the Trans-Mississippi region by enabling readers to better understand the intricacies of command. His military experience enhances the telling of the story because he added fine details not readily visible to the average observer of military operations. My hope is that this newly edited study will spur greater interest in the region and its cast of characters, while encouraging further research to broaden our collective knowledge of the war west of the Mississippi.

Michael J. Forsyth
Colonel, U. S. Army (retired)
Platte City, Missouri

Acknowledgments

As the editor of Dr. Geise's work, I would like to add the following acknowledgments as a small token of thanks to those who provided assistance to me in this effort to publish his excellent study.

First, I would like to thank the family of Dr. Geise for allowing me the privilege of editing this contribution to Civil War and Trans-Mississippi region scholarship. I feel a kinship to Dr. Geise since my own academic career closely mirrors his. I am a recently retired military officer after serving for thirty years in the US Army. I started work on my PhD shortly before retirement and am currently completing my dissertation while teaching as an assistant professor at the US Army Command and General Staff College. Thus, Dr. Geise's family provided me with a great and unprecedented opportunity to work on this project.

Next, I would like to thank Dr. Christian Keller who was my history professor during my attendance at the US Army War College. A couple of years ago he asked me to contribute a chapter to a book on Confederate strategy titled *Southern Strategies: Why the Confederacy Failed* (2021) that he was editing for the University Press of Kansas. The chapter I wrote titled "The Forgotten Trans-Mississippi Theater and Confederate Strategy" was about the failure of Confederate strategy as it concerned the Trans-Mississippi theater and why this had a catastrophic effect on its national security. This contribution opened the door to contributing to this current work.

Because of that essay Theodore P. Savas contacted me after providing a review of Dr. Keller's anthology. He asked me if I would be willing to edit the book, and of course, I eagerly accepted his invitation due to my own interest in the Trans-Mississippi region during the Civil War. Therefore, I must thank Ted and express my indebtedness to him for giving me this opportunity, to Civil War researcher and author Bryce Suderow, for bringing this manuscript to Ted's attention several years ago, and to Sheritta Bitikofer for transferring the original PDF into Word and fixing all the problems that translation entailed. Further, I must thank the folks at Savas Beatie for their assistance and editing expertise in making this project a reality, and to Lee Merideth for producing the index.

I must also thank Dr. John Modinger, my teaching partner at the Command and General Staff College, for his continuous advice to me in all projects. He is a good friend and I asked him many questions on approach and style as I worked on this particular project. Also, I have to thank the library staff at the college of whom I became closely acquainted over the course of my research for my dissertation. They assisted me on this project with sourcing notes with the same grace that they provided for my research.

Finally, I must thank my dear wife, Maryellen. As a military spouse for over thirty years with a teaching career of her own, and now a patient partner in my academic career, she has always encouraged me and kept me humble in every effort. Thank you, honey, for all that you do and making me better in every endeavor.

Michael J. Forsyth

Preface

The Confederate Trans-Mississippi Department first attracted me as a subject for study while I was a student in one of the late Professor H. Bailey Carroll's history seminars. During that course I wrote a paper on the exiled "Confederate" government of Missouri, which was subsequently published in the Southwestern Historical Quarterly and also in the Missouri Historical Review. The project whetted my interest in the Trans Mississippi, and Dr. Carroll urged me to consider the Trans-Mississippi Department as a subject for a doctoral dissertation. The present study is partially the result of his urging and his encouragement.

My purpose was to trace in some detail the evolution of unity of command and the development of improved organization and administration in the Confederate forces west of the Mississippi River, and to relate these changes to the shifting strategic situation and the general course of the war. Consequently, I have not emphasized military field operations as much as I have focused on headquarters and staff functions. As these last elements are, in a very real sense, the central nervous system of any military unit, without which it could not function, examination of them seems fully justified. This was especially so for the Trans-Mississippi Department, which provided, after July of 1863, the only viable Confederate agency west of the Mississippi, an agency that came to incorporate civilian as well as military functions. The headquarters at Shreveport, Louisiana, thus became the sole place to which all isolated Southwesterners could look for immediate overall leadership and a sense of Confederate solidarity. By filling these needs the Trans Mississippi Department assumed a unique and vital role among Confederate military departments and provided a focus for continued Confederate resistance west of the Mississippi.

The comments and observations in this short Preface about the beginnings of this study and the general direction of my work would not be complete without the acknowledgment of my deep obligation to Professor Barnes F. Lathrop. After Dr. Carroll's death, Dr. Lathrop very kindly consented to supervise this project, which had not yet begun, and he patiently endured the long months of its preparation. To his advice and particularly to his unremitting criticism this study genuinely owes most of whatever merit it possesses.

William Royston Geise

July 1974

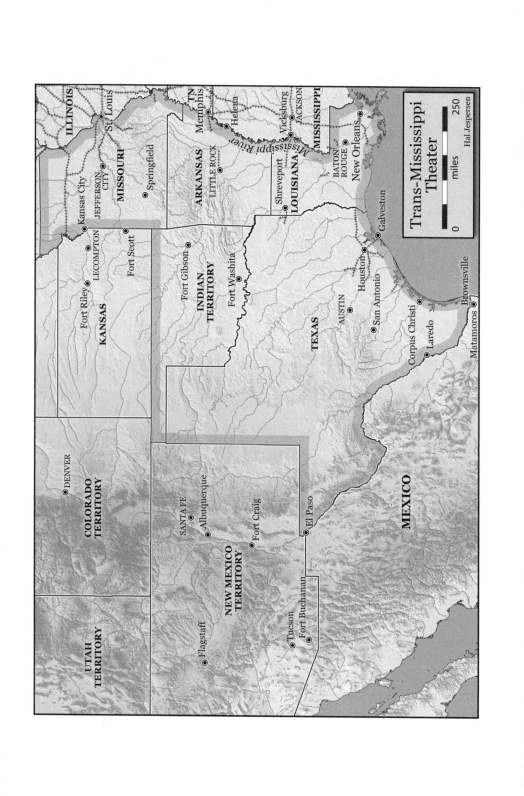

Trans-Mississippi
Theater

0   miles   250

Hal Jespersen

Chapter 1

The Confederate Northwest Frontier
May 1861 – August 1861

At THE BEGINNING of the Civil War, the Confederate War Department had no comprehensive plan for territorial organization of the vast Trans-Mississippi West. Clearly the old territorial organization of the United States Army would not, except for the Department of Texas, fit the new circumstances. The western territorial organization of the Confederate Army would have to be improvised to meet new demands.

No need existed in the spring of 1861 for a single territorial command west of the Mississippi, nor did such a need appear likely in the near future. With Confederate states on both banks of the Mississippi River from Tennessee to the Gulf of Mexico, communications and the exchange of supplies between the Confederate states east of the river and those west of it were unimpeded and presented no special problems. Indeed, the nature of the Trans-Mississippi West seemed to demand the creation of a number of area commands, both because distances were immense and communications and transportation facilities poor, and because the region comprised several distinct military frontiers, each with its special problem.

To the north along the Missouri-Arkansas border and the upper edge of the Indian Territory was the military frontier between North and South. On the southwest, in central Texas, an already-existing Indian frontier stretched along the line of abandoned Federal forts from Red River to the Rio Grande. In the extreme south, an international frontier with the neutral but uneasy Republic of Mexico followed the course of the Rio Grande. And in the southeast, finally, the Texas and Louisiana coasts would require defense.

In the first weeks of the war the progress of military organization was alarmingly uneven. Texas and western Louisiana were assigned to two well-defined military departments, permitting the recruiting, supply, and training of Confederate soldiers to begin there under recognizable patterns of military authority. But in Missouri and Arkansas, the most critical area of contact between North and South in the Trans-Mississippi, where the military demands were immediate, military organization lagged, plagued by political considerations and administrative confusion.[1]

*   *   *

THE STRATEGIC VALUE of the slave state of Missouri was obvious. It flanked the entire tier of Union states on the north side of the Ohio River, and its possession by the Confederates would render successful Federal invasion of Tennessee through Kentucky virtually impossible. Yet President Jefferson Davis and other members of his administration viewed Missouri with doubtful caution, partly because Confederate military policy was defensive, partly because the very existence of the Confederacy rested on the right of each state to determine its own future without military coercion. Military action in Missouri would have to wait until such time as Missouri might formally and voluntarily leave the Union.[2]

Considerable secession sentiment did indeed exist in Missouri among members of the state government and among the people; but in all likelihood the majority of Missouri's citizens at that time were conditional Unionists, rejecting both secession and Federal coercion of the South. In March of 1861, the Missouri State Convention, called to consider the state's future course, almost unanimously rejected secession.[3] In May the governor, Claiborne Fox Jackson, and the commander of the Missouri State Guard, Major General Sterling Price, concluded an agreement with Brigadier William S. Harney, Federal commander of the Department of the West, which provided for neutrality between Federal and state military forces. General Price then declared that the Missouri State Guard would oppose any Confederate advance from Arkansas. Since Price was an ex-governor of the state and had also been president of the Unionist-minded State Convention two months earlier,

---

1 // For a discussion of the military geographic and economic significance of the region and how the Confederate and Federal War Departments organized the Trans-Mississippi, see Michael J. Forsyth, "The Forgotten Trans-Mississippi Theater and Confederate Strategy," in *Southern Strategies: Why the Confederacy Failed*, Christian B. Keller, ed. (Lawrence, 2021), 217-259.

2 // For a discussion of the secession crisis in Missouri, see Jay Monaghan's older but still solid study *Civil War on the Western Border* (Lincoln, 1954) and Louis Gerteis, *The Civil War in Missouri: A Military History* (Columbia, 2012).

3 William E. Parrish, *Turbulent Partnership: Missouri and the Union, 1861-1865* (Columbia, 1963), 10-13; Albert Castel, *General Sterling Price and the Civil War in the West* (Baton Rouge, LA, 1993), 11.

President Davis doubted the depth of the rumored Southern sympathy among the Missouri leadership.[4]

*   *   *

TO THE SOUTHWEST of Missouri, the unorganized Indian Territory offered a likely Union invasion route from Kansas into seceded Texas and Arkansas. Even before the secession of Arkansas, on May 6 the Confederate government had become concerned about closing this potential back door to the Confederacy. Alarming rumors of an invasion through the Indian Territory had been coming from Texas for months. In January 1861, an Austin newspaper carried two such accounts in the same issue. According to one of them, Kansas guerrilla James Montgomery was readying a force of 2,000 men to raid Texas, depopulate the northern counties, kill all the men and old women, take only the "pretty young things" captive, and give every Negro freed by the expedition a white wife. Reportedly, Montgomery's guerrillas were heavily armed, each man having two Navy Colt revolvers as well as a Sharps rifle. Among the alleged backers of the raid were Wendell Phillips and Henry Ward Beecher. The other report of the same date was even more alarming. It announced that Montgomery was already on the way to Texas with 500 abolitionists and perhaps 1,000 Indians.[5] Wild and unfounded as such rumors were, they persisted in Texas newspapers as well as private correspondence during the spring of 1861, and they testify to the alarm over the unsettled conditions in the Indian Territory.

Rumors were rife, too, about the activities of Regular Army United States troops based in Indian Territory. In April, it was reported that Fort Washita, just above Red River a scant twenty-five miles from Sherman, Texas, was being reinforced from all the 'Federal posts in the Territory as well as from Fort Smith, Arkansas. The object of this reinforcement was said to be the reoccupation of the Texas frontier forts surrendered by the Federal forces in February.[6] Not until May 3, when several hundred Texas militia crossed the Red River, was it discovered that the Federal garrisons of Forts Washita, Cobb, and Arbuckle, in the southern part of the Territory, had been withdrawn northward.

---

4 Castel, *Price*, 21. // See Christopher Phillips, *Missouri's Confederate: Claiborne Fox Jackson and the Creation of Southern Identity in the Border West* (Columbia, 2000) for a discussion of Governor Jackson's effort to place Missouri within the Confederate States by leveraging the cultural relationship with the state's southern neighbors.

5 Anonymous letter titled "One of Montgomery's Confidential Men" to the Postmaster, Austin, Texas, December, 1860, and A. G. Fowler to Major John Marshall, December 10, 1860, *Austin State Gazette*, January 12, 1861.

6 A. B. to Major Marshall, April 28, 1861, *Austin State Gazette*, May 11, 1861.

By this time the Confederate government had taken several steps to control the Indian Territory. On March 5, President Davis appointed Captain Albert Pike of Arkansas as Confederate Commissioner to all the Indian tribes west of Arkansas and south of Kansas. Ten days later Congress had created a Bureau of Indian Affairs within the War Department. Finally, on May 13, former Texas Ranger Ben McCulloch, who was directly commissioned from civilian life as a brigadier general in Confederate service, was assigned to command the Indian Territory—the first Confederate military district created on the northwest frontier.[7]

McCulloch's first report to Richmond from Little Rock, Arkansas, was far from cheerful. Only a small amount of arms and ammunition was available for his command from the captured Federal arsenal at Little Rock, most of the stores having "been scattered over the state in every direction without any method or accountability." All the subsistence stores accumulated at Fort Smith had been turned over to Brigadier General N. Bart Pearce of the state militia, which meant that McCulloch would have to draw on Pearce, then pay him back in kind from future Confederate shipments. Without stating the source of his information, McCulloch reported that Senator James Lane of Kansas, a guerrilla fighter much feared in the South, was preparing an expedition aimed at the Indian Territory, and that Federal soldiers from Fort Washita, whom McCulloch had been ordered to intercept on their way north, had almost reached Fort Leavenworth, Kansas.[8]

McCulloch himself was in no position to stop the retreat of the Federal troops heading for Kansas, or implement his orders to "guard the [Indian] Territory against invasion from Kansas or else-where."[9] As yet he had no soldiers of his own to utilize. When he proceeded to Fort Smith, Arkansas, on the border of the Indian Territory, to set up his temporary headquarters, only two men accompanied McCulloch: Captain James McIntosh, a young West Pointer recently resigned from the United States Army, and William Meade Montgomery, a former quartermaster clerk who had served under McCulloch's uncle in the old U.S. Army. It would take time before the three regiments initially authorized in McCulloch's orders, one each from Arkansas, Louisiana, and Texas, could join him, and

---

7 S. Cooper to Brigadier General McCulloch, May 13, 1861, War of the Rebellion: *A Compilation of the Official Records of the Union and Confederate Armies*, 128 vols. (Washington, 1880-1901), Series I, volume 3, 575-576, hereafter *OR*. (All references are to Series I unless otherwise noted.); Walter Lee Brown, "Albert Pike, 1807-1891," unpublished PhD dissertation (University of Texas, 1955), 540-544; Jefferson Davis to the Congress of the Confederate States, December 12, 1861, James D. Richardson, ed., *A Compilation of the Messages and Papers of the Confederacy, Including the Diplomatic Correspondence, 1861-1865*, 2 vols. (Nashville, 1905), I, 149-151. // Also, see Thomas W. Cutrer, *Ben McCulloch and the Frontier Military Tradition*, (Chapel Hill, 1993) for a full biography of McCulloch.

8 Quoted in Victor M. Rose, *The Life and Services of Gen. Ben* (Philadelphia, 1888), 154-155.

9 Ibid., 130.

Ben McCulloch. *NPS*

before the pair of Indian regiments recommended by the War Department could be raised, organized, and properly armed.

It was not long before McCulloch encountered yet another obstacle to the accomplishment of his mission. He and Commissioner Albert Pike went to the Indian Territory, Pike to attempt to conclude treaties with all of the Five Civilized Tribes as well as with as many reserve and wild bands as possible, McCulloch hoping to select a military headquarters site and to establish a base of operation in the Cherokee Nation, which was strategically located in the northeastern corner of the Territory. Both Pike and McCulloch, however, were rebuffed by Principal Chief John Ross of the Cherokees. In an interview on June 5, Ross insisted on strict neutrality for the Cherokees, rejected Pike's offer of a Confederate treaty of friendship, and refused to permit a Confederate headquarters or military operations within the Cherokee Nation.[10]

Commissioner Pike went ahead to conclude successfully a series of treaties with most of the other Indians of the

Albert Pike. *NPS*

---

10 Edward Everett Dale, "*The Cherokees in the Confederacy,*" in *Journal of Southern History,* XIII (May 1947), 162-163. // For more recent scholarship on the role of the Five Civilized Tribes in the Civil War, see Clint Crowe, *Caught in the Maelstrom: The Indian Nations in the Civil War, 1861-1865* (El Dorado Hills, California, 2019).

Territory, and eventually, in August 1861, Ross and his faction would be obliged to capitulate to the Confederate cause.[11]

McCulloch, meanwhile, could only report Ross's refusal to Confederate Secretary of War Leroy Pope Walker and suggest that his district be expanded to include military control of northwest Arkansas, where Ross's attitude would compel him to operate anyway. The same day, McCulloch also wrote Chief Ross that he would respect Cherokee neutrality, but if he heard of any Northern advance through the Cherokee Nation, he would "at once advance into that Nation."[12] The old Chief understood the threat and expressed his wish to live in peace and friendship, but he reiterated his determination to remain neutral and to repel invasion by either side.[13]

By the time he wrote Ross on June 12, McCulloch had acquired sufficient military strength to carry out his threat to invade the Cherokee Nation, if necessary. On that date Colonel Thomas J. Churchill's First Arkansas Mounted Rifles, a Confederate regiment of some 700 men, reported for duty with McCulloch's command at Fort Smith. Approximately one week earlier, the Third Louisiana Infantry, commanded by a West Point colonel named Louis Hebert, had arrived 1,060 strong. Already much admired for its appearance, the regiment would prove equally admirable under fire. The third Confederate regiment destined for McCulloch's command, the Third Texas Cavalry under Colonel Elkanah Greer, was assembling at its rendezvous point in Dallas, Texas.[14] Almost two months would pass before these eager Texas volunteers, sometimes also called the South Kansas-Texas Regiment, would join McCulloch in the field. Even without them, he had a substantial and reliable force, and in an emergency he could presumably call on the military forces of Arkansas.

To establish the state troops, known as the "Army of Arkansas," the State Convention had divided Arkansas into an eastern and a western military district, each to furnish one division for its own defense and to be commanded by a brigadier general. The Convention's appointee as brigadier general of the second (or western) division was Nicholas Bartlett Pearce, a West Pointer of the class of 1850. N. Bart Pearce, as he was usually known, was directed by the Convention to begin raising state troops, to procure 2,500 stand of small arms and a battery of field artillery from the Little Rock Arsenal, and to establish his

---

11 Ibid., 165.

12 McCulloch to L.P. Walker and to John Ross, both June 12, 1861, *OR* vol. 3, 590-592.

13 John Ross to McCulloch, June 17, 1861, Ibid., 596-597.

14 Stephen B. Oates, *Confederate Cavalry West of the River* (Austin, 1961), 15.

headquarters at Fort Smith. Pearce was to cooperate with General McCulloch in defense of the state.[15]

*   *   *

ON JUNE 14, McCulloch reported to Secretary Walker that an urgent plea for military aid had just been received from Governor Jackson of Missouri. The new Federal commander at St. Louis, Brigadier General Nathaniel Lyon, was bringing pressure to bear on Governor Jackson to yield completely to Federal authority. On June 11 Lyon had repudiated Harney's neutrality agreement with the state authorities. Jackson had mobilized the State Guard, called for volunteers, and dispatched a courier to McCulloch to ask for help. Considering Jackson's situation, Chief John Ross's intransigence, and Lyon's increasing strength, McCulloch proposed that he occupy Fort Scott, Kansas, on the Missouri border. This did not mean that he intended to invade Missouri. At Fort Scott he could, as he explained to Secretary Walker, give "heart and confidence" to the Missouri rebels and also "accomplish the very purpose for which I was sent here, preventing a force from the North invading the Indian Territory." By drawing supplies from the pro-Confederate western counties of Missouri, McCulloch would soon be enabled to take any position on the Arkansas River in Kansas he chose. He again asked for command in northwest Arkansas so that he might recruit Confederate troops, but urged that Indian troops not be used outside of the Indian Territory because to do so might bring censure on the Confederacy.[16]

By June 26 Secretary Walker had received McCulloch's Fort Scott plan and forwarded his tentative approval.[17] Shortly afterward he cautioned,

> Missouri as a Southern State still in the Union requires, as you will readily perceive, much prudence and circumspection, and it should only be when necessity and propriety unite that active and direct assistance should be afforded by crossing the boundary and entering the State before communicating with this Department.[18]

McCulloch would surely have agreed with the spirit and intent of this letter had he received it earlier, but events had in the meantime persuaded him that he must, instead of

---

15 David Y. Thomas, *Arkansas in War and Reconstruction, 1861-1874* (Little Rock, 1926), 85-86; Leo E. Huff, "The Military Board in Confederate Arkansas," *Arkansas Historical Quarterly,* XXVI (Spring, 1967), 76-77.

16 Rose, *McCulloch,* 157.

17 S. Cooper to McCulloch, June 26, 1861, *OR* 3, 599-600.

18 L. P. Walker to McCulloch, July 4, 1861, *OR* vol. 3, 603; Castel, *Price,* 32.

merely occupying Fort Scott on the Missouri border, actually move into Missouri with all the force that he could muster. On the same day that Walker wrote his letter to McCulloch (July 4, 1861), McCulloch crossed over the Missouri border with Colonel Churchill's First Arkansas Mounted Rifles and 1, 200 men of General N. Bart Pearce's Division of the Army of Arkansas. Not far behind the main body was Colonel Louis Hebert's Third Louisiana Infantry. Just above the Missouri line, they rendezvoused with Sterling Price and 1, 700 mounted Missouri State Guardsmen.

For the first time in the war a Confederate army had invaded a state that in every legal sense was still in the Union. McCulloch, without authority from Richmond, had taken a bold step indeed. He had been urged on by General Price, who informed him that General Lyon had taken Missouri's capital at Jefferson City and driven Governor Jackson's and Price's forces from strategic positions on the Missouri River. Governor Jackson's forces were rumored to be trapped between General Lyon on the north and Union Brigadier General Franz Sigel on the south. Price's reports, which exaggerated Lyon's strength, had persuaded McCulloch that he must move on Missouri, not merely to extricate Jackson and his State Guard but to halt a blue avalanche before it reached Arkansas.[19]

"Citizens of Arkansas, rally to the defense of your frontier," announced McCulloch's proclamation to the citizens of Arkansas, which rhetorically demonstrated his concern over Lyon's momentum. He continued:

> The troops of Missouri are falling back upon you, if they are not now sustained, your state will be invaded and your homes desolated.
>
> All who can arm themselves will at once rendezvous at Fayetteville, where they will await further orders. All those who have arms belonging to the state, will march to the scene of action, or give their arms to those who will not desert their country in this hour of danger.... Rally promptly, then citizens of Arkansas, and let us send this Northern Horde back from whence it came!!

> Ben McCulloch
> Brig. Gen'l. Cm'dg,[20]

---

19 McCulloch to L.P. Walker, June 29, 1861, *Official Records*, Ser. I, Vol. III, 600; Ben E. McCulloch to Henry E. McCulloch, July 24, 1861, photostat in McCulloch Papers, Archives Collection, University of Texas Library.

20 *Fort Smith Times and Herald,* June 27, 1861. A separate report in the same issue said that Missouri was overrun, that Arkansas was to be invaded, that Lane and Montgomery were marching on the Indian Territory, and that Springfield, Missouri was filled with Federal troops poised to move on Fayetteville.

In his haste McCulloch ignored both protocol and the proper distinction between military and civilian authority. It was, as critics would point out, the prerogative of the governor of Arkansas, not that of the Confederate military commander of the Indian Territory, to issue proclamations to the citizens of Arkansas. To the Texas authorities McCulloch wrote of the approaching danger in such terms that on July 20, Governor Edward Clark proclaimed to the citizens of Texas that although he had already offered ten regiments of Texas volunteers to President Davis for service in Missouri or Arkansas, he nevertheless urged that all Texans take the extra precaution of arming themselves.[21]

In spite of the excitement surrounding its beginning, McCulloch's first excursion into Missouri proved to be little more than a forced march of some five days' duration. From their rendezvous point the combined Confederate, Arkansas, and Missouri forces of McCulloch, Pearce, and Price marched north toward Neosho, a small southwestern Missouri town, where General Sigel had been reported menacing Governor Jackson's line of retreat. Having arrived there and captured a Union detachment of about 100 men without a fight, General McCulloch learned that Sigel's men, mostly Union Home Guards, had been defeated by Jackson's troops on July 5 at Carthage twenty miles north of Neosho. Sigel had retreated in the direction of Springfield, opening the way for Jackson's withdrawal to the south. Soon thereafter Jackson and his men were met upon the road, and the temporary crisis appeared to be over. Governor Jackson was safe, and General Lyon was still many miles to the north of Springfield. General McCulloch withdrew to Camp Jackson, near Maysville, Arkansas, not far from the Missouri border. He explained to Secretary Walker on July 9: "Having made the movement [into Missouri] without authority, and having accomplished my mission, I determined to fall back to this position and organize a force with a view of future operations."[22]

McCulloch's prudent decision took into account the situation of his own and the Missouri forces. His inexperienced troops required extensive training, were short of arms and ammunition, and until Colonel Greer's Third Texas Cavalry should arrive, were below authorized strength. As for the condition of the Missourians, McCulloch had been appalled by their unsoldierly appearance and conduct on the march to Neosho. Most of them had not yet even been assigned to companies and regiments and were poorly armed with shotguns and squirrel rifles. Furthermore, McCulloch distrusted the military abilities of their largely

21 *Austin Texas State Gazette*, July 29, 1861. Separately in the same issue, Texans were advised that their old Kentucky rifles bored out to the caliber of the Minie ball would have a range of 400 yards and be useful in repelling invaders.

22 McCulloch to L. P. Walker, July 9, 1861, *OR* 3, 606. // For an excellent tactical study of this small but fascinating and important battle, see David C. Hinze and Karen Farnham, *The Battle of Carthage: Border War in Southwest Missouri, July 5, 1861* (Savas Publishing, 1997).

political leaders. A brief respite from active operations would give the Missourians time to organize military units. Should they again require support, McCulloch's camp was within two days' marching distance of their encampment at Cowskin Prairie in the extreme northeast corner of the Indian Territory.

After McCulloch's withdrawal to Arkansas, General Lyon's Union forces of some 5,000, (believed by McCulloch to be 10,000), had gone into camp seventy miles north of Maysville at Springfield, where wagon roads led north to the railheads at Rolla and Sedalia. Although McCulloch credited Lyon's army with superior strength, it was actually on the verge of dissolution because the short-term enlistments of the volunteers ran out. Ignorant of Lyon's true situation, McCulloch was keenly aware of what be considered the continuing threat to both Arkansas and the Indian Territory posed by the Federal army. Provided he did not receive orders to the contrary, McCulloch was determined to blunt that threat by attacking as soon as the troops of Price and Pearce were sufficiently well organized.[23] He was less than aggressive when it came to the capture of Missouri for the Confederacy, but was aggressive indeed in his designs for the defense of Confederate territory. On July 18, he expressed to the war secretary his determination to march against Lyon in the next few days. He was doubtful of the reliability of his supporting troops, particularly the Missourians, but the time was propitious since he had "reliable information" that no hostile force threatened the Indian country.[24]

While there is no hint in McCulloch's correspondence that he had any objective in Missouri beyond a limited offensive operation to destroy General Lyon's threatening army, General Price, as commander of the Missouri State Guard, had much more extensive designs. Unlike McCulloch, Price was eager for the recovery of his home state from Federal control, a goal to which he would cling throughout the war. In the last two weeks of July 1861, as McCulloch made up his mind to resume operations in Missouri, Price had special reasons for desiring action. At Cowskin Prairie, where he was camped, his army would soon disintegrate from scarcity of supplies. Moreover, the Missouri State Convention was preparing to reassemble under a new president, and Price, who had presided over the Convention in March, hoped to disrupt or at least discredit their proceedings.[25]

On July 29, McCulloch's Confederates, Pearce's Arkansas militia, and Price's Missouri State Guard assembled at Cassville with a total of some 12,000 men. On August 1, they marched north with the intent of destroying Lyon's army. McCulloch's doubts about the reliability of the Missouri troops were quickly confirmed. Before leaving Cassville

---

23 Ibid.

24 McCulloch to L. P. Walker, July 18, 1861, Ibid., 610-612.

25 Castel, *Price*, 33.

McCulloch discovered that Price had brought with him some 2,000 unarmed men he had promised to leave behind at Cowskin Prairie. When McCulloch ordered that all unarmed men stay at least one day's march behind the main body, Price, as an independent commander, boldly rescinded the order. Even worse, on the second day's march from Cassville, near Dug Springs, the advance guard of the combined army, a ragged mob of Missourians euphemistically known as Brigadier General James S. Rains's Division, fell back in great panic on the main body after receiving a single Union cannon shot in their vicinity. The incident disgusted McCulloch. "It was at this point I saw the total inefficiency of the Missouri mounted men under Brigadier General Rains," he later wrote in exasperation to Secretary Walker.[26]

The next day, August 3, discouraged by the misconduct of Rains' troops and worried about the shortage of subsistence stores, which was particularly severe among the Missouri troops, McCulloch was ready to abandon the campaign. At this juncture, realizing the gravity of the situation and anxious to continue the campaign to recover at least a part of their state, the Missouri generals, led by Price, offered McCulloch overall command of the combined armies. At first he refused, little desiring the sole responsibility for the retreat that seemed inevitable. On August 4, however, a message arrived from Major General Leonidas Polk, commanding Department Number Two east of the Mississippi River, that Polk had ordered Brigadier General Gideon J. Pillow with 12,000 troops to invade Missouri by way of New Madrid. Heartened by this news, McCulloch agree to take command of the combined Missouri, Arkansas, and Confederate forces and continue the march on Springfield.[27]

---

26   Ibid., 36; Rose, *McCulloch*, 169.

27   Castel, *Price*, 37-38; Rose, *McCulloch*, 170. // The events described in this chapter led to the battle of Wilson's Creek. Two additional sources for more on the battle include Ed Bearss, *The Battle of Wilson's Creek* (Springfield, 1992), and William Riley Brooksher, *Bloody Hill: The Civil War Battle of Wilson's Creek* (Gaithersburg, 1999). Ed Bearss was the former Chief Historian of the National Park Service and his work was considered the benchmark for the event for many years. See also a recent study by Thomas W. Cutrer entitled *Theater of a Separate War: The Civil War West of the Mississippi River, 1861-1865*, (Chapel Hill, 2017). In Chapter 2, Cutrer describes the 1861 Confederate effort to coordinate the simultaneous offensive moves into southwest and southeast Missouri by McCulloch and Pillow. This book is an excellent source for gaining an overarching understanding of how the war unfolded in the Trans-Mississippi across the duration of the war. However, reviews point out that while well written, the book contains a bevy of errors including dates. (For a representative critical review, see Donald S. Frazier, June 20, 2018, *The Civil War Monitor*, posted online at www.civilwarmonitor.com/book-shelf/cutrer-theater-of-a-separate-war-

The almost simultaneous forward movements of McCulloch and Pillow into Missouri resulted from coincidence rather than conscious design. Each was a local response to northern pressure, initiated by the separate decision of an independent commander, uncontrolled by any central system of command. Prior to August, apparently few if any communications had passed between General McCulloch in northwestern Arkansas and General Polk in Memphis, Tennessee. As commander of Department Number Two, the sprawling central territorial command on the northern frontier of the Confederacy, General Polk was charged primarily with the defense of Tennessee and the Mississippi River. It was for this purpose and not from concern over McCulloch's situation that Polk sent Pillow's men across the Mississippi River into Missouri.

Unplanned though it was in origin, a coordinated Confederate invasion of Missouri from both its southwestern and southeastern quarters appeared to be underway by August 4, 1861. In each of those regions some 12,000 rebel soldiers were advancing with an unparalleled opportunity to take this pivotal state and turn the right flank of the Union-line along the Ohio River. Success would require the utmost cooperation between separate commanders and commands. As the first week of August 1861 ended, it remained to be seen whether the Confederates would, despite the glaring defects in their military organization on the northwestern frontier, prove equal to the opportunity.

2017.) An updated edition is due out in paperback in 2022. The book remains a solid reference source that provides a holistic view of events west of the river.

Chapter 2

Divided Command
and Divided Counsels in Missouri

August, 1861

William J. Hardee. *LOC*

The SPONTANEOUS AND uncoordinated nature of the Confederate movements into Missouri in the first days of August 1861 was the result of the War Department's piecemeal creation of independent military commands on the Confederacy's northwest frontier. Three different Confederate commanders had operational jurisdiction over parts of northern Arkansas, and none of the three officers had a superior closer than Richmond, Virginia. One was Ben McCulloch, whose primary charge was the Indian Territory. A second was Leonidas Polk, whose main concern was defending the Mississippi River valley. The third was Brigadier (soon to be Major) General William J. Hardee, whose role remains to be examined.

Hardee had been assigned on June 25, six weeks after McCulloch's assignment to Indian Territory, to command a military district embracing Arkansas west of the White and Black

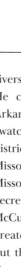

Leonidas Polk. *LOC*

rivers and north of the Arkansas River. He called it the "District of Upper Arkansas."[1] His orders required him to "watch over and protect" both his district and the adjacent part of Missouri. The requirement respecting Missouri seemed curious in light of the Secretary of War's admonition to McCulloch a week later to exercise the greatest prudence regarding Missouri; but the inconsistency typified the War Department's tendency both then and later to deal with McCulloch and Hardee as though they were totally isolated from each other.

Indeed, the creation of Hardee's command in the geographic area in which McCulloch had been forced to operate since June 5, and for command of which he had already appealed to Richmond, indicated the War Department had forgotten McCulloch, especially since an Arkansas regiment then being raised for him by Colonel Thomas C. Hindman, a prominent Helena lawyer, was assigned by the Department to Hardee. General Hardee was also authorized to raise 3,000 men in northern Arkansas, apparently without any notice to McCulloch, vitally interested though he might be.[2]

Much of the confusion soon to arise in Arkansas could be blamed on poor staff work in Richmond. The Arkansas counties east of Hardee's district between the Mississippi River and the White and Black rivers were inserted into General Polk's Department Number Two. Polk's area was a huge command extending as far east as northwest Alabama and as far south

1   S. Cooper to Hardee, June 25, 1861, *OR* vol. 3, 598.

2   Walker to Hindman, May 25, 1861, Hindman to Walker, May 29, 1861, R. H. Chilton to Hindman, June 11, 1861, ibid., 587, 588, 590. // Dr. Geise's military experience is prominent here in this passage in that he is illustrating the lack of unity of command in the Confederate organizational structure. The division of command caused many lost opportunities for the Confederate army, especially early in the war. Unity of command remains an enduring principle of war and joint operations and as codified in current military doctrine. See JP 3-0, *Joint Operations* (Washington, DC, 2017), 1-2 and GL-17.

Sterling Price,
Missouri State Guard. LOC

as the Red River in Louisiana. Its intent was to provide a coordinated defense of both sides of the Mississippi Valley.[3]

General Polk set up his headquarters at Memphis, Tennessee, in mid-July.[4] A few days later Hardee took formal command of his separate Arkansas district, establishing his headquarters just 400 yards from the Missouri state line at Pitman's Ferry, Arkansas.[5] Above the Missouri line and outside the Confederate territorial commands stood elements of the Missouri State Guard, poorly trained and equipped, but nonetheless allied to the Confederate cause and increasing in numbers.

Besides Major General Sterling Price's state troops in southwest Missouri, another Missouri State Guard force had been raised in July in southeast Missouri by Meriwether Jeff Thompson, erstwhile mayor of Saint Joseph and newly elected brigadier general and commander of the First Military District of the Missouri State Guard.[6] An ardent secessionist and eager to cooperate with the Confederates, Thompson nevertheless made it clear that he considered himself and his perhaps 2,000-man force subject only to the direct orders of Missouri's Governor Jackson.

To recapitulate, by late July 1861, an unbroken line of Confederate territorial commands extended (on paper at least) from the Arkansas-Missouri border on the east at the Mississippi River to the far western corner of the Indian Territory—but there was no single chain of command. Separate channels ran from the headquarters of Polk, Hardee,

3 Special Orders No. 88, Adj. and Insp. Gen. Office, Richmond, July 4, 1861, ibid., vol. 4, 362. // See Huston Horn, *Leonidas Polk: Warrior Bishop of the Confederacy* (Lawrence, 2019). General Polk is an enigmatic figure in Confederate military history. A close friend of President Jefferson Davis, he used this relationship to advance his agenda throughout the war with mostly harmful effects for the Confederate cause.

4 General Orders No. I, Hdqrs., Department No. 2, Memphis, July 13, 1861, ibid., 368-369.

5 McCulloch to Walker, July 30, 1861, Hardee to Polk, July 28, 1861, ibid. 622-625, 618-619.

6 // See Doris Land Mueller, *M. Jeff Thompson: Missouri's Swamp Fox of the Confederacy* (Columbia, 2007) for more information on this forgotten figure in Confederate military history.

and McCulloch directly to Richmond, and the independent aggregations of Missouri State Guards under Price and Thompson, both of whom ostensibly reported directly to the Governor of Missouri, only added to the confusion.

The weakness of this divided command is illustrated in proposals made to Hardee by the Confederate McCulloch and the Missourian Price just prior to their joint expedition against Lyon at Springfield. About July 20, McCulloch had informed Hardee by courier that he planned to advance on Springfield at the end of the month and suggested that Hardee simultaneously make a demonstration at Rolla, Missouri, the southern terminus of the Southwestern Railroad. This suggestion Hardee declined on the valid grounds that he had less than 2,300 men, all untrained, badly equipped, undisciplined, and almost totally without supporting transportation.[7]

Almost simultaneously with General McCulloch's dispatch another arrived, this one from General Price, suggesting that Hardee join in the forthcoming attack on Springfield itself. Hardee once more declined, citing reasons similar to those he had given McCulloch.[8] Inasmuch as Springfield and Rolla are almost 100 miles apart, Price and McCulloch had clearly not bothered, though almost on the eve of their proposed joint expedition to Springfield, to agree or perhaps even to consult on the possible role of nearby supporting troops.

Similar detachment was evident in the relations between McCulloch and Hardee, the two officers most directly responsible for the defense of upper Arkansas. This detachment was at least suggested in the arrangements Hardee attempted to make to receive N. Bart Pearce's Arkansas Brigade into his command. Having reached an understanding with the Arkansas Military Board that the troops, arms, and munitions of the state be turned over to him,[9] he instructed Colonel Thomas Hindman on August 8 to proceed to Pearce's brigade and muster its members into Confederate service, marching the infantry by the shortest route to Hardee's headquarters at Pitman's Ferry and stationing the cavalry at various points along the Arkansas frontier.[10]

Obviously Hardee did not know that at that moment the Arkansas brigade of General Pearce was camped with McCulloch's army at Wilson's Creek, Missouri, just forty-eight hours away from the bloody battle of the same name. Again that same August 8, Hardee revealed in a letter to the President of the Arkansas Military Board that he did not know whether McCulloch meant to persist in his plan of attacking Springfield or perhaps had

---

7   McCulloch to Walker, July 30, 1861, Hardee to Polk, July 28, 1861, ibid. 622-625, 618-619.

8   Hardee to Price, July 27, 1861, ibid, 616; Price to Comdg. Officer, Pocahontas, Ark., July 19, 1861, Mrs. Mason Barret Collection of Albert Sidney and William Preston. Johnston Papers, 1803-1900, Tulane University Library.

9   Hardee to Cooper, July 17, 1861, *OR* vol. 3, 609.

10   Hardee to Hindman, August 8, 1861, ibid., 638.

already done so.[11] Granting that 150 miles of rough terrain separated McCulloch and Hardee, and that the disorganization of Hardee's troops as well as his brief period in command may have precluded his conducting joint operations with McCulloch, the apparent failures of both McCulloch and Hardee to establish regular courier service between their two headquarters can only be explained by the absolute independence of their commands.

One participant who recognized the danger of divided command in the Trans-Mississippi even as it was yet developing was Missouri's Governor Claiborne Fox Jackson. Having cast his lot with the Confederacy, Jackson had much to lose if his state were lost. After narrowly escaping entrapment by Franz Sigel at Carthage, Jackson had gone to Memphis to confer with General Polk and to urge him—successfully, as it turned out—to invade Missouri. On August 8, Jackson wrote from Memphis to one of Missouri's commissioners in Richmond, Edward Carrington Cabell, to warn President Davis and his cabinet of the pitfalls of the division of command that existed between Hardee, McCulloch, and Price. "Circumstances may require that these three distinct commands should be united and that they should act in concert, though separately, for the accomplishment of a common object," stressed Jackson, who continued:

> As affairs now stand, though I do not specially apprehend it, it is possible there may be some distraction in counsel, jealousy of command, and consequent inefficiency and inaction. It has occurred to me that if President Davis would appoint a major-general for all that district of country lying west of General Polk's district, and if he could go into Missouri accompanied by me, I could require and compel by my orders as complete cooperation on the part of the State troops as if they had been transferred to the Confederate service and were under his command. Thus all military operations would be completely under the control of one head.[12]

Even though he was a civilian, Governor Jackson had a better grasp of the muddled command situation in Arkansas than the Confederate generals in the field, and a better solution for the problem than the War Department in Richmond. Apparently in an effort to encourage the acceptance of his plan of command and to raise Richmond's interest in the cause of Missouri, Jackson sent along a state declaration of independence that he had issued a short time before.[13]

11 Hardee to H. M. Rector, August 8, 1861, ibid., 636-637.

12 Jackson to Cabell, August 8, 1861, *OR* vol. 3, 639.

13 Cabell to Davis, August 21, 1861, Jefferson Davis Collection, Louisiana Historical Association Collection, Tulane University Library. Cabell forwarded Governor Jackson's letter to President Davis with the remark that he was also forwarding the Missouri Declaration of Independence. Then came a penciled P.S.: "I handed the paper containing the proclamation & Declaration of Independence to a friend, who has mislaid it, I shall probably tomorrow be able to send it to the President."

Jackson's communication to Richmond would have little effect, but his consultations with General Polk at Memphis were more fruitful. Under Jackson's urging, and impressed with his reports exaggerating the available troop strength across the river, Polk formulated as early as July 23 the tentative plan to send Brigadier General Gideon J. Pillow and 6,000 men to New Madrid, Missouri, where they would be reinforced by Missourians under Thompson and a column from Arkansas under Hardee. Pillow would then either get immediately between Lyon and St. Louis or, in Polk's words, "to proceed to St. Louis, seize it, and taking possession of the boats at that point, to proceed up the river Missouri, raising the Missourians . . . and at such point as may appear most suitable to detach a force to cut off Lyon's return from the West." Having dealt with Lyon, Pillow's army, in a kind of grand right wheel, during their return march to Tennessee, was to enter Illinois and take Cairo in the rear.[14]

This was grandly optimistic thinking. The plan, like later ones schemed for the invasion of Missouri, was based on a gross overestimation of the troop strengths and logistical resources available.[15] By July 28, Polk had received more accurate information from Price's adjutant general, who was visiting in Memphis. Unfortunately, there were only about one-half as many men as Governor Jackson had reported available for an immediate full-scale campaign in Missouri. Consequently, Polk reported to Secretary Walker that he would now drop his plan for a movement to the Missouri River and direct instead that New Madrid be occupied and fortified as a base for future operations in Missouri. He still believed, however, that if Missouri was to be saved the time was close at hand, and Polk proposed that he be permitted to draw troops from Tennessee and the lower South for more vigorous operations in that state.[16]

Polk's feelings were shared by a number of southwestern civilian leaders, both east and west of the river. Their desire for a military concentration in Missouri was clearly expressed to Confederate Congressman David M. Currin by prominent Memphis citizen Robertson Topp. "As I came from Richmond a few days since I met on the entire road from Richmond to Memphis a vast number of soldiers," began Topp, who continued:

> I learn that companies from Mississippi, Louisiana, and elsewhere arriving here are sent on eastward. It occurs to me that the true policy would be in view of the great stake we are playing for in Missouri, to turn all the forces now organized in Tennessee, Mississippi, Louisiana, Texas, and elsewhere upon Missouri so that we could throw an overpowering

---

14 Polk to Walker, July 23, 1861, *OR* vol. 3, 612-614. // See Nathaniel C. Hughes, Jr., *The Life and Wars of Gideon J. Pillow* (Knoxville, 2011).

15 Pillow to Polk, August 2, 1861, Hardee to Polk, July 30, 1861, Abstract from return of the troops of the Upper District Arkansas, commanded by Brig. Gen. W. J. Hardee, August 31, 1861, ibid., 626-627, 620, 690.

16 Polk to Walker, July 28, 1861, ibid., 617-618.

force upon Missouri and crush out abolitionism in Missouri, and thereby break up their contemplated movement on the South in the fall.[17]

Secretary Walker responded to Polk on August 8 that the War Department was inclined to accept Polk's military decisions and that he could raise as many troops as he could support. About a major effort in Missouri Walker wrote nothing, but his silence, whatever it signified, was too late to have any effect. A Confederate invasion of southeast Missouri had already begun. In the first days of August both Pillow and Hardee had entered the state, though lack of transportation had prevented Hardee from bringing with him his whole force. Pillow's first objective was New Madrid; Hardee's was Greenville, whence he planned to advance on Ironton, the southern terminus of the St. Louis-Iron Mountain Railroad. On advancing Hardee enthusiastically announced to Polk that "a brave movement" into Missouri would do much to prevent an offensive movement of the enemy into Tennessee and that he would unite with General Pillow in any movement to free Missouri.[18]

Despite Hardee's enthusiasm, no greater degree of cooperation developed between him and Pillow in southeast Missouri than did between McCulloch and Price in the southwestern part of the state. Hardee believed his and Pillow's proper objective to be the railhead at Ironton. The destruction of enough track above that place would prevent enemy reinforcement and supply of southeast Missouri. From Ironton, his and Pillow's forces could next move west to the railhead at Rolla, cutting Lyon's line of retreat from Springfield. After disposing of Lyon they could advance on St. Louis.

General Gideon Pillow at New Madrid along the Mississippi River also wanted to advance, but he thought the first step should be the seizure of Birds Point and Cape Girardeau to protect his right flank and rear as he moved north from New Madrid. What followed was a series of conflicting messages from the headquarters of Polk, Pillow, Hardee, and Thompson. Hardee insisted that Pillow move northwest from New Madrid to join him at Greenville for the attacks on Ironton and Rolla and eventual rendezvous with Price and McCulloch. As long as Pillow operated along the Mississippi River, his line of communication could be disrupted. Pillow insisted that Hardee move either to New Madrid or to Benton so they might combine for an attack against Cape Girardeau. A glance at the

---

17 Topp to Currin, August 20, 1861, ibid., vol. 4, 395-396. // Topp's observation is astute for several reasons. Missouri's geographic position had great potential advantages to both sides. For the South it would impede movement on the Mississippi River, thus preventing its use as a highway to invade the South. Further, control of Missouri would place a Confederate presence astride the flank of a Northern state, Illinois, threatening Union territory. For the North, control of Missouri pushed the Confederate army away from the river and secured Illinois' flank. This would set the conditions for future Union operations in the Deep South utilizing the Mississippi as a route to invade. It is interesting that civilian observers like Governor Jackson and Topp were making these connections, but it seemed to allude Confederate generals.

18 Hardee to Polk, August 4, 1861, ibid., vol. 3, 629.

map of southern Missouri suggests, superficially at least, that Hardee's plan was the sounder, since it removed the Confederate forces from the enemy infested river area, cut off Lyon's principal escape route to St. Louis through Rolla, and put Pillow and Hardee within easier marching distance of Price and McCulloch.[19]

By August 15-16, General Polk in Memphis felt that because of possible Federal threats to New Madrid, not to mention Knoxville, Pillow ought to fall back into Tennessee. Polk, however, left the decision to Pillow. Having just received positive news of McCulloch's August 10 victory over Lyon at Wilson's Creek, Pillow stubbornly replied that now was the time to press the enemy at all points in Missouri and demanded reinforcements from Polk. "For God's sake," he wrote, "don't hold me back or cripple me for a want which will wait on you until the work of emancipating Missouri is completed."[20] During this emergency while confusing and bickering communications passed between Pillow, Polk, and Hardee, a part of Pillow's forces advanced as far as Benton, Missouri, about fifteen miles south of Cape Girardeau.

Even if Hardee had joined Pillow at Benton, which he declined to do, their mutual cooperation would likely not have improved very much. Pillow complained to Secretary Walker on August 21 that in the event of a junction Hardee would be the senior officer present. "Why is it that I have been placed in position and ranked by nearly every General officer of the Confederate Army when it is known that I ranked every officer now in that Army in my long term of service in the Mexican War?" Pillow also complained about his superior, complaining that Polk's "varying views and countermanding orders" were crippling him.[21] It was true that Polk had not been firm enough nor explicit enough in his instructions to Pillow.

Pillow's tone changed abruptly on August 25. Bowing to Hardee's estimate of the situation, and to the belief of some of his own brigade and regimental commanders that an attack on Cape Girardeau was too hazardous, Pillow agreed to abandon his plans. Further, he requested General Polk's instructions and promised to abide by them.[22]

On August 26, Polk advised both Hardee and Pillow to fall back. He suggested Hardee withdraw to New Madrid, but Hardee instead chose to return to his Arkansas base at Pitman's Ferry. Pillow was ordered to dispose his forces at Island Number Ten and Union City, Tennessee. He should, if possible, urged Polk, get M. Jeff Thompson to garrison the best positions on the Missouri shore with Missouri State Guardsmen. Polk believed that all

---

19 Pillow to Polk, August 1, 2, 1861, ibid., 626-627, Hardee to Polk and to Pillow, both August 7, 1861, ibid., 633-634.

20 Polk to Pillow, August 15, 16, 1861, Pillow to Polk, August 16, 1861, ibid., 650-651, 653-654, 654-655.

21 Pillow to Walker: August 21, 1861, ibid., 666-667.

22 Pillow to Polk, August 25, 1861, ibid., 677-679. 684.

forward movement in southern Missouri should cease.[23] Thus by the end of August 1861, the promising if unplanned opportunity for a simultaneous Confederate assault on Missouri from both southwest and southeast had vanished in an atmosphere of confusion and bitterness. There would be no more talk in Confederate circles of a "brave movement" into Missouri in 1861 or of falling on the enemy's flank in Illinois.

The failure in Missouri aroused concern in Richmond. The War Department, by direction of President Davis, asked for an explanation of the events in southeast Missouri, and Davis wrote personally to his friend General Polk requesting enlightenment.[24] Polk's reply stressed divided command as the overriding deficiency that had hampered all the military operations undertaken. He recommended both sides of the Mississippi Valley be placed under the most experienced general available with all the existing western commands under his jurisdiction. For this high post Polk recommended Albert Sidney Johnston.[25]

Polk's recommendations, which had been made by others as well, were now in effect adopted by the Richmond authorities. The responsibilities of the commander of Department Number Two were expanded on September 2 to include the entire state of Arkansas and all military operations in Missouri.[26] On September 10, General Albert Sidney Johnston was assigned to command Department Number Two, which was further extended to include military operations in Kentucky, Kansas, and the Indian Territory.[27]

Johnston's assignment would have little effect on events unfolding west of the river.[28] From existing correspondence, it appears as though the president and secretary of war had expected active military operations in Missouri to continue. But the opportunities that had existed in the first two weeks of August had vanished by September when Union troops poured into the state. What was even more important in the long run was General Polk's decision to march his troops into Columbus, Kentucky, on September 3, a political and military blunder that violated Kentucky's outward neutrality and triggered the Unionist legislature to invite Northern troops in to drive out the Confederates. Polk's thrust

---

23 Polk to Hardee and to Pillow, August 26, 1861, ibid., 682-684.

24 Cooper to Polk, August 28, 1861, ibid., 684-685: Nathaniel Cheairs Hughes, Jr., *General William J. Hardee, Old Reliable* (Baton Rouge, 1965), 79.

25 Polk to Davis, August 29, 1861, *OR* vol. 3, 687-688.

26 Special Orders No. 141, Adj. and Insp. Gen. Office, Richmond, September 2, 1861, 691.

27 Special Orders No. 149, Adj. and Insp. Gen. Office, Richmond, September 10, 1861, ibid., vol. 4, 405.

28 // One of the reasons Johnston's appointment had "little effect" is that he chose to make his headquarters in the field with a part of the Confederate forces posted at Bowling Green, Kentucky. Thus, Johnston became absorbed by events to his immediate front rather than taking a holistic view of the defense of the vast Department No. 2. Polk's earlier move into Columbus, Kentucky, made Johnston's task all the more complex.

prompted the occupation of Paducah, Kentucky, at the mouth of the Tennessee River, by Brigadier General Ulysses S. Grant on September 6. These episodes abruptly shifted the Confederate war effort in the West from Missouri to Kentucky. Subsequent Confederate operations in southeast Missouri, in the vicinity of Belmont and New Madrid, were mere extensions of the war unfolding east of the river, dictated by the need for a flank guard of the Kentucky line of defense.

The focus would remain east of the Mississippi for the remainder of the war.

Chapter 3

Continued Command Problems on the Northwest Frontier and a New Year's Promise of Solution

August 1861 - January 1862

While CONFEDERATE HOPES in southeast Missouri had risen in the final week of August 1861 before fading at month's end when attention was diverted east of the river, those of General Price remained high. He and McCulloch had won a victory over Lyon at Wilson's Creek on August 10, which opened the way to the Missouri River.

The battle's details are beyond the scope of this study, but under McCulloch's overall command, Price's Missourians, Pearce's Arkansans, and McCulloch's Confederates from Louisiana, Texas, and Arkansas had driven Lyon's army from the battlefield south of Springfield. The dedicated General Lyon was among the Union dead, his body left abandoned on the field during the hasty withdrawal. The Confederates were too exhausted and disorganized to take up immediate pursuit, and the Union troops were permitted to retire toward the rail head at Rolla where they might entrain for St. Louis. Eager to turn this tactical success to strategic advantage, Price approached McCulloch three days after the battle to urge a joint advance to the Missouri River. McCulloch firmly declined his suggestion.

More than four months later McCulloch later explained to the new secretary of war, Judah P. Benjamin, the reasons for his decision.[1] There were many. His orders strictly limited him to the defense of upper Arkansas and the Cherokee Nation, and he felt that his entire

---

1 McCulloch to Benjamin, December 22, 1861, *OR* vol. 3, 743-749.

force was required for that mission, inasmuch as Pearce's Arkansas militia had been called up only for the current emergency and would probably disband because Lyon's army had been turned back. McCulloch doubted willingness of the Arkansas troops to enlist in the Confederate Army upon termination of their state service.[2]

A major concern centered on logistics and supply. McCulloch's ammunition had been almost completely exhausted by the battle and there was not a sufficient amount for an extended campaign.[3] Finally, McCulloch claimed that by August 13 he knew from General Hardee that Gideon Pillow had fallen back and that he could expect no help from them. This last claim is doubtful because it is hard to see how news of Pillow could have reached McCulloch or Price by August 13.[4] McCulloch's other reasons for not advancing were sound. No doubt his decision was made easier by his well-known antipathy toward the Missourians in general, and especially toward Price.[5]

Price's desire to advance was not blunted by McCulloch's hard-headed refusal to cooperate. The Missouri general was convinced that the people of his state would rise against the Federal occupation were he to reconquer even a portion of the state, and that once he reached the Missouri River, some 50,000 recruits from the pro-Confederate river

---

2   General N. Bart Pearce, disgruntled because he would not remain in command of his men if they transferred to Confederate service, detached them from McCulloch's army on August 21 and marched them back to Arkansas, where they were mustered out of state service at Fayetteville on August 29. Since all but eighteen or twenty declined immediate enlistment in the Confederate Army, McCulloch was left on August 30 with only about 2,500 soldiers fit for duty in his entire command. Ibid.; Huff, "Military Board in Confederate Arkansas," *Arkansas Historical Quarterly,* XXVI, 80-81; Rose, *McCulloch,* 162; Fort Smith *Times and Herald,* August 30, 1861; McCulloch to Walker, September 2, 1861, *OR* vol. 3, 691-693.

3   This is not surprising since the average number of rounds that McCulloch's soldiers carried into the battle of Wilson's Creek was only twenty-five. Castel, *Price,* 40. Further, if McCulloch advanced to the Missouri River, his ammunition supply line from Fort Smith, already 150 miles long, would be increased by an additional 250 miles of rough roads, while the enemy could rely on the railroads and rivers for resupply.

4   The letter from Hardee to which McCulloch referred must have been one written on August 13 and not received by McCulloch until August 24. McCulloch to Hardee, August 24, 1861, *OR* vol. 3, 672.

5   McCulloch's distrust and dislike of Price and the Missouri troops, and Missourians in general, is implicit in his report to Secretary Benjamin and explicit in a letter to Hardee. To Benjamin he mentioned Rains's panic at Dug Springs "to show the unorganized condition of the Missouri forces, and what great risk we ran of a panic being communicated to the fighting men of the army by having such material among them." McCulloch also expressed resentment that Price had officially claimed the capture at Wilson's Creek of a Union battery that had in fact been overrun and captured by the Third Louisiana, and that Missouri camp followers had robbed the dead of weapons. McCulloch to Benjamin, December 22, 1861, ibid., 743-749. To Hardee, McCulloch wrote, "I dare not join them [Missourians] in my present condition, for fear of having my men completely demoralized." As for the attitude of the Missouri civilians, "we had as well be in Boston." McCulloch to Hardee, August 21, 1861, ibid., 672; Castel, *Price.* 48-49.

counties and from northern Missouri would flock to his army. Price knew many of his men were anxious to reclaim their distant homes from Federal control. An advance into the heart of the state was important for the morale of his troops and perhaps even necessary to hold them together.[6]

The chances that an advance by Price could achieve the results he desired, beyond the improvement of morale, were not good. To influence public opinion in Missouri and to acquire the hoped-for number of recruits would require taking and holding a section of the Missouri Valley for an indefinite time. Of the 9,500 men in Price's army, the majority were cavalry—an arm that was not suited, even when well-trained, to take and hold ground for an extended period. With no established supply depots and an enormous need for forage, Price's mounted army could not long occupy any single position for any length of time and must, out of necessity, keep moving or starve. Furthermore, although Price had not known on August 13 that he could expect no help from any of the Confederate commanders, he did know it when he finally moved north from Springfield on August 25. Any advance he would make could only be an exceedingly risky hit-and-run raid with little chance of long-term success.

By the time Price started north, Major General John C. Fremont, commanding the United States Army's Western Department at St. Louis, had close to 40,000 disposable troops in Missouri as well as possession of the rail and river lines of communication to the threatened Missouri River area.[7] Only a lethargic failure to reinforce in sufficient time Colonel James A. Mulligan's Illinois regiment at Lexington enabled Price to take that Missouri River town on September 20 after a two-day siege.[8]

Price's campaign was at least partially vindicated at Lexington, where he received some 10,000 recruits in addition to taking large amounts of ordnance and commissary supplies in the town.[9] Nevertheless, Price could afford to remain at Lexington only ten days, for on September 26 Fremont left St. Louis with some 38,000 men with a plan to cut off Price's retreat. Once again Union lethargy aided Price, for had he been hotly pursued his army

---

6   // This was a common refrain from Sterling Price throughout the war and documented by Missouri Governor Thomas C. Reynolds who wrote a post-war biography of the general. This manuscript went unpublished for 142 years until discovered and published by the Missouri History Museum. The book, published in 2009, provides primary source insight on the personality, motivations, and leadership of Price in a refreshingly honest assessment. Further, Reynolds provides a glimpse into the inter-workings of the state government-in-exile and the Trans-Mississippi region at large. See Thomas C. Reynolds, *General Sterling Price and the Confederacy*, Robert G. Schultz, ed. (St. Louis, 2009).

7   Castel, *Price*, 57; Thomas W. Knox, *Camp-Fire and Cotton Field: Southern Adventure in Time of War. Life with the Union Armies and Residence on a Louisiana Plantation* (New York, 1865), 94-95.

8   Castel, *Price*, 56; Francis B. Wilkie, *Pen and Powder* (Boston, 1888). 43.

9   Castel, *Price*, 56-57.

might well have been destroyed at the Osage River, which, for lack of boats, his troops took three days and three nights in crossing.[10]

Although Price's campaign produced substantial booty as well as many temporary recruits, it had no significant effect on the course of the war in Missouri. The recruits as well as some of his veterans drifted away as Price marched south, so that an army swollen to near 20,000 at Lexington had dwindled to only about 7,000 at the Osage River crossing.[11] To Price's bitter disappointment, the predicted general rising of the Confederate people of Missouri had not occurred. He would not penetrate so deeply into Missouri again in force for three long years, and at that late date he would not escape the disaster he had perhaps deserved in the fall of 1861.

General Price's retreat from Lexington stopped at Neosho in the far southwestern corner of the state on October 20. There, a rump session of the Missouri Legislature passed a few days later an ordinance of secession and Missouri was admitted to the Confederacy on November 28.[12] Although something of a legal fiction even in Confederate eyes, this action transformed Price's orphaned State Guard into the militia of a Confederate state and cleared the way for acceptance of its members by the Confederate Army.

The headstrong Price continued to insist on a full-scale Confederate invasion of Missouri. At least twice, once on October 16 and again in November, he wrote General Albert Sidney Johnston urging an attack on St. Louis. To the first request Johnston replied cordially, congratulating Price on his victory at Lexington but pleading more pressing demands on his resources than an attempt on St. Louis.[13] To the second request Johnston apparently did not reply. Price sent a similar request to President Davis, perhaps hoping he would put pressure on Johnston. Nothing came of it.[14]

Price also continued to urge McCulloch to join him in an all-out campaign against the Federals in Missouri, but once again nothing came of his pleas.[15] What did follow was a series of substantial but fruitless advances and withdrawals in southwest Missouri by both Confederate and Union forces, with no major fighting. General Fremont occupied

---

10   Ephraim McD, Anderson, *Memoirs; Historical and Personal, Including the Campaigns of the First Missouri Confederate Brigade* (St. Louis, 1868), 86-87.

11   Ibid., 80, 88; Castel, *Price*, 57.

12   According to Castel, *Price*, 59, a quorum was not present at this Neosho session of the Missouri Legislature. Anderson, *Memoirs*, 94 claims a quorum was present, and the Little Rock *Daily State Journal*, November 22, 1861, offered particulars, stating that twenty-three senators and seventy-seven representatives were present, with only nineteen and sixty eight, respectively, being necessary for a quorum.

13   Price to Johnston, October 16, 1861, Johnston to Price, October 31, 1861, Price to Johnston, November 7, 1861, *OR* vol. 3, 719-720, 729, 731-732.

14   Price to Davis, November 10, 1861, ibid., 734-736.

15   Price to McCulloch, October 23, 1861, ibid., 722.

Springfield briefly, apparently intent on an invasion of Arkansas, but his successor, Major General David Hunter, was ordered by Abraham Lincoln himself to retire toward Rolla and Sedalia in the second week of November. McCulloch then marched to Springfield, and Price took up an advanced position fifty-five miles to the north near Osceola on the Sac River.[16] By the first week of December, however, McCulloch had again withdrawn to Arkansas, this time to Cross Hollows.

Camp Benjamin at Cross Hollows, endowed with two grist mills and a fine spring and creek, was an excellent place for wintering McCulloch's army. Most of his 7,600 men were comfortably quartered in wooden huts with brick chimneys, and the camp was conveniently located only eighteen miles from the supply depot at Fayetteville. The town of some 4,000 contained an accumulation of commissary and quartermaster supplies as well as manufacturing facilities for ammunition, gun carriages, and army wagons.[17] The headquarters and other miscellaneous elements of the army were billeted in the Van Buren–Fort Smith area, where the communication line of the Arkansas River could be used.

Ordered by Secretary of War Benjamin to explain his conduct in Missouri, McCulloch obtained permission in December to report to Richmond in person, leaving command of his troops to Colonel James McIntosh. Thus it was McIntosh who received Price's last request for a winter campaign in Missouri in 1861. Price wrote on December 6 that Lane, Montgomery, and Charles Jennison, with their bands of Kansas Jayhawkers, were marauding through the state's western counties. Price requested aid to repel them, destroy the railroads, and disrupt Federal river communications. The reply of the young West Pointer McIntosh to the old militia general was a cold one. McIntosh cited the lateness of the season, the impassability of Missouri roads in winter, the troubles in Indian Territory with the dissident Creek chieftain, Opothleyahola, and the probable need for his troops to help defend Memphis in the near future as obstacles to any cooperation with Price. In a letter to General Samuel Cooper, the Confederacy's adjutant general, McIntosh termed the Missouri general's proposal "almost madness."[18]

Without support from the nearest Confederates, Price was forced to retire from his advanced position near Osceola. On Christmas Day his forces, about 10,000 strong, went into comfortable winter quarters at Springfield.[19] They were less than 100 miles north of McCulloch's main camp at Cross Hollows and the Confederate supply depot at Fayetteville. The nearest Federal troop concentrations were at least 100 miles away in the Rolla and Sedalia areas, east and north, respectively, of Springfield.

16 Castel, *Price*, 59-60.

17 William Watson, *Life in the Confederate Army. Being the Observations and Experiences of an Alien in the South during the American Civil War* (New York, 1888), 234.

18 Castel, *Price*, 62; Rose, *McCulloch*, 162-164.

19 Anderson, *Memoirs*, 139.

* * *

BY THE FIRST December of the war, active campaigning to establish the northern border of the Confederate Trans-Mississippi West had thus temporarily ceased, but the bickering between Southern commanders had not. General McCulloch's report to Secretary Benjamin of December 22 explaining his conduct in Missouri is full of recriminations against Price and his Missourians. Price, in his turn, bitterly complained to General Polk on December 23 that both McCulloch and McIntosh had obstructed him in Missouri. The controversy erupted in the newspapers, the Missouri *Army Argus* taking Price's side, and the Fayetteville *Arkansian* and the Richmond *Whig* publishing articles favoring McCulloch.[20]

It had become abundantly clear by December that the assignment of responsibility to General Johnston for all military operations in Arkansas and Missouri had not eliminated divided command on the northwest frontier. McCulloch had totally ignored Johnston and had continued to correspond directly with Richmond.[21] In fact, McCulloch was so completely out of touch with Johnston that the latter finally complained to Secretary Benjamin that he had "been unable to obtain any reports from that [McCulloch's] command, and do not know its number and condition." Johnston added that he had in consequence refrained from issuing any orders to McCulloch.[22] Beset with serious problems in Kentucky and Tennessee, he had little time to spare for Missouri and Arkansas.

Johnston's preoccupation with his command east of the river did not escape criticism in the Trans-Mississippi West. On November 18, Senator Robert W. Johnson of Arkansas wrote him a reproachful letter that included the following:

> If disaster falls in your division it must be at your door, onerous as your duties are, unless it shall appear that you have fully comprehended the whole field of operations and made every effort, not for means, but for adequate means, to sustain such high and imposing interests. You have not even a major-general West of the Mississippi River; a country as broad as all Austria, Prussia, and German.[23]

---

20 Castel, *Price*, 63; Rose, *McCulloch*, 183-192.

21 // This is partially attributable to Johnston's previously noted myopic focus on events to his immediate front in Kentucky. Further, Confederate commanders in the field routinely communicated directly with the president or War Department undermining the chain of command. This practice during the war caused much unnecessary friction among commanders and railed against unity of command. Finally, the tyranny of distance and primitive communications of the nineteenth century also made it difficult for commanders to communicate as in the case of McCulloch and Johnston.

22 Johnston to Benjamin, January 5, 1862, *OR* vol. 7, 820-821. 563.

23 Senator Johnson to Johnston, November 18, 1861, ibid., vol. 4, 562-563.

At least one paper commented on Johnston's failure to exercise command beyond the river. According to the Little Rock *Daily State Journal*, vigorous action in Missouri had been expected from Johnston. Instead, argued the *Journal* (somewhat inaccurately), he had ordered Hardee into Kentucky, leaving only 600 men to protect the important Pitman's Ferry region on the Missouri border.[24]

McCulloch had done nothing to cooperate with Johnston, but he did recognize that a single firm leader was needed west of the river, one able to devote full attention to the northwestern frontier. He had written to Secretary Benjamin on November 8 urging that one man be placed in command of his and Price's armies. Expressly eliminating himself and Price from consideration, he suggested Major General Braxton Bragg, then in command of the Department of Alabama and West Florida.[25] By December the War Department was considering both a new commander and a new command structure for the Trans-Mississippi. A rumor reached the area that a new Department of Missouri and Arkansas was to be created with Henry Heth (who was then a colonel) in command.[26] Heth was indeed the first man selected for the post, but he refused. Richmond turned Braxton Bragg. McCulloch was in the capital at the time and may have influenced the selection.

Whatever the influences involved, Benjamin on December 27, 1861, after "long and anxious" consultation with the president, tendered Bragg command of a new Trans-Mississippi Department embracing Arkansas, Missouri, northern Texas, and the Indian Territory. General Johnston's department would be restricted to the east bank of the Mississippi, although in the event of joint operations along the river, Johnston, as the senior officer, would assume command. In turn, Bragg's Department of Alabama and West Florida would be turned over to Major General E. Kirby Smith. Benjamin emphasized the "supreme" importance of Missouri. When Johnston was sent to command the Western Department, he explained, it was assumed he would take personal charge in Missouri and Arkansas, but that he had been diverted by the course of events in Kentucky and Tennessee. Johnston's inattention had not been too costly while the incompetent Fremont commanded Union forces in Missouri, but since Fremont's removal the situation had become critical. The war secretary's tone was urgent, and he asked for Bragg's immediate answer by telegraph.[27]

After more than half a year of divided command, of logistical neglect, and of administrative confusion, the remedy of unified command seemed about to be applied to the painfully chaotic condition of the Trans-Mississippi West. Unfortunately, the reorganization was not to take place. About the time that Benjamin was penning his letter to Bragg, Federal reinforcements were landing at Ship Island and Biloxi, Mississippi,

---

24 Little Rock *Daily State Journal*, November 2, 1861. Actually, Hardee left behind at Pocahontas near Pitman's Ferry some 2,000 men under Colonel Solon Borland. Ibid., January 7, 1862.

25 McCulloch to Benjamin, November 8, 1861, *OR* vol. 3, 733-734.

26 Castel, *Price*, 67.

27 Benjamin to Bragg, December 27, 1861, *OR* vol. 6, 788-789.

threatening his own Department of Alabama and West Florida. Bragg asked to be removed from consideration for the Trans-Mississippi command in the second week of January 1862.[28]

With Bragg unavailable the decision in Richmond was to continue the Trans-Mississippi frontier as a satellite of the Western Department, as Department Number Two had come to be known, rather than to create another military department. Henceforth, Missouri, Arkansas, Louisiana above Red River, and Indian Territory would be designated the Trans-Mississippi District of the Western Department. The new district commander was to be Major General Earl Van Dorn, the former commander of the Department of Texas and more recently an infantry division commander in Virginia. Before assuming his new command, Van Dorn was to report in person to General Johnston for special instructions regarding the movement of a part of McCulloch's forces east to New Madrid for defensive operations along the Mississippi River.[29]

In this reordering of commands the War Department seems to have overlooked the military structure it had earlier created in the Indian Territory. Back in November, a Department of the Indian Territory had been established under Brigadier General Albert Pike. The War Department, however, created a Trans-Mississippi District that included the Indian Territory without either relieving Pike or redesignating his department.[30] Subsequently, this blunder would prove a source of extreme embarrassment, for Pike insisted on continuing to report directly to Richmond as a department commander.

The reorganization of January 1862, did promise to solve the most vexing command problem on the northwest frontier, namely the unresolved conflict between Price and McCulloch. Both would now be subject to the orders of Van Dorn, whose energy and dash promised a renewal of offensive operations in Missouri. Indeed, as Van Dorn traveled west in January, his thoughts were on the eventual capture of St. Louis. He discussed his plans for a Missouri campaign with General Johnston at Bowling Green, Kentucky, and he wrote his wife enthusiastically, "I must have St. Louis—then huzza!"[31]

The opportunities of August 1861 had faded, but as the new year began the northwestern limits of the Confederacy had still not been decided in battle. Martial enthusiasm remained high with the hope that the Confederate northwest frontier might yet lie along the Missouri River.

28 Benjamin to Bragg, January 5, 12, 1862, ibid., 794, 803.

29 Johnston to Benjamin, January 5, 1862, Benjamin to Johnston, January 12, 1862, ibid., vol. 7, 820-821, 826; Special Orders No. 8, Adj. and Insp. Gen. Office Richmond, January, 10, 1862, ibid., vol. 8, 734.

30 Special Orders No. 234, Adj. and Insp. Gen. Office, Richmond, November 22, 1861, ibid., 690; Walter Lee Brown, "Albert Pike, 1809-1891" (unpublished Ph.D. dissertation, University of Texas, 1955), 597-598, 623.

31 Castel, *Price*, 68; Robert G. Hartje, *Van Dorn: The Life and Times of a Confederate General* (Nashville, 1967), 105.

Chapter 4

Texas: The First Year

Texas, THE HEARTLAND of the Confederate Trans-Mississippi, received unified Confederate military command quite early, in April 1861. Even before this, however, important military steps had been taken by the secessionists.

Following adoption of an ordinance of secession by the State Convention on February 1, 1861, the secessionists were quick to seize military control of the state. After Ben McCulloch occupied San Antonio with a force of irregular Texas cavalry, Major General David E. Twiggs, the commander of the· Department of Texas, surrendered all United States forces and property in the state to the Convention on February 18. In addition to posts and public buildings and approximately $1,229,500 of quartermaster, commissary, and ordnance stores, the surrender included about 3,100 officers and men of the 1st, 3rd, and 8th Infantry Regiments, the 2nd Cavalry, and the 1st Artillery.[1]

Permitted to retain their small arms, these United States troops were required to leave the state by way of the Gulf Coast instead of overland lest they reassemble in New Mexico or Indian Territory. The posts they evacuated on the northwest frontier began to be occupied before the end of February by the First McCulloch Texas Mounted Rifles under Colonel Henry E. McCulloch, brother of Ben, and those on the lower Rio Grande by Colonel John S. "Rip" Ford's Second Texas Mounted Rifles.[2]

---

1 *San Antonio Herald*, February 23, 1861, quoted in *New York Times*, March 8, 1861; *New York Times*, February 27, 1861.

2 // There are many published sources on the Civil War in Texas. The following is a representative example of some sources that contain military history, perspectives on the social impact of the war, and the economic upheaval. See Ralph A. Wooster, *Civil War Texas* (College Station, 1999); Ralph Wooster and Robert Wooster, eds., *Lone Start Blue and Gray: Essays on Texas in the Civil War* (Austin, 2015); and Charles D. Grear, ed., *The Fate of Texas: The Civil War and the Lone Star State* (Fayetteville, 2008).

The problem of defending the land frontiers of the state was laid before the Confederate Secretary of War by the Texas delegation to the Provisional Confederate Congress in a letter dated March 30, 1861:

> Our frontiers may be divided into three sections, each presenting its peculiar aspect. 1st. That portion bounded by the Rio Grande, from the mouth of that river to New Mexico; 2nd, the frontier settlements in the state from Preston on Red River, to the Rio Grande; and 3rd, the northern boundary of the State on Red River, from the southwest corner of Arkansas up to Preston.[3]

The delegation recommended permanently garrisoning the army posts on the lower Rio Grande and maintaining a cavalry force on the upper Rio Grande where the settlements were subject to Indian depredations. For the second frontier, the land between the Rio Grande and Red River, the delegation recommended roving cavalry detachments capable of rapid concentration against marauding Indian bands that scattered too quickly to permit elaborate preparations for pursuit. The delegation saw no need for defenses along the Red River from Preston eastward, "as our neighbors on that line are highly civilized and agricultural tribes of Choctaws and Chickasaws, who are in friendship with Texas and the Confederate States."[4]

Though the Texas delegation did not mention the Gulf Coast, which constituted a sea frontier extending from Sabine Pass on the Louisiana border to Brazos Santiago near the Mexican border, much concern was felt within the state over the complete lack of coastal defenses, particularly at Galveston. Twelve guns captured at Fort Brown by Colonel Ford's state volunteers in February were mounted at Galveston shortly thereafter, and in March the State Convention authorized the erection of entrenchments at Sabine Pass, Matagorda Island, Aransas Pass, and Port Isabel.[5]

The inhabitants of north Texas were less confident of their security than was the Texas delegation at Montgomery. In consequence of many rumors of Union invasion from Kansas, 500 volunteer horsemen under Colonel William C. Young crossed the Red River on May 2 into Indian Territory. There, they were agreeably surprised to find that the three forts in the lower Territory—Washita, Arbuckle, and Cobb—had been abandoned shortly before by their Federal garrisons. The Chickasaws in the vicinity soon agreed that the Texas volunteers should garrison Forts Washita and Arbuckle until the arrival of Confederate troops. At Fort

---

3 John Hemphill and W. S. Oldham to Walker, March 30, 1861, in *Austin State Gazette*, May 27, 1861. Preston, an important Red River crossing in 1861, was in northern Grayson County a few miles northwest of present Denison. It was submerged in 1944 with the filling of Lake Texoma.

4 Ibid.

5 Alwyn Barr, "Texas Coastal Defense, 1861-1865," *Southwestern Historical Quarterly*, XLV (July, 1961), 1-4.

Earl Van Dorn. *NPS*

Cobb, the reserve Indians allied themselves with Colonel Young and promised to give warning of any United States expedition starting from Kansas for Texas.[6]

The new Confederate Department of Texas came about under orders of April 11, 1861, that directed Colonel Earl Van Dorn to assume the command. En route from New Orleans to San Antonio to take over, Van Dorn employed a number of volunteers he had recruited in Galveston to capture both the Union steamer *Star of the West* and several hundred Union troops waiting at Indianola to embark for the North. Immensely popular in Texas because of these exploits, Van Don assumed command of the Department at San Antonio on April 29. Soon afterward he rounded up at San Lucas Springs, sixteen miles west of San Antonio, the last contingent of Union troops in Texas, most of them men from the 8th United States Infantry on their way to the coast for evacuation. Their capture, like that of the other Federal troops, seemed to violate the terms granted by the state authorities to David Twiggs that February. Van Dorn, however, was a Confederate officer, and he considered the state agreement no longer in effect after the outbreak of hostilities between the United States and the Confederate States.[7]

6   *Austin State Gazette,* June 8, 15, 1861.

7   Hartje, *Van Dorn,* 83-85. // See also, Arthur B. Carter, *The Tarnished Cavalier: Major General Earl Van Dorn, CSA* (Knoxville, 1999), a more updated biography of Van Dorn than the one used by Dr. Geise. Carter utilized previously unpublished sources to portray the general in a different light, including more sordid aspects of his character. Scholars and buffs of the war will enjoy a recently published series of volumes with essays about generals in the Trans-Mississippi. Lawrence Lee Hewitt and Thomas E. Schott, eds., *Confederate Generals in the Trans-Mississippi: Essays on America's Civil War,* 4 volumes published to date (Knoxville, 2010-2019). Volume 3, in particular, contains an essay about Van Dorn's actions that pulls the curtain back even further on this ill-fated general. See Joseph G. Dawson III, "Major General Earl Van Dorn and "a Most Unpromising Field for Operations": Observations of Confederate Generalship in the Trans-Mississippi," 1-34.

When Van Dorn turned his attention to bringing the defenses of Texas under Confederate jurisdiction, the two lines he established on May 24 closely paralleled those previously set up by the state. Colonel Henry E. McCulloch's First Texas Mounted Rifles, now a Confederate regiment, was to be supported by a battery of field artillery and garrison the line from the Red River south to the junction of the Main and North Concho rivers (the site of present San Angelo). Colonel Ford's 2nd Texas Mounted Rifles, also being received into the Confederate Army, was to occupy the Rio Grande frontier. Ford's command was to be supported by a battery and a company of artillery, as well as a company of infantry. Lieutenant Colonel John R. Baylor, Ford's second in command, was to command temporarily the western end of the Rio Grande line running from Camp Wood (near present Leakey) to Fort Bliss.[8]

Colonel McCulloch's men on the frontier line extending south from the Red River were organized to make regular patrols that met at mid-point between the permanent stations, which were about one day's ride apart.[9] These troopers must have been reasonably well prepared for the duty assigned them if the enlistment requirements for one of the companies, that of Captain James Buckner Barry, were enforced throughout the unit. McCulloch had directed Barry to enlist only healthy men of good moral character between the ages of eighteen and forty-five. It was desirable that the recruit be a good shot and a good rider, and he must possess a suitable horse not more than ten years old. Each man was to have a Texas-style saddle and a saddle blanket, a Colt six-shooter, a double- barreled shotgun or short-barreled rifle, a heavy blanket, and a cloth-covered half-gallon canteen. In no case was a "known professional gambler or habitual drunkard" to be enlisted.[10] Concern for the soldiers' morality appears frequently in the correspondence of McCulloch's regiment; even playing of cards for entertainment, without stakes, was expressly prohibited.[11]

---

8 *Austin, State Gazette,* June 8, 1861.

9 William. W. Heartsill, *Fourteen Hundred and 91 Days in the Confederate Army; A Journal Kept by W, W. Heartsill for Four Years, One Month and One Day or Camp Life Day by Day of the W. P. Lane Rangers from April 19. 1861 to May 20. 1865* (1876; reprint edited by Bell Irvin Wiley; Jackson, Tennessee, 1954), 15. See also, 105 of James Buckner Barry, "Reminiscences," a typescript bound volume in Barry Papers, 1847-1947, Archives Collection, University of Texas Library.

10 McCulloch to Barry, March 27, 1861, Barry Papers.

11 Typescript copies in Barry Papers of Special Orders No. 44 appended to Special Orders No, 40, Hdqrs. 1st T.M.R., in the Field near Camp Cooper, June 18, 1861; Regimental Orders No. 12, Hdqrs. 1st T. M. R,, Camp Jackson, July 13, 1861; Regimental Orders No. 20, Hdqrs., 1st T .M. R., Fort Mason, Texas, December 5, 1861. Information that a certain Lieutenant Price had laid out a race track at Camp Cooper brought stern admonitions from McCulloch and a warning from McCulloch's second in command, Major Edward Burleson, that "This 'horse racing' and 'hog killing' business at your camp will be investigated at the proper time and by the proper tribunal." Captain Barry's explanation that the race track was intended to exercise the horses placated

In addition to performing their regular patrols, the troopers on this frontier were occasionally sent out in company or battalion strength to scout areas where Indian bands had been reported. The patrols triggered a number of severe Indian fights. One company of this regiment had the additional duty of guarding the Federal prisoners at Camp Verde about sixty miles west of San Antonio. These prisoners, members of the 8th U.S. Infantry who had been captured by Van Dorn, were treated with surprising leniency, having complete liberty within a quarter mile of the camp's flag pole. Many of McCulloch's troops appear to have suffered from extreme boredom in their isolated frontier stations and longed for the action and glory they felt were to be had east of the Mississippi River. Much of their considerable leisure time was spent hunting and fishing and, in spite of the regulations, gambling.[12]

The mission of Colonel Ford and his 2nd Texas Mounted Rifles on the line of the Rio Grande was more complicated than Colonel McCulloch's responsibilities because it involved Mexican relations, coastal defense, and frontier protection. Already well known in the Rio Grande Valley, Colonel Ford immediately set about cultivating friendly relations with the officials and merchants in Matamoros across the river from his headquarters at Brownsville. He also adopted a policy of treating Mexican-Americans and Mexicans residing north of the border as having the same interests as Anglo southerners and thus enlisted the support of important Mexican-American citizens. This policy served him particularly well in stamping out the roving bands of the anti-Confederate guerrilla chieftain Juan Nepomuceno Cortina, for it was Captain Santos Benevides and his Mexican-American company who defeated Cortina near Redmond's Ranch and ended the over-the-border raids of this guerrilla in 1861. Further, Benevides urged the Mexican general commanding the line of the Rio Grande to thwart any further efforts of Cortina that would create friction between the Confederates and Mexico.

Later, when the United States Navy blockaded Texas, Colonel Ford visited Matamoros to make arrangements to open up trade with Europe through that city. He also advised the

---

McCulloch, but he directed that the race track be disposed of since the horses had enough to do in drilling and scouting. Burleson to Barry, October 3, 1861; McCulloch to Barry, October 27, November 27, 1861, ibid.

12 DeWitt Clinton Thomas, Sr., "Reminiscences," 11-12. The "Reminiscences" are in the form of a typescript prepared by James B. Thomas, September 18, 1964 in the Archives Collection, University of Texas Library. Prior to August, these 8th U.S. Infantry prisoners were treated even more leniently. First quartered at San Pedro Springs in the vicinity of San Antonio, officers were restricted to the limits of the Confederacy, enlisted men to Bexar County. About the second week of July 1861 they were transferred to Camp Van Dorn on Salado Creek, also in the San Antonio area. There, they were restricted to a distance of one mile from camp. In late August they were moved to Camp Verde, where McCulloch's men guarded them, and late in the year they were dispersed to several frontier military posts. Most of them were eventually paroled. Leon Mitchell, Jr., "Prisoners of War in the Confederate Trans Mississippi" (unpublished Ph.D. dissertation, University of Texas, 1961), 4-9.

important cotton exporters Richard King and Mifflin Kenedy to put their vessels under Mexican registry, even though this precluded Confederate control of them, so that they would be free of Federal interference. Ford was keenly aware that supplies from abroad depended upon friendly Mexican neighbors, and that Mexican friendship, in turn, would be bolstered by a lucrative trade through Matamoros.

In the southeast along on the coast, Ford decided to abandon Brazos Island and strengthen Fort Brown at Brownsville. He reasoned that the island, which lacked fresh water, rations, and artillery, might be seized by a single United States revenue cutter, whereas Fort Brown could be put in condition to withstand a siege and protect the potentially valuable supply route into Mexico. Brush around the fort was cleared for fields of fire and repairs begun that included new protective works against artillery bombardment.[13]

To secure the far western end of the Rio Grande, as ordered by General Van Dorn, a battery of field artillery and four companies of Ford's regiment under Lieutenant Colonel John R. Baylor began occupying Fort Bliss in late June. Because of the great stretch of rugged and barren land separating Forts Brown and Bliss, Ford would have little if any communications with or control over these troops.[14]

The Union blockade of the Texas coast began with the appearance of the U. S. S. *South Carolina* off Galveston on July 2, 1861. The Union warship soon captured and armed three small schooners, allowing her captain to extend the blockade east to Sabine Pass. Apparently in response to popular demand for a strengthening of the Galveston defenses, Van Dorn requested three prominent citizens of the city—William Pitt Ballinger, John S. Sydnor, and M. M. Potter—to bear to Richmond an urgent appeal for six ten-inch Columbiads and six thirty-two pounders with the projectiles and other equipment necessary to serve them. Many months later, after an agonizing series of transportation breakdowns, some of these cannon would arrive at Galveston.[15]

*   *   *

MEANWHILE, ON JULY 8, a Confederate brigadier general named Henry H. Sibley had been ordered to Texas—not to supersede Van Dorn, who was now a brigadier, but rather to form an independent brigade of two full regiments of cavalry, a battery of howitzers, and

---

13 Discussion of Ford's activities in the Rio Grande Valley is based on an account in John Salmon Ford, *Rip Ford's Texas*, edited by Stephen B. Oates (Austin, 1963), 323-329.

14 Martin Hardwick Hall, *Sibley's New Mexico Campaign* (Austin, 1960), 25-26; Ford, *Rip Ford's Texas*, 326.

15 Barr, "Texas Coastal Defense," *Southwestern Historical Quarterly*, XLV, 7; M. M. Potter to his brother, July 24, 1861, William Pitt Ballinger Papers, Archives Collection, University of Texas Library; William P. Ballinger, Diary, August 7, 1861 - February 22, 1862 (type script copy), first entry, ibid.

Henry H. Sibley. *LOC*

whatever other units he felt necessary. Sibley's mission was to drive the Federals from New Mexico, where he was to establish a military government. Fresh from service in New Mexico as a United States Army officer, Sibley had convinced President Davis that a Confederate invasion there had every opportunity of success.[16]

By the second week of August Sibley had established his headquarters at San Antonio and had begun recruiting troops. Colonel Baylor's detachment of the 2nd Texas Mounted Rifles, meanwhile, already in New Mexico, had attacked and captured the superior Union forces of Major Isaac Lynde in the Mesilla Valley. From Mesilla, just above El Paso, on August 1 Baylor proclaimed all of New Mexico below the thirty-fourth parallel to be the Confederate Territory of Arizona and assumed the position of military governor.[17]

Sibley's activities appeared likely to strain the slender military resources of Texas. In June, the Richmond War Department had requisitioned twenty companies of Texas infantry from Van Dorn, presumably for service east of the river.[18] In July, Governor Clark of Texas had offered ten regiments of Texas volunteers to President Davis for service in the emergency in Missouri and Arkansas.[19] Other officers had received independent authorization from the War Department to raise units of one kind or another. As a result, Sibley's recruiting efforts constituted yet another drain on Texas manpower, especially since he had broadly interpreted his orders and had prudently decided to raise three regiments of cavalry instead of two. At the same time, concern was increasing in Texas over the weakly defended Gulf coast.

That Richmond was also concerned about the almost unprotected coastline seems evident from two military assignments made at this juncture. On August 14, Paul Octave

---

16 Cooper to Sibley, July 8, 1861, *OR*, vol. 4, 93; Hall, *Sibley's New Mexico Campaign*, 30-33. // See Jerry Thompson, *Confederate General of the West: Henry Hopkins Sibley* (College Station, 1996).

17 Ibid., 26-28.

18 Cooper to Van Dorn, June 12, 1861, *OR*, vol. 4, 91-92.

19 Austin, *Texas State Gazette*, July 27, 1861.

Hebert, a cousin of the Colonel Hebert commanding the 3rd Louisiana in Missouri, was appointed a brigadier general and directed by Secretary Walker to assume command of the Department of Texas, relieving Van Dorn, who had been ordered to report to Richmond immediately[20] and to turn over temporary command of the Department of Texas to the next senior officer. Thus, temporary department command devolved upon Colonel McCulloch of the 1st Texas Mounted Rifles at San Antonio. Walker asked Hebert to go first to Galveston and to devote special attention to the defenses of the Texas Coast.[21] He was given the assistance of Commander William W. Hunter of the Confederate States Navy to supervise construction of fortifications.

Hebert's selection was a logical one. The top graduate of the West Point class of 1840, he had also taught engineering at the Academy and had subsequently served in the Mexican War. As a former Chief Engineer of Louisiana and also a former governor of that state, he was well acquainted with the Gulf Coast and could be expected to pay close attention to the situation there.[22]

Indeed, Hebert's keen interest in that area, coupled with poor administration in Department Headquarters, produced an anomalous command situation in Texas for a time. Apparently, Hebert's first general order of September 18 regarding his assumption of command and returning McCulloch to his regiment was not published and distributed to the units of the Department.[23] A month later McCulloch at San Antonio wrote plaintively to the secretary of war that he continued to style himself "Commander of the Department of Texas" because Hebert had never formally assumed command, nor apparently even communicated with him.[24] Not until October 26 did General Hebert's headquarters staff at Galveston get around to acknowledging their mistake by issuing a new general order confirming the original one.[25]

Because of this oversight there were, in effect, two department commanders in Texas during September and October 1861. Hebert at Galveston paid no attention to interior Texas, although he issued a number of orders and proclamations concerning the coast.[26]

20 Special Orders No. 123, Adj. and Insp. Gen. Office, Richmond, August 14, 1861, *OR* vol. 4, 98.

21 Walker to Hebert, August 14, 1861, ibid., 97-98.

22 Allen Johnson, *et al*, eds., *Dictionary of American Biography* (22 vols. in 11, New York, 1957-1958), Part 2, Vol. IV, 492-493.

23 General Orders No. I, Galveston, September 18, 1861, *OR* vol. 4, 106.

24 McCulloch to Cooper, Headquarters, Department of Texas, San Antonio, October 17, 1861. ibid., 122-123.

25 General Orders No. 7, Military Department of Texas, Galveston, October 26, 1861, in General Orders, Department of Texas, October, 1861 – November, 1862, Chapter II, Vol. 112, Military Departments, Record Group 109, National Archives.

26 Orders Nos. 19 and 20, Military Department of Texas, Galveston, October 2, 1861, "To the Men of Texas," October 7, 1861, Hebert to Benjamin, October 24, 1861, *OR* vol. 4, 113, 115-116, 126-127.

McCulloch at San Antonio, meanwhile, was distressed at receiving no instructions from Hebert concerning Sibley. On September 20 McCulloch warned Hebert that supplying Sibley would nearly strip the department of quartermaster supplies and also of transportation unless Sibley's wagon trains were provided by contract.[27] Apparently, McCulloch received no answer to his complaints.

Sibley, too, was was troubled by the confusing situation. Shortly before his departure for New Mexico in November he reported to Richmond that his brigade was understrength because he had to compete with calls for men for regiments going east of the Mississippi. Because of Texas' fears of a coastal invasion, Sibley was also short of arms. The command structure in Texas compounded already existing problems. According to Sibley, there was for several weeks no responsible officer to issue his ordnance and other supplies. The department's assistant quartermaster and acting ordnance officer, Major Sackfield Maclin, had left the San Antonio headquarters to seek out the missing commanding general in Galveston, and not long afterward the erstwhile department commander, Colonel McCulloch, had gone to the same destination.[28]

Nonetheless, on November 18 Henry Sibley set out for New Mexico. Two of his regiments had already preceded him, and the third regiment was soon to follow. A casual observer, impressed by the appearance of the men, described one of the regiments on the march:

> I met the Second Regiment of Sibley's Brigade on their way from San Antonio. It made a grand appearance as the Horsemen filed past by twos . . . each company followed by its train of Wagons and the whole set off by the pretty little flags of two companies of lancers who rode in single file by the side of the other companies – The Regiment with its wagons, etc., strung along the road for at least a mile.[29]

By the time Sibley's regiments departed for New Mexico, General Hebert, still at Galveston, had become deeply pessimistic about his ability to hold the coast. He reported to Richmond that he would attempt to hold Galveston because of its value as a cotton port, but he added that because of shortages of men and arms, probably Galveston and the whole Texas coast were indefensible.[30]

Hebert had begun organizing the defenses of the city. He had created the Military District of Galveston on October 1 and placed Colonel John C. Moore in command of the

27 McCulloch to Hebert, September 20, 1861, ibid., 107-108.

28 Sibley to Cooper, November 16, 1861, ibid., 141-143; Hall, *Sibley's New Mexico Campaign*, 34-35.

29 Travis [Hensley] to Julia [Hensley], San Antonio, November 9, 1861, Hensley Beaumont Papers, Heirs of Julia Hensley Collection, Dallas Historical Society.

30 Hebert to Benjamin, October 24, November 15, 1861, *OR* vol. 4, 126-127, 139-140.

troops there, designated the First Brigade, Texas Volunteers.[31] By November, Hebert appears to have succeeded in raising a garrison of about 5,000 men. He also ordered his chief quartermaster to procure munitions in Mexico in exchange for cotton. He had also asked the citizens of Galveston to donate $5,000 to pay for building earthworks, and had the railroad bridge connecting with the mainland planked so that troops might be marched over it. Nevertheless, by November he estimated glumly that he needed at least 15,000 more men to defend the Texas coast and two additional general officers, one to command along the coast, and the other along the Rio Grande.[32]

In reality the coast stood in no great danger of major attack, nor would it for another year. Although small boat forays were attempted against isolated points, the United States naval forces then operating off the Texas coast were unimpressive. In September and October only the main channel at Galveston was blockaded, and that by one frigate. Neither the west entrance, with ten feet of water, nor the Brazos River mouth, which had six feet and gave access to Galveston by canal, were blockaded, and small vessels passed freely in and out. None of the Texas ports west of Galveston was blockaded.[33]

Hebert appears to have allowed his fears to render him ineffective as a commander. The new Texas governor, Francis R. Lubbock, who took office November 6, later explained that the general "appeared somewhat bewildered at the magnitude of the task assigned him and not to have matured, at least at the beginning of my administration, any definite line of policy."[34] Word of Hebert's pessimism had spread to the people of Galveston by late November and near panic prevailed in that city, as evidenced by a steady stream of families and furniture leaving by train and boat.[35]

While the people of the coast daily expected invasion from the sea, in north Texas strong rumors of an old threat—invasion from Kansas or Indian Territory—revived in November and December. Colonel William C. Young of the Eleventh Texas Cavalry was sufficiently disturbed to write directly to Secretary of War Judah P. Benjamin that Forts Washita, Cobb, and Arbuckle in Indian Territory were no longer occupied by troops and that nothing but some 3,000 reserve Indians stood between north Texas and the wild Comanches and the disaffected Creeks. Young feared that in the event of either a Unionist

31 Orders No. 19, Military Department of Texas, Galveston, October 2, 1861, General Orders No. 12, Headquarters, Military Department of Texas, Galveston, November 11, 1861, ibid., 113, 138.

32 Hebert to Benjamin, October 24, November 15, 1861, ibid., 127, 139-140.

33 Frank Lawrence Owsley, *King Cotton Diplomacy: Foreign Relations of the Confederate States of America* (Chicago, 1931), 258.

34 Francis Richard Lubbock, *Six Decades in Texas or Memoirs oi Francis Richard Lubbock, Governor of Texas in War-Time. 1861-1863: A Personal Experience in Business, War and Politics,* ed. by C. W. Raines (Austin, 1900), 346.

35 William P. Ballinger, Diary, November 29, 1861; Lubbock, *Six Decades,* 347.

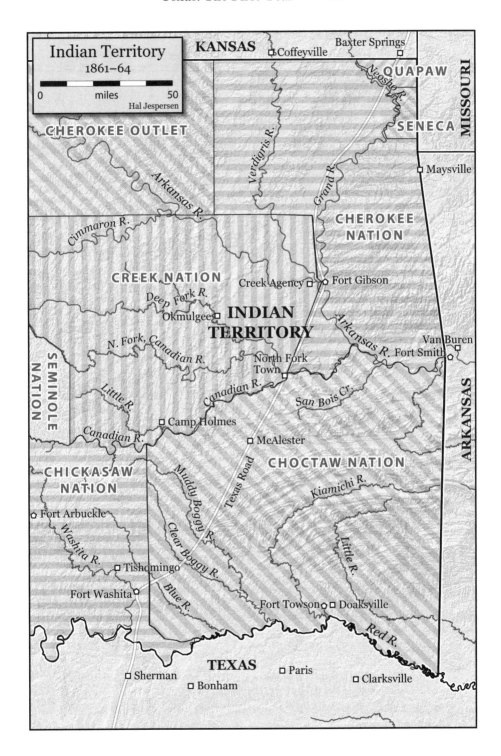

Indian Territory
1861–64

0   miles   50
Hal Jespersen

KANSAS
☐ Coffeyville
Baxter Springs ☐
QUAPAW
Neosho R.
MISSOURI
SENECA
CHEROKEE OUTLET
☐ Maysville
Verdigris R.
Arkansas R.
Grand R.
CHEROKEE NATION
Cimmaron R.
CREEK NATION
Creek Agency ☐ ☐ Fort Gibson
Deep Fork R.
Okmulgee ☐ INDIAN TERRITORY
N. Fork, Canadian R.
Arkansas R. Fort Smith
Van Buren ☐
North Fork Town ☐
SEMINOLE NATION
Little R.
Canadian R.
San Bois Cr.
ARKANSAS
Camp Holmes ☐
☐ McAlester
Canadian R.
CHOCTAW NATION
Kiamichi R.
CHICKASAW NATION
Muddy Boggy R.
Texas Road
Little R.
☐ Fort Arbuckle
Washita R.
Clear Boggy R.
☐ Tishomingo
Blue R.
Fort Washita ☐
Fort Towson ☐ ☐ Doaksville
Red R.
TEXAS   ☐ Paris
☐ Sherman   ☐ Clarksville
☐ Bonham

Opothleyahola. *Oklahoma Historical Society*

or a Comanche invasion, the reserve Indians, instead of standing, would be stampeded upon north Texas, adding fury and momentum to the advance.[36]

The anxiety in northern Texas was generated by Confederate difficulties with Opothleyahola and his dissident Creeks in the Indian Territory and by the activities of Senator James H. Lane of Kansas. Opothleyahola, an old and revered chief, was the leader of the Unionist Creek faction and his home in the Creek Nation had become a rallying point for large numbers of dissident Creeks and Seminoles within the Indian Territory. By early November, several thousand persons had gathered there. When he learned that Confederate Colonel Douglas H. Cooper planned to attack his camp, Opothleyahola organized his people and led them in flight toward Kansas. Cooper followed in hot pursuit with Texans and Indian troops. A series of savage skirmishes between Cooper's men and the Indians broke and scattered Opothleyahola's forces, ending all threat from them by mid-December.

Senator Lane, who had consistently urged the invasion of Texas, traveled in late November to Washington, where he seems to have convinced President Abraham Lincoln, Secretary of War Edwin M Stanton, and Major General George B. McClellan of the practicality of invading the Lone Star State from Kansas. Soon thereafter, the Little Rock *Daily State Journal* reported that Lane had been assigned 20,000 men and even named three of the regiments said to be involved. That Lane's scheme was favorably received in Washington seems to have been true, but it never materialized. The Union commander in Kansas was too concerned with protecting his isolated department to approve a Jayhawking expedition into Texas. Nevertheless, Lane's rumored activities during the winter of 1861 and 1862 kept the frontier people of north Texas on edge.[37]

---

36 Young to Benjamin, November 3, 1861, *OR* vol. 4, 144-145. // Benjamin had replaced Walker as secretary of war on September 17, 1861.

37 Albert Castel, *A Frontier State at War: Kansas, 1861-1865* (Ithaca, 1958), 78-79; Little Rock *Daily State Journal*, January 25, 1862. // Jayhawkers were anti-slavery guerrilla fighters from Kansas.

In far west Texas, meanwhile, Sibley energetically carried forward his plans for the conquest of New Mexico. At Fort Bliss on December 14 he assumed command of all Confederate forces in far west Texas and the territories of Arizona and New Mexico and grandly designated his command the Army of New Mexico. Sibley proclaimed martial law, and in a general order on December 20, directed that Colonel Baylor continue as military and civil governor of Arizona.[38] Characteristically, Sibley failed to notice that in assuming to command at and above Fort Quitman, Texas, he was infringing upon Colonel McCulloch's newly created Western Military District of Texas. This oversight, of a type all too common in Confederate military administration, fortunately created no friction between the two commanders, for McCulloch in distant San Antonio could have no real control over the region.[39]

Colonel Baylor, who had been in New Mexico for some months, boasted in a letter home to his wife after Sibley's arrival, "There is Texians enough here to eat up all the Yankees in New Mexico."[40] Unfortunately for Sibley and the Confederacy, Baylor's quip did not remain true, for more Yankees soon arrived. Initially, however, Sibley succeeded in occupying both Santa Fe and Albuquerque, and one of his detachments even held distant Tucson.

A defeat in late March 1862 at Glorieta Pass crippled Sibley's effort, and in April Union forces thwarted his attempts to capture the key posts of Fort Union and Fort Craig. By April 11, Sibley was slowly retreating from New Mexico with his haggard men much in want of food and clothing. The shortages his troops had suffered at the beginning of the expedition plagued them to the end, for no provision had been made for resupply of his troops from the Department of Texas.[41]

Along the other frontiers of Texas, defensive preparations advanced but slightly during the first months of 1862. On the Gulf Coast, an additional five cannon—probably the weapons procured by the Ballinger-Sydnor-Potter mission to Richmond—were mounted that January.[42] At Pass Cavallo, the entrance to Matagorda Bay, a detachment of 180 Confederates served and guarded a battery of four twenty-four pounders, two twelve-

---

38 Hall, *Sibley's New Mexico Campaign*, 45-46; General Orders No. 12, Hdqrs. Amy of New Mexico, A.G.O., Fort Bliss, Texas, December 20, 1861, *OR* vol. 4, 159.

39 B. E. Benton to McCulloch, December 31, 1861, ibid., 164.

40 Baylor to his wife, January 12, 1862, typescript copy in volume titled "Miscellaneous Personal Letters," John R. Baylor Transcripts, Archives Collection, University of Texas Library.

41 // Sibley's command fought with Union forces under Brigadier General John P. Slough at the Battle of Glorieta Pass (March 26-28) and had to retreat after cavalry destroyed the Confederate wagon train that held most of Sibley's supplies and ammunition. For more on this small but decisive battle, see Don E. Alberts, *The Battle of Glorieta: Union Victory in the West* (Texas A & M Univ Press, College Station, TX, 1998).

42 Barr, "Texas Coastal Defense," *Southwestern Historical Quarterly*, XLV, 8.

pounders, and one six-pounder.[43] Sabine Pass was protected by a small fort containing two old twelve-pounders captured in the Mexican War and two eighteen-pounders.[44] Although a few other places along the Texas coast were guarded by a field piece or two, the places mentioned comprised the principal strong points. Considering how woefully weak they were, it was fortunate for the Confederacy that the Lincoln administration did not mount an invasion.

The main Federal objective along the lengthy Gulf of Mexico coast would of course prove to be New Orleans, Louisiana. Indeed, by February 1862 the Confederate high command was so sure the Texas coast would not be invaded that it directed General Hebert to remove all troops not actually serving guns and send them forthwith to General Van Dorn, who was by this time at Little Rock, Arkansas, commanding the Trans-Mississippi District of the Western Department.[45]

After almost a year of patrolling the Indian frontier between Red River and the Rio Grande, the men of Colonel Henry McCulloch's old regiment, the First Texas Mounted Rifles, began concentrating at Fredericksburg, Texas, for their discharge in late March, their term of service having expired. Their place on the frontier had been assumed by the Frontier Regiment of Texas State Troops, an organization authorized by the state legislature in December 1861. The dates of discharge of the various companies of the Mounted Rifles differed because of different dates of original muster. Consequently, some four companies of the regiment were still stationed at Fort Mason when news of the Confederate Conscription Act of April 16 finally reached them. Their anger at having their voluntary term of service extended by compulsion culminated in a two-week mutiny at that post. Their outrage seems to have subsided gradually, without coercion, after an election of new officers.[46]

Along the lower Rio Grande the military situation changed very little, but the small villages of Brownsville, Texas, and Matamoros, Mexico, were transformed into bustling centers of supply. In April of 1862, a traveler in Brownsville observed a great many people from interior Texas gathered in the town with plenty of cotton to sell. Twenty-four large foreigner merchantmen lay at anchor off the mouth of the Rio Grande waiting to exchange

---

43 Lester N. Fitzhugh, "Saluria, Fort Esperanza and Military Operations on the Texas Coast, 1861-1864," *Southwestern Historical Quarterly*, LXI (July, 1957), 69.

44 K. D. Keith, "Military Operations, Sabine Pass, 1861-63," *Burke's Texas Almanac and Immigrant's Handbook for 1883, With Which is Incorporated Hanford's State Resister* (Houston, 1883), reprinted in Program of Sixty-Seventh Annual Meeting, Texas State Historical Association, April 26-27, 1963.

45 Benjamin to Hebert, February 23, 1862, *OR* vol. 6, 830.

46 James Buckner Barry, "Reminiscences," 105-1/2; T. C. Frost to Barry, April 11, 1862, Barry Papers.

their cargoes for Southern cotton, and Confederate notes were being discounted 40 percent, the Brownsville merchants in their newfound prosperity preferring specie.[47]

The Texas Military Board, which had been established as a war financing body in January of 1862, began to function as a supply agency by appropriating 2,000 to 4,000 bales of cotton on April 29 to be used to purchase arms, ammunition, clothing, accouterments, and medical supplies in Mexico. Apparently their agent, John Marks Moore, was highly successful in locating the desired items, and all but the Mexican gunpowder proved to be of good usable quality. In this way, a source of supply had thus been opened up across the Rio Grande.[48]

During a year of war Texas had sent out troops that provided good and needed service elsewhere, but the state itself remained militarily weak and almost defenseless on its multiple frontiers.[49] Fortunately for the Confederacy, no serious military threat had materialized during that time frame. The department had suffered from a confusion of purposes and a lack of firm overall military leadership. General Hebert, who was more suited by experience for an engineer staff assignment than for a complicated field command, appears to have been an ineffective martinet. He was personally unpopular with both troops and citizens, and obviously unequal to his task.[50]

What was probably the most ill-advised early decision relating to Texas, however, was made not by Hebert within the state but by President Davis in distant Richmond. It was the chief executive who allowed General Sibley to mount his fruitless and costly expedition into New Mexico, an effort that may well have affected adversely the entire Trans-Mississippi West.[51]

47 Travis Hensley to wife, Brownsville, April 3, 13, 1862, Hensley Beaumont Papers.

48 F. R. Lubbock, Governor and President Military Board, to Moore, April 29, 1862 and Moore to Honorable Investigating Committee of the Military Board, November 3, 1862, John Marks Moore Papers,1838-1925, Dallas Historical Society.

49 // This was a common theme throughout the war in the Trans-Mississippi in which the Confederate government routinely stripped the states west of the river of men and resources for the purpose of bolstering the armies in Virginia and Tennessee to the east. This decision led to discontent among the citizens of the Trans-Mississippi states, and their political leaders took note expressing their dissatisfaction with the government in Richmond. At times the Davis administration feared that the western Confederate states might themselves secede from the Confederacy.

50 // This is another recurring problem west of the river. Poor military leadership plagued the region and it became a dumping ground for generals who failed in action east of the river.

51 // Dr. Geise is among the first scholars to point this out as it pertains to the Trans-Mississippi region. Allowing Sibley to attempt an offensive in the far West adversely affected the fate of the Trans-Mississippi, especially the effort to hold Missouri for the Confederacy and prevent the Union forces from using the Mississippi River as a highway of invasion. The Confederate policy of dispersing forces across various points was at odd with concentration, and represented a dilemma for the central government. Should the Davis administration attempt to defend every mile of

Confederate Senator Williamson S. Oldham of Texas thought as much and commented about the decision not long after the war:

> But if one will look at the map, a glance will satisfy him that the field of contest for the possession of Arizona and New Mexico was Missouri. Had the Confederate States succeeded in the struggle and held Missouri, the territory west of that state, even including Kansas, would necessarily have gone with that state. To hold Missouri required a concentration of the forces west of the Mississippi. It has always seemed to me, that our authorities by some means had inverted a primary military principle "concentrate your forces and fight the enemy's detachments," for in most cases we fought the enemy concentrated with our detachments.[52]

Senator Oldham's last comment was particularly applicable to the Trans-Mississippi operations. The concept of concentration of force at crucial points was an old and tried one in warfare, but the almost indispensable prerequisite, which Oldham did not mention, was unity of command. Effective concentration normally requires a single chain of command to a competent and energetic commander. In Missouri and Arkansas, the chain was lacking and command chaos had rendered concentration of force impossible until the assignment of Van Dorn to the area in February of 1862. In Texas, a single chain of command did exist almost from the beginning, but the general in charge (Hebert) lacked the necessary competence and energy.[53]

Confederate territory, or concentrate in a specific area? As seen in the previous note, when the administration did shift forces east of the river, the population and political leaders in the West felt ignored. However, an attempt to defend everywhere would create a weakness that the stronger Union forces could (and did) exploit by punching a hole through the weakly held Confederate frontier. The Confederate national authorities never adequately resolved this dilemma.

52 William Simpson Oldham., "Memoirs." The "Memoirs," as here used, are a typescript volume in William S. Oldham Collection, 1843-1865, Archives Collection, University of Texas Library. // This is an astute observation by Senator Oldham.

53 // This last paragraph exhibits Dr. Geise's military experience. Poor command arrangements led to a lack of unity of command. Thus, Confederate leaders could not concentrate when required in a rapid manner. The author's experience enabled him to recognize this and emphasize the finer points of command that often make the difference between success and failure in military operations.

Chapter 5

Increasing Isolation and a New Command
in the Trans-Mississippi West
January 1862 – May 1862

In CONTRAST TO the slow passage of events during the first year of the war in Texas, the tempo on the northern Trans-Mississippi frontier quickened in late January 1862.

General Van Dorn formally assumed command of the Trans-Mississippi District on January 29, eager for an invasion of Missouri. Once he established his headquarters at Pocahontas, Van Dorn issued a series of orders to concentrate Confederate troops in Arkansas at Pitman's Ferry on the northeastern border. He cancelled all leaves and asked for strength and condition reports from all of his major units. In addition, he ordered General Albert Pike to march his troops from the Indian Territory to Lawrence County in southwestern Missouri to protect the lead mines there and to provide support for Sterling Price's Missourians at Springfield.[1] From Governor Henry M. Rector of Arkansas, Van Dorn requested ten infantry regiments and four companies of artillery as soon as possible. "With them I hope to guard this State of Arkansas—prevent invasion, and with the co-operation of troops from Texas, Louisiana, and Missouri," wrote the general, "I hope to drive the enemy from the down-trodden state of Missouri."[2]

Van Dorn outlined his plans to Price in letters dated February 7 and 14. Price, reinforced by McCulloch's infantry under the command of Colonel McIntosh, was to move northeast from Springfield while Van Dorn's troops, augmented by McCulloch's cavalry,

---

1 Castel, *Price*, 68; Special Orders Nos. 4-6, 9-11, Hdqrs. Trans-Miss. District, Dept, No. 2, Little Rock, Jacksonport, January 29, February 2, 7, 8, 1862, all in Maj. Gen. Earl Van Dorn's Command, January-May 1862, Chapter II, Vol. 210, Military Departments, Special Orders, Record Group 109, National Archives. 1862.

2 Little Rock *Daily State Journal,* January 31, February 2.

proceeded north from Pitman's Ferry. The two forces would combine near the Missouri village of Salem for a joint march on St. Louis. After the capture of city, outposts would be thrust across the Mississippi to the Illinois shore. Van Dorn set March 20 as the tentative date for the opening of his ambitious campaign.[3]

Despite the importance and boldness of his plan, Van Dorn remained singularly unconcerned about the concentration of enemy troops at Rolla, Missouri, under Major General Samuel Ryan Curtis. Van Dorn suggested merely that Price not stir up Curtis, or, alternatively, that Curtis be kept off balance until the two Southern commands could unite. Evidently Van Dorn did not know that Price had recently sent repeated and almost desperate warnings to Colonels Hebert and Mcintosh and to Governor Rector that the enemy was concentrating at Rolla to drive him from Springfield, and would do so if he were not immediately reinforced. Finally, on February 8 Price dispatched a similar warning to Van Dorn.[4]

It was already too late. Curtis began his advance on February 9, and three days later Price's outnumbered Missourians reluctantly abandoned Springfield without a fight and began falling back to Arkansas. In informing Van Dorn of this development on February 13, Price dryly remarked that Van Dorn would probably not be visiting Springfield on the 15th as he had intended.[5] Just below the state line Price's troops met advance elements of McCulloch's command marching to their support. In some confusion, McCulloch's oncoming Confederates reversed their direction and joined the Missourians in their withdrawal south.[6] A brief stop was made in Fayetteville, where the army warehouses were opened and some 500,000 pounds of pork, bacon, and ham were distributed to the hungry troops. Apparently the soldiers made warming fires of the food they could not eat or carry.[7] McCulloch and Price, not yet under Van Dorn's immediate control, took this brief opportunity to quarrel once more. McCulloch argued that all the remaining supplies should be burned, whereas Price contended that to do so would force the pursuing Federals to loot the surrounding countryside, which they subsequently did.[8]

---

3 Castel, *Price*, 68; Van Dorn to Price, February 7, 14, 1862, *OR* vol. 8, 748-752.

4 Price to Hebert, January 21, 26, 31, February 9, 1862; Price to McIntosh, January 26, 31, 1862; Price to Rector, January 31, 1862, Price to Van Dorn, February 8, 9, 1862, all in Mrs. Mason Barret Collection of Albert Sidney and William Preston Johnston Papers, 1803-1900, Tulane University Library.

5 Price to Van Dorn, February 13, 1862, ibid.

6 Many uncomplimentary remarks passed at this meeting. Missourians jeered at by members of the Third Louisiana for running retorted, "The Arkansas pickets are now driven in, and they [the Louisianians] would have to fight." No doubt many of the Missourians felt as if they had been serving merely as an outpost line to protect the Confederates in Arkansas. Anderson, *Memoirs*, 156.

7 Rose, *McCulloch*, 199.

8 Knox, *Campfire and Cottonfield*, 128-129.

The Confederates continued their retreat until February 22, when they reached the Boston Mountains. Here McCulloch made camp next to the telegraph road to Van Buren with Price camped three miles to the west. The aggressive Federal pursuit had provoked almost daily cavalry skirmishes, but Curtis halted at Fayetteville and prudently withdrew his main body north of Sugar Creek to a strong natural position at the base of Pea Ridge. On March 1, the Union troops began throwing up field fortifications. Advance Federal elements were left at Cross Hollows and at Bentonville.

Van Dorn at Pocahontas, meanwhile, learned on February 22 of Price's withdrawal. Two days later he set out to take personal command in northwest Arkansas. He had already decided that if he succeeded in repulsing Curtis he would "push on," presumably to St. Louis.[9] He arrived at Price's headquarters on March 2 and assumed command of the combined armies of Price and McCulloch, which he promptly named the "Army of the West." Although McCulloch's troops seem to have received Van Dorn with little enthusiasm, Price's Missourians turned out to provide cheers, a band, and a forty-gun salute for the occasion.[10]

At a strategy conference the next day, the cautious Ben McCulloch presented a plan calculated to achieve Confederate success in northwestern Arkansas with minimum risk. Curtis's army was wholly dependent for resupply on the wagon trains shuttling steadily from the Rolla railhead to the Springfield supply base and thence to Arkansas. McCulloch proposed that he take most of the cavalry, some 5,000 strong, and destroy the wagons en route to Curtis from Springfield. After that, the cavalry might raid Springfield, destroy the supply base there, and then fall on the wagon trains moving south from Rolla. Van Dorn's main body, meanwhile, would remain on the defensive and avoid a general engagement until the cavalry's return, at which time Curtis's demoralized and hungry army could be attacked with every chance of success.[11] As a lifetime cavalryman Van Dorn should have appreciated this proposal for a classical utilization of the speed and mobility of cavalry. Instead, he seems to have been obsessed with the idea of an immediate crushing attack upon Curtis with every man of his command.[12]

9 Castel, *Price*, 68-69; Van Dorn to Colonel W. W, Mackall, February 24, 1862, *OR* vol. 8, 755.

10 Castel, *Price*, 69-70; Rose, *McCulloch*, 200.

11 Rose, *McCulloch*, 224. For Union evidence that shortages left some of Curtis's soldiers threadbare and shoeless in the freezing weather at this time, see David Lathrop, *The History of the Fifty-Ninth Regiment, Illinois Volunteers . . .* (Indianapolis, 1865), 88.

12 // The phrase "lifetime cavalryman" is a bit of a misnomer. Though Van Dorn was a cavalryman in the United States Army when he resigned his commission to offer his services to his native state of Mississippi, he had become a cavalry officer a mere six years previous. Van Dorn's poor standing at West Point earned him a commission as an infantryman upon graduation from the academy in 1842. Before transferring to the cavalry in 1855, Van Dorn spent thirteen years as an infantryman including service in the Mexican War and Third Seminole War. His superb service

McCulloch's suggestion was not adopted, and on March 4 Van Dorn set in motion his entire Confederate command toward the enemy. The main body, consisting of Price's and McCulloch's troops, marched in heavy snow up the Van Buren-Fayetteville Telegraph Road. Albert Pike's Indian Brigade paralleled the main body on adjacent roads to the west, joining up in the vicinity of Elm Springs north of Fayetteville. It is not within the scope of this study to detail the tactics of Pea Ridge. Van Dorn sought a battle of annihilation by flanking Curtis to the north in an attempt to get astride his line of retreat. The fighting that followed just a few miles below the Missouri border included some 26,500 combatants. For multiple reasons, not the least of which were Van Dorn's failures to reconnoiter properly and keep his army well in hand, his plan faltered and the combatants ended with a two-day drawn battle. Southern losses totaling some 2,500 from all causes, including Ben McCulloch and James McIntosh, both of whom had been killed. Curtis suffered nearly 1,400 casualties. Running low on ammunition and supplies, Van Dorn decided to leave the field to his enemy. The result was a major Confederate strategic defeat.[13]

Van Dorn's bedraggled army retreated slowly to Van Buren. Most of the men reached that town within about ten days. They suffered severely from the cold, many of them sorely missing the coats and blankets they had dropped when they stripped for action on March 7. Many were nearly starved, and they straggled widely from their units in search of food. As one witness of that retreat later remarked, "everything like military order of march was at an end."[14] Fortunately, Van Buren contained a well-stocked commissary. There the soldiers also found their missing quartermaster wagons with the blankets, tents, and other camp utensils left behind on the eve of battle.

Luckily for the defeated Rebels, Curtis's army was also disorganized by Pea Ridge and in no condition to pursue them. Instead, Curtis's soldiers spent two days after the battle resting, burying the dead, and wandering about the deserted battlefield in search of

---

record in that branch earned him a billet in the vaunted 2nd Cavalry Regiment when it was formed in 1855.

13 Anderson, *Memoirs*, 176-181; S. B. Barron, *The Lone Star Defenders: A Chronicle of the Third Texas Cavalry, Ross' Brigade* (New York and Washington, 1908), 70; Wiley Britton, *The Civil War on the Border*, 2 vols. (New York, NY, 1899), vol 1, 256-274; Castel, *Price*, 75-76; Washington Lafayette Gammage, *The Camp, the Bivouac and the Battlefield: Being a History of the Fourth Arkansas Regiment from its First Organization Down to the Present Date* (Little Rock, AR, 1958), 26; Lathrop, *Fifty-Ninth Illinois*, 95; Rose, *McCulloch*, 210-211; William Watson, *Life in the Confederate Army* (New York, NY, 1888), 303-305. // For an excellent single source study on the battle of Pea Ridge, see William L. Shea and Earl J. Hess, *Pea Ridge: Civil War Campaign in the West* (Chapel Hill, 1992). Shea and Hess disagree with the consensus view that the battle was a tactical stalemate. They provide a thorough assessment of the action from a tactical and a strategic level in the concluding chapter on pages 307-318. I agree with Shea and Hess that Van Dorn's decision to leave Curtis in control of the field was an acknowledgment of his tactical defeat. The authors clearly state on page 282 that the battle of Pea Ridge was a "stunning tactical" Union victory in addition to a strategic triumph.

14 Watson, *Life in the Confederate Army*, 320.

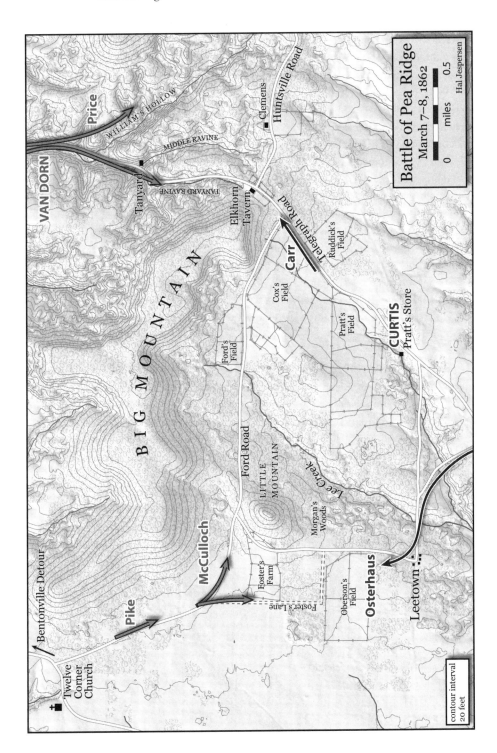

Battle of Pea Ridge
March 7–8, 1862

Hal Jespersen

0   miles   0.5

contour interval
20 feet

souvenirs. Curtis withdrew his army northward just above the Missouri border for additional rest and reorganization. Van Dorn's retreat left Arkansas virtually defenseless, and Union forces now controlled the border state of Missouri, and would for the next two years.[15]

Van Dorn spent the time at Van Buren patching up his battered army, restoring its spirits, and preparing it for future field operations. There was even time for ceremony, during which the bodies of McCulloch and McIntosh were given elaborate military burials in the Fort Smith government cemetery.[16]

Van Dorn assumed that, rather than having suffered a significant defeat, he had been only temporarily thwarted at Pea Ridge and had actually struck a paralyzing blow against the enemy. On March 18, he wrote General Johnston that he intended to strike the enemy again at New Madrid in order to relieve General Beauregard across the river, or, if that proved unfeasible, to march on St. Louis.[17] Van Dorn was not simply boasting. His Army of the West remained essentially intact, and the morale of his soldiers was by no means broken by the heavy fighting at Pea Ridge. Moreover, Curtis's withdrawal to Missouri, where he would spend almost a month recuperating, allowed Van Dorn sufficient time to reorganize and redeploy his army. Before the end of March Van Dorn had moved his headquarters to Jacksonport and begun preparations to move his army to the Pocahontas-Pitman's Ferry neighborhood, which he had selected as the assembly area for a drive into southeastern Missouri.

It was all for naught. Van Dorn set his cherished plans for an invasion of Missouri in motion but was obliged to drop them abruptly because of Union pressures in Tennessee. The Confederate situation east of the Mississippi was a desperate one. The fall of Forts Henry and Donelson in mid-February resulted in the collapse of General Albert Sidney Johnston entire extended front and the abandonment of Nashville, which fell later that same month. On March 23, Johnston ordered Van Dorn to move his entire command immediately by the shortest possible route to Memphis.[18]

The effect of the receipt of this directive was vividly illustrated in Van Dorn's own orders. On March 28 he directed four officers to reconnoiter the routes to Pocahontas, paying particular attention to their suitability for moving large bodies of men and heavy artillery pieces. These orders were abruptly revoked and they were instead instructed to

15 Lathrop, *Fifty-Ninth Illinois*, 95-101; Knox, *Campfire and Cottonfield*, 145.

16 General Order, Fort Smith, Arkansas, March 9, 1862, photostat in McCulloch Papers, Archives Collection, University of Texas Library; Order of Proceedings, Fort Smith, Arkansas, March 10, 1862, ibid.; *William Edward Woodruff, With the Light Guns in '61-'65: Reminiscences of Eleven Arkansas, Missouri and Texas Light Batteries in the Civil War* (Little Rock, 1903), 65. The body of McCulloch was subsequently disinterred and re-buried with at Austin on April 10, 1862. See Austin *Texas State Gazette*, April 12, 1862.

17 Van Dorn to Johnston, March 18, 1862, *OR* vol. 8, 789-790.

18 Johnston to Van Dorn, March 23, 1862, ibid., Vol. 10, Pt. II, 354; Castel, *Price*, 81.

select campsites and suitable embarkation areas at Des Arc and Duval's Bluff on the White River.[19] No time was wasted in transporting the Army of the West to the east side of the Mississippi. Most of the troops in the Van Buren-Fort Smith area started for the embarkation points about April 1. A number of units unable to reach Des Arc or Duval's Bluff because of high water were embarked at Little Rock.[20] All cavalry commands enlisted for only twelve months were ordered dismounted (in effect converted to infantry), the reasons assigned being insufficient transport and forage. Their horses, wagons, and teams were to be conducted by the least fit officers and men of each regiment or battalion to depots to be established along Red River.[21]

In addition to moving the entire Army of the West, as much military material as possible would also be transported across the Mississippi. All ordnance stores were to be removed from the arsenal at Little Rock, and the movable machinery transferred to Vicksburg. The quartermaster at Little Rock had orders to send to Memphis all good quartermaster wagons, camp, and garrison equipment. Everything unserviceable was consigned to the depots along the Red River. After reserving 50,000 rations for troops passing through Arkansas on their way east, the commissary at Little Rock was to ship remaining stores to Memphis. Even the surgeons in charge of the hospitals at Little Rock—almost the only military installations left along the Arkansas River—were directed to forward their recovered patients as quickly as possible to the army east of the Mississippi.[22]

Arkansas was being practically stripped of all immediately available military resources, Two Arkansas militia companies were ordered to patrol along the White and the Black rivers and would receive Confederate logistical support from Little Rock. Apparently the only

19 Special Orders Nos. 36 and 37, Trans-Miss. Dist., Jacksonport, March 28, 1862, both in Maj. Gen. Earl Van Dorn's Command, January-May, 1862, Chapter II, Vol. 210, Military Departments, Special Orders, Record Group 109, National Archives.

20 Anderson, *Memoirs*, 187-190; Barron, *Lone Star Defenders*, 79; Gammage, *Camp, Bivouac and Battlefield*, 35; Watson, *Life in the Confederate Army*, 339-340.

21 Special Orders No. 43, Hq. Trans-Miss. Dist., Des Arc, April 8, 1862, in Maj. Gen. Earl Van Dorn's Command, January-May, 1862, Chapter II, Vol. 210, Military Departments, Special Orders, Record Group 109, National Archives. A little more than a month after the dismounting of these units a report, "Confederate States Forces, General Braxton Bragg commanding Army of the Mississippi," June 30, 1862, *OR*, vol. 10, Pt. 1, 789-790, which designates units including dismounted cavalry but not strength figures, shows what appears to be twelve regiments and one battalion of dismounted cavalry in the Army of the West east of the Mississippi. Comparing unit designations in this report with the unit designations and strength figures given in Oates, *Confederate Cavalry West of the River*, 37 would seem to indicate that roughly 6,000 of the 11,601 cavalrymen crossing the river were dismounted.

22 Special Orders No. 39, 48, 51, 52, Hq. Trans-Miss. Dist., Des Arc, April 5, 11, 14, 15, 1862. All are in Maj. Gen. Earl Van Dorn's Command, January-May, 1862, Chapter II, Vol. 210, Military Departments, Special Orders, Record Group 109, National Archives.

regular Confederate troops left in the state were a few units in the process of forming.[23] Brigadier General John Selden Roane was left in command at Little Rock, but his assignment orders implied that his principal responsibilities were to forward promptly troops then en route from Texas and elsewhere to the army east of the river, and to establish the Red River depots and collect animals, wagons, and stores in them.[24]

On the western boundary of Arkansas remained the forces under Albert Pike, some 3,400 men available for duty. Pike, however, insisted that Indian Territory was a separate department and that he was responsible only for its defense. Van Dorn ordered him to protect northwestern Arkansas, and assigned additional troops coming up from Texas to do so. Instead of obeying Van Dorn's order, Pike withdrew south through Indian Territory before finally stopping at Nail's Bridge on the Blue River some forty miles north of Sherman, Texas. Supplies there adequate, and Pike claimed he could command the roads north to Forts Smith, Gibson, Washita, Arbuckle, and Cobb, and south to Sherman, Bonham, and Preston, Texas. Just west of the river crossing on the Missouri-Texas Road he erected field fortifications named Fort McCulloch in honor of the fallen officer.[25]

As noted, it was the beleaguered Albert Sidney Johnston in Tennessee who made the strategic decision that removed Van Dorn's army from Arkansas. Johnston explained to President Davis that he had not approved Van Dorn's plan for an advance to New Madrid because of the nature of the country between Jacksonport and New Madrid and the lack of subsistence there. Van Dorn, he continued, was not menaced by an enemy in Arkansas and would be of more immediate use at Memphis. Johnston might well have been influenced in his decision by the views of his subordinates, Generals Beauregard and Bragg, for at least a month earlier both officers had strongly expressed their convictions that the military requirements of other areas had to be subordinated to the defense of the Mississippi Valley in Kentucky and Tennessee.[26]

---

23 John M. Harrell, "Arkansas," in Clement A. Evans, ed., *Confederate Military History*, 12 vols. (Atlanta, 1899), vol. X, 97; Woodruff, *With the Light Guns*, 66.

24 Special Orders No. 45, Des Arc, April 9, 1862, in Maj. Gen. Earl Van Dorn's Command, January-May, 1862, Chapter II, Vol. 210, Military Departments, Special Orders, Record Group 109, National Archives.

25 Brown, "Pike," 673-678; Harrell, "Arkansas," *Confederate Military History*, X, 98.

26 Johnston to the President, March 25, 1862, *OR* vol. 10, pt. II, 361; Bragg to Benjamin, February 15, 1862, ibid., vol. 6, 826-827; Beauregard to S. Cooper, February 23, 1862, First Inclosure, "Confidential Circular," February 21, 1862, ibid., vol. 7, 899-900. // This decision following on the heels of the defeat at Pea Ridge ceded Missouri and Arkansas to the Union by enabling their forces to eventually isolate the Trans-Mississippi Confederacy and most of its resources. The decision is questionable because Van Dorn did not reach Johnston's army in time to help him with active operations in general, and his attack at Shiloh in early April in particular. Further, the decision to strip the Trans-Mississippi District was politically fraught. The governors of these states felt deserted by Richmond and were less enthusiastic about support the Confederacy going forward.

Johnston's explanation was probably acceptable to Richmond for both the president and the secretary of war had already endorsed the idea that most of the resources of the Gulf Coast and western areas were needed in Tennessee. Troops from western Virginia, the Department of Alabama and West Florida, Department Number One, and the Department of Texas had already been ordered there by the War Department.[27] Johnston, however, had merely ordered Van Dorn's army to Tennessee; the details of the near-complete stripping of Arkansas's military materiel were probably worked out by Generals Beauregard and Van Dorn at a conference shortly after Van Dorn's receipt of Johnston's orders.[28]

With Arkansas apparently abandoned by the military forces of the Confederacy, near panic began sweeping the northern part of the state. General Curtis added to the fear by starting a new campaign. On April 30, advance elements of his army crossed the Arkansas border with the band playing "Arkansas Traveler" and proceeded southeast down the White River toward Batesville. On May 6, Curtis reported to Major General Henry W. Halleck from Batesville that because high water prevented any movement farther east, he now contemplated an attack on Little Rock. Halleck responded by ordering Curtis to Little Rock, where he was to assume the duties of military governor of Arkansas. On May 18, Curtis's troops began marching over washed-out roads toward the Arkansas capital.[29]

Not only was Arkansas being invaded, but the whole Confederate Trans-Mississippi was threatened with isolation by the almost complete Confederate loss of control of the lower Mississippi River in April and May. A clamor began west of the Mississippi for attention and assistance from Richmond, especially in Arkansas. As early as April 15, Senator Robert W. Johnson and four other prominent Arkansans petitioned President Davis to halt Van Dorn's evacuation of Arkansas, to return the military supplies already sent east of the river, and to unify all the Confederate states west of the Mississippi under one military department.[30]

Anne J. Bailey's article "The Abandoned Western Theater: Confederate National Policy Toward the Trans-Mississippi Region," in *Journal of Confederate History*, V (1990), 35-54, provides an excellent overview of how Confederate national policy abandoned the region and eventually led to the loss of the Mississippi Valley, as Dr. Geise duly notes.

27 Bragg to Benjamin, February 15, 1862, Benjamin to Bragg, February 8, 18, 1862, ibid., 823-824, 826-827, 828.

28 Beauregard to Van Dorn, March 23, 1862, Van Dorn to Johnston, March 29, 1862, ibid., vol. 10, Pt. II, 354, 371.

29 A Committee of the Regiment, *Military History and Reminiscences of the Thirteenth Regiment of Illinois Volunteer Infantry in the Civil War in the United States, 1861-1865* (Chicago, 1892), 176-188, 195-196. // General Halleck, who was in charge of the Department of Missouri, was given the states of Ohio and Kansas along with oversight of General Don C. Buell's Army of the Ohio in March of 1862, and his entire command was renamed the Department of the Mississippi.

30 Harrell, "Arkansas," *Confederate Military History*, X, 99-101. // The Arkansas senator's recommendation was indeed prescient.

Thomas C. Hindman. *LOC*

Arkansas governor Henry Rector was sufficiently alarmed to call for 4,500 state volunteers coupled with the threat to resort to state conscription if the quota were not filled by May 25. Rector was so incensed by the seeming abandonment of his state that he issued a proclamation threatening secession from the Confederacy on the grounds that Arkansas had been "placed . . . beyond the pale of protection."[31] President Davis, uneasy at this news, attempted on May 20 to counteract the discontent by urging Van Dorn to prepare an address to the people of his Trans-Mississippi District assuring them that as soon as General Halleck was checked in Tennessee, the Army of the West would return to protect them. The situation moved Davis to suggest that Sterling Price, whom he mistrusted, sign the address as well as Van Dorn.[32]

Meanwhile, an Arkansas delegation had visited General Beauregard at the headquarters of his Western Department in Corinth, Mississippi. On May 26, at their "earnest solicitation," Beauregard directed Major General Thomas C. Hindman, a citizen of Arkansas, to assume command of the Trans-Mississippi District of the Western Department. The energetic Hindman began his journey to Arkansas almost immediately, pausing at Memphis, Helena, and Napoleon to pick up $1,000,000 in Confederate currency and various military supplies. Hindman utilized a direct supply method within his district: whatever he needed, he impressed. By May 31 he had established his headquarters at Little Rock, and soon his firm, even heavy, hand would be felt throughout Arkansas.[33]

---

31 Ibid.; Huff, "Military Board in Confederate Arkansas," *Arkansas Historical Quarterly*, XXVI, 88; Lubbock, *Six Decades*, 388-389.

32 Davis to Van Dorn, May 20, 1862, in Jefferson Davis Collection, Louisiana Historical Association Collection, Tulane University Library.

33 General Orders No. 59, Headquarters, Western Department, May 26, 1862, *OR*, vol. 10, Pt. II, 547; *Thirteenth Illinois Volunteer Infantry*, 194; Harrell, "Arkansas," *Confederate Military History*, X, 103-104. // See Dianne Neal and Thomas W. Kremm, *The Lion of the South: General Thomas C. Hindman* (Macon, Georgia, 1997) for more on General Hindman's career including his efforts to shore up

Paul Octave Hebert. *LOC*

However, much the assignment of Hindman might serve to allay the fear and to improve the Confederate military posture in Arkansas, it could not solve the problem of near-isolation that faced the Trans-Mississippi as a whole. Even before the assignment of Hindman the Arkansans were joined in their demands by leaders in the other Trans-Mississippi states. While on a mission to Richmond, Guy M. Bryan, an influential Texan who was aide-de-camp to Brigadier General Paul Octave Hebert and a nephew of Stephen F. Austin, urged in a letter to the Texas Delegation in the Confederate Congress that Texas, Arkansas, and Louisiana be combined in a single department under a competent senior general with a major general to command in each state. Because of the increasing difficulty of communication across the river, he added, branches of the War and Treasury departments ought to immediately be established west of the Mississippi.[34]

At almost the same time, Governor Thomas O. Moore of Louisiana began to insist that something be done. The fall of New Orleans in late April 1862 had created a situation of the utmost gravity in Louisiana. The parishes above that city on the west bank of the river lay almost completely exposed to Federal depredations. Moreover, Union admiral David G. Farragut's naval operations along the river threatened to soon cut all communication between eastern and western Louisiana as well as between northern Louisiana and Mississippi. Alarmed by these developments, Governor Moore telegraphed President Davis on May 4 to suggest that the area west of the Mississippi River be placed in a single department under a general with "plenary powers." To strengthen the war effort, the civilian governors should subordinate themselves to the commanding general when necessary or, as Moore phrased it, make "all their efforts auxiliary to his."[35]

the defense of Arkansas. Beauregard's choice of Hindman was excellent as Hindman was able to turn a dire situation around within a matter of months in Arkansas.

34 Bryan to the Congressmen of Texas, May 2, 1862, *OR*, vol. 53, 804-805.

35 Moore to Davis, May 4, 1862, ibid., 805. // It is interesting to note that several political leaders, such as Governors Rector and Moore, were suggesting that the military create a unified department west of the Mississippi long before this actually came to fruition. Had this happened

The suggestions of Bryan and Moore were unprecedented in their invocation of extraordinary military authority. Moore, who was facing a dire emergency in Louisiana, was especially insistent. On May 7 he inquired whether the president had received his previous message, and the following day repeated his suggestion by telegraph. General Bragg was his personal choice for the commanding general of the new department, he suggested, but either Sterling Price or Bragg would please the people and the army.[36]

President Davis had replied on May 5 to Governor Moore's first urgent message assuring him that even before the fall of New Orleans he had decided to form a department west of the Mississippi. The loss of that city made it imperative to do so, added Davis, but action would have to wait because of the expected great battle to be fought in Tennessee.[37] More than three weeks passed without such a battle having materialized, but the War Department issued orders on May 26 defining a new Trans-Mississippi Department to include Missouri, Arkansas, Indian Territory, Louisiana west of the Mississippi, and Texas.[38]

In place of immediately providing a department commander, however, General Robert E. Lee wrote General Hebert that Major General John Bankhead Magruder would soon be assigned to the department, but Hebert should assume command during the interim.[39] Lee obviously could not know that on that same day he wrote, General Beauregard had ordered Thomas Hindman to Arkansas to assume command of the Trans-Mississippi District. When Hebert learned, as he soon did, that Hindman was commanding in Arkansas, he made no attempt to extend to that state the jurisdiction conferred upon him by Lee's letter.

Throughout June and July of 1862, Hindman at Little Rock and Hebert at Houston functioned independently of one another, one as district commander above the Red River, and the other as district commander below it, while the embryo military department awaited the arrival of a commanding general who might marshal and coordinate all the military resources in the Trans-Mississippi in an attempt to restore full communications and cooperation with Confederate forces east of the river or, failing that, organize the Department to survive in isolation.[40]

---

sooner the Confederacy may have presented a more durable defense of the Mississippi Valley to challenge Union operations in the region.

36 Moore to Davis, May 7, 8, 1862, ibid., 805-806; Jefferson Davis Bragg, *Louisiana in the Confederacy* (Baton Rouge, 1941), 253.

37 Davis to Moore, May 5, 1862, *OR* vol. 53, 805.

38 General Orders No. 39, War Dept. Adjt. and Insp. Gen. Off., Richmond, May 26, 1862, ibid., vol. 9, 713.

39 Lee to Hebert, May 26, 1862, ibid.

40 // The lack of a unified command created the command frictions that plagued military operations in the region. This demonstrates a failure at the highest level of the Confederate government to repair the fractured command situation so that the Confederacy could mount a credible defense as Dr. Geise clearly articulates.

Chapter 6

Hindman and Hebert Divide Command While the Trans-Mississippi Department Awaits a Department Commander

June – July 1862

"I HAVE COME here to drive out the invader or to perish in the attempt." Such was the announcement of Thomas Hindman upon assuming command at Little Rock, Arkansas, on May 31, 1862. He meant what he said. An early accident had left the physically small man with one leg shorter than the other, but the injury had no effect on the size of his willpower and determination. The general quickly came to grips with the many problems facing him in his new Trans-Mississippi responsibility.[1]

During his journey from Memphis to Little Rock via the Mississippi and Arkansas rivers, Hindman directed all northbound steamboats he met on the Mississippi to turn back to Arkansas, and ordered the burning of large quantities of cotton along the river lest it fall into enemy hands. With Major General Samuel Curtis threatening the state capital, Hindman's first needs were men and supplies. At Little Rock, he found that Brigadier General John Selden Roane had collected some 1,500 Texas cavalrymen, eight companies of unarmed Arkansas infantry, and a six-gun battery of field artillery—all short of supplies. The supplies that Governor Rector had assembled under his call for state volunteers Hindman took over by threatening to conscript the state troops and impress their supplies. Without permission from higher authority, Hindman began enrolling men in his new formations in Arkansas who were absent from their units (for whatever reason) operating east of the Mississippi River. Further, he authorized the organization of men not subject to

---

1 T. C. Hindman to the Soldiers and Citizens of the District, May 31, 1862, *OR* vol. 13, 830; Harrell, "Arkansas," *Confederate Military History*, X, 105.

conscription into independent local companies, and gave permission to certain persons, apparently including the soon-to-be notorious William C. Quantrill, to raise guerrilla forces in Missouri.[2]

Hindman divided Arkansas into districts to provide an administrative structure for his efforts. Each district commander was charged with the supervision of every conscript enrolling officer within his area and given a staff consisting of a bonded quartermaster and a bonded commissary to see to the gathering of supplies. Orders were issued on June 23 to seize all cotton. Only ten pounds per person, including slaves in each household, was exempted to provide material for clothing. Two days later all arms and ammunition in the hands of civilians were ordered collected. District commanders were to submit detailed reports of the resources and potential supplies within their districts. Shops were set up, particularly around Arkadelphia, for the manufacture of shoes, harnesses, gun carriages, and other items of military use. A chemical laboratory was established at Little Rock to assist the ordnance department and to provide medicine. General Roane was dispatched to north Louisiana to establish similar procedures and facilities.[3]

Simultaneously, Hindman applied stringent measures to enforce his orders and to suppress the lawlessness and defeatism that had spread throughout northern Arkansas after the Confederate evacuation. Persons found hoarding cotton were to be brought to Little Rock for trial as traitors. Confederate notes were to be accepted at par for all transactions, and profiteering was prohibited. Price control lists were issued for the more common products including bacon (twenty-five cents a pound), eggs (fifteen cents a dozen), and potatoes (one dollar a bushel).[4]

Hindman trod heavily on civilian sensibilities and indeed on constitutional rights by initiating on June 17 a system intended to prevent "offenses against the government" and "offenses against the community." A provost marshal general and staff for Arkansas and northern Louisiana were appointed at district headquarters. Beneath him were four divisions, each under a provost marshal. Then came county or parish provost marshals, who could, in turn, appoint captains of local independent companies as their assistants. The independent companies were to act as police. Persons accused of "offenses against the government" would be heard by the local provost marshal and either dismissed or

---

2 *Report of Major General Hindman of His Operations in the Trans Mississippi District* (Richmond, 1864), 8-11; Reports of Maj. Gen. Thomas C. Hindman, C.S. Army, of operations May 31-November 3, 1862, Richmond, June 19, 1863, *OR* vol. 13, 28-44; Daniel O'Flaherty, *General Jo Shelby, Undefeated Rebel* (Chapel Hill, 1954), 130.

3 *Report of Major General Hindman*, 9-11; Reports of Maj. Gen. Thomas C. Hindman, C.S. Army, of operations, May 31-November 3, 1862, Richmond, June -19, 1863, *OR* vol. 13, 28-44; Special Orders 4 and 11, Headquarters Trans-Miss. Dist., Little Rock, June 3, 9, 1862, in District of Arkansas, Trans-Mississippi Department, Departmental Records, Record Group 109, National Archives.

4 General Orders No. 4 and Special Orders No. 4, Headquarters Trans-Miss. Dist., Little Rock, June 2, 3, 1862, ibid.

forwarded to the next higher level for a further hearing. The district provost marshal general would make the final decision in cases reaching his level. "Offenses against the government" meant "furnishing the enemy with supplies—giving him information in any manner—encouraging the organization of tory bands—spreading discontent or disaffection—acting as spy or guide for the enemy—the depreciation of Confederate money—evasion of or resistance to the 'Conscript Act' or other evidence of disloyalty." "Offenses against the community," which included unauthorized impressments, marauding, theft, disturbing the peace, and extortion, might be tried by the local provost marshal who was enjoined to proceed promptly and avoid "technicalities." Citizens were not to travel without a passport from the local provost marshal nor to leave the District without a passport from the provost marshal general. On June 30, Hindman tightened all these measures by proclaiming martial law throughout the district.[5]

Hindman's enforcement of military order and discipline was no less strict than his regime for civilians. During his brief tenure as a semi-independent commander, a military commission of three officers was convened at Little Rock to try serious military offenses. As a result of their deliberations, six soldiers were executed in the presence of the troops for desertion and a civilian received the same punishment for inciting soldiers to desert. According to Hindman, these executions had the desired effect: "The spirit of desertion was crushed."[6]

Harsh and controversial as his methods were, Hindman's determination paid off handsomely by saving Little Rock and northern Arkansas from Federal occupation. He deliberately spread rumors for Curtis to pick up, exaggerating Confederate strength and hinting at reinforcements on the way from Corinth. He actively pushed his outnumbered cavalry against the Federal elements nearest Little Rock, which caused them to fall back east of Bayou des Arcs. He ordered the Confederate gunboat *Maurepas* in White River to steam upriver, a move that threatened the rear of the Federal advance and forced it back to Curtis's headquarters at Batesville. This gave Hindman a good line of defense along the White River and its tributary, the Little Red. A Federal fleet that attempted in mid-June to ascend White River to reinforce and supply Curtis. The effort failed to reach him and the ships withdrew downriver with heavy damage to the large ironclad *Mound City*. Curtis evacuated Batesville and began moving down the east bank of White River toward the supporting Union fleet, which he was unable to contact. During the ensuing series of skirmishes, a Federal success near Clarendon convinced Hindman to withdraw his main line of defense westward to Bayou

---

5 General Orders No. 17, Headquarters Trans-Miss, Dist., June 17, 1862, *OR* vol. 13, 835; General Orders No. 18, Headquarters Trans-Miss. Dist., June 30, 1862, and Regulations for the Government of the Provost Marshal's Department, Office Provost Marshal General, Little Rock, July 7, 1862, both in District of Arkansas, Trans-Mississippi Department, Departmental Records, Record Group 109, National Archives.

6 *Report of Major General Hindman*, 17.

Meto. Even so, the prospect of continued stiff Confederate resistance, coupled with falling water in the White River that interfered with Federal supply and reinforcement, caused Curtis to remove to the Mississippi at Helena where he could be readily supported. He would remain there for the rest of Hindman's tenure as senior Confederate commander in Arkansas. Starting with almost no resources, by July 1862 Thomas Hindman had relieved the threat to Little Rock, at least for the time being.[7]

Successful though he was in defending Arkansas, General Hindman's policies made him bitter enemies. He exercised unauthorized powers when he felt it necessary, and quickly sought added responsibilities, which suggested to Adjutant General Cooper in Richmond that he be given command of the entire Confederate Trans-Mississippi. Still, Hindman's unshakeable self-assurance gave offense. When publicly accused of illegal activities in Arkansas, he admitted that occasional injustices might have been done, but insisted that on the whole, "the greatest good of the greatest number of loyal citizens was promoted."[8] The senior officer in the best position to judge Hindman's accomplishments, Major General Theophilus H. Holmes, concluded that Hindman had performed "the most strenuous exertions" and employed "an indispensable exercise of despotic power" to save Arkansas from invasion and to provide time for Confederate reorganization.[9]

*   *   *

TO THE INDIAN TERRITORY, midsummer brought a rather aimless Federal invasion that came to be known as the Indian Expedition. It began on June 25 and ended, after some sharp skirmishing, with Federal withdrawal above the Kansas line in late July. Ostensibly the object had been to return exiled loyal Indians to their homes. The actual effect was a wave of

---

7 Discussion of military movements is based principally on ibid., 12-16; Reports of Maj. Gen. Thomas C. Hindman, C.S. Army, of operations May 31-November 3, 1862, Richmond, June 19, 1863, *OR* vol. 13, 28-44, and in minor detail on Report of Commander Winslow, U.S. Navy, Commanding U.S.S. *Cincinnati*, regarding the abandonment of the position at St. Charles on account of low water, U.S. Gunboat *Cincinnati*, June 25, 1862, Report of Commander Winslow, U.S. Navy commanding U.S.S. *Cincinnati*, announcing arrival at mouth of White River convoying transports, and intended return to Memphis, U.S. Gunboat *Cincinnati*, June 27, 1862, Report of Flag-Officer Davis, U.S. Navy, regarding the hindrance to operations in White River on account of falling water, U.S. Flag-Steamer *Benton*, June 27, 1862, *Official Records of the Union and Confederate Navies in the War of the Rebellion*, 30 vols. (Washington, D.C., 1894-1927), Ser. I, Vol. 23, 181-184, hereafter cited as *ORN*; Harrell, "Arkansas," *Confederate Military History*, x, 108-115, and John N. Edwards, *Shelby and His Men: or the War in the West* (Cincinnati, OH, 1867), 64-69.

8 Hindman to Cooper, June 9, 1862, *OR* vol. 13, 832-833; *Report of Malar General Hindman*, 18; Edwards, *Shelby and His Men*, 107-110.

9 Holmes to S. J. Hinsdale or H. S. Holmes, March 25, 1863, Correspondence of Genl. T. H. Holmes, 1861-1864, Chapter II, Vol. 358, Record Group 109, National Archives.

retaliatory vengeance against the remaining Unionist Indians after the Federal force withdrew.

During this brief invasion the Confederate commander of Indian Territory, General Pike, appears to have spent more time writing indignant letters to Richmond and Little Rock than conducting active operations. The thrust of Pike's complaint was already familiar; his department was independent and it should not be subject to the commander of the Trans-Mississippi District. For a time, he obeyed Hindman's orders. Under one, he forwarded a regiment of Arkansas infantry and a battery of field artillery to help defend Little Rock, and under another had grudgingly—and in piecemeal fashion—moved the bulk of his command northward toward Fort Gibson.

Pike was especially outraged by two appointments made by Hindman without reference to him. The first was Major N. Bart Pearce, who was assigned to Fort Smith as commissary, quartermaster, and ordnance officer with responsibility for supplying the Indian Territory. To Pike, this was both an encroachment on the functions of his own staff and a subordination of the interests of the Indian Territory to those of Arkansas. He threatened to arrest Pearce if he entered the Territory. The other offending assignment was that of Colonel James J. Clarkson to command the troops in the Indian Territory above the Arkansas River. Clarkson was a Missouri officer, not a Confederate officer. He was officially ranked by the Indian colonels, who were Confederate officers, of three of the regiments Clarkson was to command. Pike attempted to nullify Hindman's order with one: in the chain of command in the Territory, only Confederate officers would be obeyed.[10]

These antagonisms and others between Hindman and Pike produced an open collision. After Hindman ordered Pike to Fort Smith to assume command in northwest Arkansas, Pike on July 12 submitted a letter of resignation. Hindman promptly forwarded it to Richmond with his approval and dispatched an order to Pike relieving him of command. Upon receipt of this order Pike published a circular address to the Indians that blamed Van Dorn and Hindman for the poor support the Indians had received from the Confederacy. Colonel Douglas H. Cooper, who had assumed command upon Pike's relief, proceeded to suppress the circular and ordered Pike's arrest, reporting to Hindman that Pike was either insane or a traitor. Hindman immediately requested Richmond disapprove Pike's resignation and ordered him brought to Little Rock for trial. Before he could be taken into custody, however, Pike decamped for Texas.[11]

10 *Report of Major General Hindman*, 18-21; Brown, "Pike," 682-691; Pike to Randolph, July 4, 5, 1862, Pike to Secretary of War, July 6, 20, 1862, Pike to Hindman, July 15, 1862, Pike to Davis, July 31, 1862, *OR* vol. 13, 850-869; Abstract of Orders to Brig. Gen. A. Pike and Abstract of Letters from Bg. Gen. A. Pike to Maj. Gen. T. C. Hindman, both in Papers of Various Confederate Notables, Major General T. C. Hindman, Record Group 109, National Archives.

11 Brown, "Pike," 691-695; *Report of Major General Hindman*, 19-21. // The problem of personality clashes causing command friction was the bane of the Trans-Mississippi region. This clash between

Later, Pike would take the lead in demanding a Congressional inquiry into Hindman's conduct in Arkansas. To President Davis he wrote that Hindman was "an Arkansas politician looking for future civil honors" as a reward for defending his state, a man who had no interest in the welfare of the Indians, while Pike himself as negotiator of the Indian treaties, felt a moral obligation to the Indians.[12]

The accusation that Hindman sought political advantages seems obviously unjust, for his actions and public utterances in Arkansas had hardly been calculated to endear him to the electorate. In fairness to Pike, on the other hand, it must be said that he constantly expressed sympathy and concern for the tribes under his jurisdiction, fretted over the scanty supplies and monies furnished them, and worried that the interests of white Arkansas would be put ahead of their interests. He had, according to his own testimony, never wanted military command of the Indian Territory and would have preferred a civilian position among the Indians. However that might be, his stubbornness about military orders was a constant embarrassment to Hindman, and his inactivity was a drag on operations in the Trans-Mississippi District.

*   *   *

IN TEXAS, MEANWHILE, Brigadier General Paul Hebert had begun well before the summer of 1862 to subdivide his huge command to achieve better military administration. An Eastern District and a Western District were created with the dividing line running north from the eastern shore of Galveston Bay up the left bank of the Trinity River to Alton, near present Denton, then north along the eastern edge of the Cross Timbers to Red River. Whether actual operational headquarters were established at this time for both these districts is unclear, Brigadier General Henry E. McCulloch (the deceased Ben McCulloch's brother) appears to have functioned temporarily as commander of the Western District at San Antonio.

More important were the subdistricts created in areas of heavy troop concentration and directly involved in the problems of military training, defense, and supply. In June the separate "Sub Military Districts" of Houston and of Galveston were consolidated in the "Sub Military District of Houston," which extended eastward along the coast from Harris and Galveston counties to the Louisiana border. The "Sub Military District of the Rio Grande,"

Pike and Hindman is a microcosm of the problem, which did not facilitate success. Rather, such clashes made Confederate operational and strategic failure more likely.

12 Pike to Davis, July 31, 1862, *OR* vol. 13, 860-869.

with headquarters San Antonio, was loosely defined as including all "military posts, west and south of San Antonio, including the posts at Victoria and Saluria."[13]

On June 18, Hebert, acting apparently upon instructions brought from Richmond by his aide, Major Guy M. Bryan, assumed command of that part of Louisiana west of the Mississippi and south of the Red River. He had by then already sent a battalion of mounted men to New Iberia in the Bayou Teche country. At the same time he began styling his slightly enlarged command the "Trans Mississippi District South of Red River." This cumbersome term stayed in use only until August 9 when, upon learning that Brigadier General Albert G. Blanchard had been ordered to Louisiana, Hebert relinquished his command there and reverted to calling his command the Department of Texas.[14]

Hebert seems to have been instructed in one of the dispatches that Bryan brought from Richmond to cooperate fully with Hindman in Arkansas. Certainly he did his best. An order of June 18 directed all troops en route to northeast Texas to march to Little Rock; regiments still organizing to proceed as soon as possible by routes already designated; and post quartermasters and commissaries to facilitate these movements.[15]

At Tyler, General McCulloch, who had been put in charge of collecting and forwarding the troops to Hindman's hard pressed command in Arkansas, took particular care to satisfy the latter's requirements. When Hindman on July 10 ordered that all such troops be dismounted, McCulloch supplemented the order by directing that Texas cavalry send their mounts home upon reaching the Red River.[16]

By early August, Hebert was able to report that eight mounted regiments, thirteen infantry regiments, one battery of field artillery, and one legion (Waul's) from Texas had joined Hindman in Arkansas or were on "their way to him." Several additional battalions and companies still in Texas were also destined for Arkansas. Hindman's estimate of the Texas

---

13 Special Orders No. 33, Adj't. and Insp. Gen's. Office, Richmond, February 10, 1862, General Orders No. 3, Hdqrs. Sub-Mil. Dist. of Rio Grande, San Antonio, April 24, 1862, Special Orders No. 819, Headquarters Department of Texas, Houston, June 3, 1862, ibid., vol. 9, 699, 708-709, 717.

14 Fannie Baker Sholars, "Life and Services of Guy M. Bryan" (unpublished master's thesis, University of Texas, 1930), 111-112; Hebert to Lee, June 18, 1862, OR vol. 9, 719; General Orders No. 1, Hdqrs. Trans-Miss. District South of Red River, Houston, June 18, 1862, ibid.; General Orders No. 56, Headquarters Dept. of Texas, San Antonio, August 9, 1862, in General Orders, Department of Texas, October, 1861-November, 1862, Chapter II, Vol. 112, Military Departments, Record Group 109, National Archives.

15 General Orders, No. 2, Hq. TM Dist. S. of R.R., Houston, June 18, 1862, ibid.

16 General Orders No. 46, Headquarters Department of Texas, June 2, 1862, OR vol. 9, 717; General Orders No. 49, Headquarters Department of Texas, June 20, 1864, in General Orders, Department of Texas, October, 1861-November, 1862, Chap. II, Vol. 112, Military Departments, Record Group 109, National Archives; General Orders No. 5, Headquarters Tyler, Texas, June 12, 1862, OR vol. 9, 718; Special Orders No. 26, Trans-Miss. Dist., Little Rock, July 10, 1862, Special Order [unnumbered], Read quarters Tyler, ·Texas, July 19, 1862, both photostats in McCulloch Papers.

contribution at about the same time confirmed Hebert's and was indeed slightly higher, showing twenty-one regiments of infantry and dismounted cavalry, four regiments of cavalry, and three field artillery batteries.[17] Whatever the precise numbers, Hindman later spoke gratefully of the support of both Hebert and McCulloch as "prompt, liberal, and patriotic." Indeed in the long record of bickering between neighboring generals in the Confederate Trans-Mississippi, this was one of the few examples of unstinting cooperation.[18]

Helpful as he might be to Hindman, Hebert, by interference in civilian affairs and encroachments upon civil authority, created much bitterness within the District of Texas. In May of 1862, he prohibited the export of cotton by private citizens except under conditions imposed by the military authorities. Commanders of coastal batteries were to enforce the prohibition in their areas (presumably the Union blockade left them little to do). The other route for exportation was across the Rio Grande into Mexico. There, Brigadier General Hamilton P. Bee, commanding the "Sub Military District of the Rio Grande," took charge, issuing permits only on condition that the exporter give bond to return a part of the value of his cotton in army supplies. Charges of favoritism and corruption resulted from this practice. Hebert also prohibited the export of cattle from Texas except by state or Confederate agents.[19]

On May 21, Hebert imposed martial law on thirteen counties in the Houston-Galveston area, and nine days later extended it to the whole state. His orders also outlined the general duties of provost marshals. The provost marshal system does not appear to have been as thoroughly organized in Texas as in Arkansas, but provost marshals were appointed down to the county level and given considerable authority. They were to register all white males above sixteen years of age and to control travel by a passport system. To prevent profiteering, they were to establish local price controls. General Bee was directed by Hebert to supervise the provost marshals.[20]

---

17 The discrepancies are perhaps to be accounted for by Waul's Legion, which contained all three arms, and Hindman's inclusion of some of the independent units that Hebert indicated were still on Texas soil. Hebert to H. H. Sibley, August 8, 1862, *OR* vol. 9, 729-731; *Report of Major General Hindman*, 23.

18 Ibid., *11.* // As Dr. Geise notes, this was a rare instance of cooperation between Confederate commanders west of the Mississippi.

19 General Orders No. 36, Headquarters Department of Texas, Houston, May 6, 1862, in General Orders, Department of Texas, October, 1861-November, 1862, Chapter II, Vol. 112, Military Departments, Record Group 109, National Archives; Oldham, "Memoirs," 360-362; Austin, *Texas State Gazette*, September 17, 1862. // For a profile of the leadership of General Bee, see Richard H. Holloway, "He is the Poorest Excuse for a General that I Ever Saw," in Hewitt and Schott, eds., *Confederate Generals West of the Mississippi* (Knoxville, 2019), vol. 3, 35-59.

20 General Orders No. 45, Headquarters Department of Texas, Houston, May 30, 1862, *OR* vol. 9, 715-716; General Orders No. 41, Headquarters Department of Texas, Houston, May 21, 1862, General Orders No. 7, Headquarters TMD S. of R. R., San Antonio, July 8, 1862, both in General

Hebert's orders further provided that civil administration of the law be suspended only where necessary, but judicial machinery was set up to try cases arising under martial law. On June 16, a military commission was appointed at Houston to hear such cases, and on July 2 a similar commission was actually convened at San Antonio. The San Antonio commission, which ruled on some fifteen cases during the next three months, mostly of suspected Unionists, was generally inclined toward leniency if the accused agreed to enlist in the Confederate Army.[21]

It was the threat of enemy action that brought martial law on Galveston and the neighboring coastal region, but actual military operations in Texas were minimal during June and July of 1862. Union efforts to break up the coastal trade provided a few minor clashes, but Union forces were too weak to attempt a bridgehead. In far west Texas, the last exhausted remnants of the Confederate Army of New Mexico departed El Paso for San Antonio in mid-July leaving the way open for an uncontested Federal reoccupation of Forts Bliss, Quitman, and Davis in the Trans-Pecos region.

Though the military outlook was not particularly bright, Hebert and Hindman had set up a viable administration in Texas and Arkansas by the summer of 1862, but northern and western Louisiana, included in the districts of Hindman and Hebert, continued in a state of near chaos almost devoid of Confederate troops, supplies, and funds. Governor Thomas O. Moore, established temporarily at Opelousas, continued to press Richmond for better organization west of the river. Resentful of Hindman's and Hebert's neglect of his state, he grew especially furious when in late June a party of Hindman's soldiers commandeered supplies in a state warehouse at Alexandria. Moore warned that if they did it again, the next time they would meet the bullets of the state militia. On July 8, he complained to Secretary of War Randolph that Hindman's headquarters at Little Rock and Hebert's in Texas were as inaccessible to him as Richmond, and he urged that a district commander be assigned to Louisiana.[22]

Brigadier General Albert Blanchard had already been ordered to Louisiana on June 21, but not as district commander. His duties seem to have been limited to superintending conscription and setting up camps of instruction. After reaching Monroe just four days after Moore's letter of complaint, he too reported that western Louisiana was practically

Orders, Department of Texas, October 1861-November, 1862, Chapter II, vol. 112, Military Department, Record Group 109, National Archives; Oldham, "Memoirs," 348.

21 Alwyn Barr, ed., "Records of the Confederate Military Com mission in San Antonio, July 2 – October 10, 1862," *Southwestern Historical Quarterly*, lxx (July, 1966), 93-99; General Orders No. 55, Headquarters Department of Texas, Houston, June 16, 1862, in General Orders, Department of Texas, October, 1861-November, 1862, Chapter II, vol. 112, Military Departments, Record Group 109, National Archives; McCulloch to Samuel Boyer Davis, March 3, 25, 31, 1862, *OR* vol. 9, 701-702, 705-706.

22 Moore to Randolph, July 8, 1862, ibid., vol. 15, 773-774.

Theophilus H. Holmes. LOC

undefended. Blanchard was also embarrassed: he found Thomas Hindman's deputy, Brigadier General Selden Roane, in command at Monroe, which was where he had expected to establish his own headquarters, and Blanchard was uncertain whether he was subject to the orders of Hindman.[23]

The plight of Louisiana was receiving attention in Richmond. Available there was a promising officer, Richard Taylor, a Louisiana sugar planter, son of Zachary Taylor, and brother of President Davis's first wife. The general was recuperating from partial paralysis brought about by rheumatoid arthritis suffered as a brigade commander during the fighting outside Richmond. Upon General Lee's recommendation Taylor, who had just been promoted to major general, was by orders of July 28 and 30 assigned to "duty in" [i.e., command of] the "District of Western Louisiana in the Trans-Mississippi Department." He was to command the troops serving in the southern part of the district, and to do everything possible to harass the enemy along the Mississippi.[24]

By the time Taylor was sent to Louisiana a decision had also been reached on the larger question of a commander for the whole Trans-Mississippi Department. On July 16, Major General Theophilus H. Holmes was assigned to the important position. His appointment had been made after considerable presidential procrastination. Davis's original choice for the position back in May had been Major General Magruder, but as he later explained to the

---

23 Special Orders No. 143, Adjt. and Insp. General's Office, Richmond, June 21, 1862, Blanchard to Randolph, July 17, 1862, ibid., 760, 799.

24 Richard Taylor, *Destruction and Reconstruction, Personal Experiences of the Late War* (New York, NY, 1955), xxv; Special Orders No. 174, Adjt. and Insp. General's Office, Richmond, July 28, 1862, Cooper to Taylor, July 30, 1862, *OR* vol. 15, 789, 791. // For more on Taylor, see generally, T. Michael Parrish, *Richard Taylor: Soldier Prince of Dixie* (Chapel Hill, 1992). Although supremely competent as an officer, Taylor had a tendency to irritate superiors, peers, and subordinates alike. Though Taylor would make great contributions to the defense of the Trans-Mississippi, his irascible personality would cause unnecessary frictions within the command, making cooperation among the leaders for the higher cause difficult to achieve.

governors of the Trans-Mississippi states, he had been delayed because he could not spare any first-rate general until after the Seven Days' Battles, and for other reasons "of a nature which cannot now be divulged."[25]

Davis's reasons that could not be divulged because they probably related to Sterling Price. Van Dorn had telegraphed from Mississippi on June 9 requesting the president to delay final appointment of Magruder because of the great esteem in which Price was held west of the Mississippi.[26] Price traveled to Richmond on leave that June. He met considerable popular enthusiasm as a western hero, and there was even idle talk in political circles of making him commander-in-chief and the next President of the Confederate States. Price's reception by President Davis was, however, not warm and perhaps chilly. Besides command of the Trans-Mississippi Department, Price wanted the Missouri troops returned west of the Mississippi. Davis acknowledged that they had been transferred east of the river without his prior knowledge or approval, but he flatly refused to return them immediately or to give Price command of the Trans-Mississippi. Price talked angrily of resigning and both he and his adjutant general publicly threatened that the Missourians would go their own way. He was finally mollified by a promise to return the Missouri troops to Arkansas as soon as the military situation permitted, and the offer of appointment as Magruder's second-in-command west of the river.

Nothing came of Price's visit to Richmond and the promises made to him. He could not become second-in-command to Magruder because charges of misconduct at the battle of Malvern Hill prevented Magruder's assuming command of the Trans-Mississippi Department. By the time the charges were found groundless, Holmes had been appointed in Magruder's stead. Holmes's appointment led Price and his supporters to suspect the president of double-dealing, suspicions that seemed confirmed when Price was not returned to the Trans-Mississippi for many months and most of his Missouri troops never were. Davis's decisions seem attributable, however, not to intentional deceit but to the military situation in the Mississippi Valley, his distrust of Price's loyalty and capacity for independent command, and on his own partiality toward and confidence in his old friend Theophilus Holmes.[27]

25 Special Orders No. 164, Adj. and Inspector General's Office, Richmond, July 16, 1862, ibid., vol. 13, 855; Harrell, "Arkansas," *Confederate Military History*, x, 126-127; Davis to Lubbock, Jackson, Moore, and Rector, September 12, 1862, *OR* vol. 13, 879-880.

26 Van Dorn to the President, June 9, 1862, ibid., 831-832.

27 Discussion of Price's bid for command is based principally on Castel, *Price*, 87-91. / / See Walter C. Hildermann, *Theophilus Hunter Holmes: A North Carolina General in the Civil War* (Jefferson, North Carolina, 2013). The appointment of Holmes to command a unified Trans-Mississippi Department is one of the worst military decisions Davis made during the war. Holmes was nearly deaf, low in energy, lacked administrative skills, and did not possess the strategic vision required to cope with the difficult situation west of the Mississippi. Holmes' only qualification for this command appears to have been his friendship with President Davis.

*   *   *

AT THE TIME President Davis was choosing a commander for the Trans-Mississippi, he was also conceiving the idea that a conference of the governors of the Trans-Mississippi states should be held to formulate recommendations for the better defense and administration of their states. Davis's request for such a conference was brought to Governor Francis Lubbock of Texas by Major Guy M. Bryan, Hebert's aide-de-camp, who had been sent to Richmond and seems to have talked with the president several times about affairs west of the river.[28]

To satisfy the President's wishes Lubbock invited the Trans-Mississippi governors to a meeting on July 26 at Marshall, Texas. This conference, which proved to be the first of an annual series, was attended by only two of the governors: Claiborne Jackson of Missouri, who was then living in north Texas, and Lubbock himself. Henry Rector of Arkansas was prevented from attending by serious illness in his family, and Governor Moore felt that his presence was needed in Louisiana. Both subsequently approved the proceedings. Also present at Marshall were Major Bryan and Charles S. West, Secretary of State for Texas.

The conference issued a prepared address to the people of the Trans-Mississippi states urging their continued strong support of the Confederacy. A letter to President Davis made three specific recommendations: immediate appointment of a commanding general for the whole department, more money for departmental operations, and provision for 20,000 to 30,000 stand of small arms for the weaponless troops in the area. The request for money emphasized the difficulties of fiscal agents in crossing the Mississippi and suggested a treasury branch west of the Mississippi to issue bills as needed. This interesting suggestion, probably Bryan's, would be adopted a year later.[29]

After the Marshall meeting, it remained for Major Bryan to travel to Louisiana and Arkansas to secure the signatures of the absent governors on the documents produced by the conference, and then on to Richmond to present the recommendations to the president. He carried also a letter from Governor Lubbock to Davis explaining more explicitly the wishes of the governors. Lubbock was especially vivid in describing the kind of commander wanted by the governors (news of Holmes's appointment not yet having arrived):

A general, cool, brave, energetic, and with the ability to command our vast country, should be immediately sent here. There should be but one head, with ample· power to control all of

---

28 "Autobiographical Sketch of Guy M. Bryan, 1896," in Guy M. Bryan Papers, Archives Collection, University of Texas Library; Lubbock, *Six Decades*, 389; William P. Ballinger Diary, June 22, 1862.

29 // Dr. Geise wrote about these conferences in articles published *Southwestern Historical Quarterly*, one of which is noted in the bibliography titled "Missouri's Confederate Capital in Marshall, Texas." He is one of a very small group of scholars that has chronicled those proceedings.

the territory west of the Mississippi, including jurisdiction over all of the sub-military districts, and he should be fully authorized to do all things connected with the defense of the country.[30]

At almost the same time Lubbock wrote from Texas, General Holmes, who was in Vicksburg preparing to cross the river, issued a general order assuming command of the department.[31] Holmes, a West Point classmate of Davis's, was already at the age of fifty-eight an old man and a seriously deaf one as well. Thus far in the war he had been a barely adequate commander of the District of North Carolina, and an unimpressive infantry division commander during the Seven Days' Battles before Richmond.[32] Davis overlooked his friend's shortcomings and thought of him as a loyal and experienced soldier. Holmes himself, however, seriously doubted his capacity to command such a huge and semi-independent department, and he wrote almost pitifully to his boyhood acquaintance, Governor Moore, that he wished "to God" the president had entrusted the command to abler hands than his. Apparently he had accepted the responsibility with considerable misgivings and only at the urging of his friend Davis.[33]

It was an unfortunate decision, both for the department and for the Confederacy. Despite his personal bravery and his good intentions, it became apparent almost immediately that "Granny" Holmes was not the "general, cool, brave, and energetic . . . with the ability to command our vast country" for whom Lubbock and the other Trans-Mississippi governors had hoped.

30 Discussion of governors' conference at Marshall is based principally upon Lubbock, *Six Decades*, 389-395. / / Holmes was antithetical to the description in this passage as he brought none of these talents to the job in the Trans-Mississippi.

31 General Orders No. 1, Vicksburg, July 30, 1862, *OR* vol. 13, 860.

32 Douglas Southall Freeman, *Lee's Lieutenants: A Study in Command*, 3 vols. (New York, 1942-1945), vol. 1, 96-97, 581-586, 614.

33 Holmes to Moore, August 3, 1862, typescript in vol. III, 1862-1863, Thomas O. Moore Papers, 1832-1878, Department of Archives and Manuscripts, Louisiana State University.

Chapter 7

General Holmes Fails to Create a Department

August 1862 – February 1863

Major GENERAL THEOPHILUS Holmes arrived in Little Rock, Arkansas, in early August 1862. On the 12th he fixed his headquarters there, and on the 20th subdivided his department into districts with boundaries differing somewhat from those of the earlier districts. The District of Texas, with Brigadier General Louis O. Hebert in command, consisted of Texas and the so-called Territory of Arizona, the District of Louisiana under Major General Richard Taylor included all of Louisiana west of the Mississippi River, and the District of Arkansas, still under Major General Thomas Hindman, consisted of Arkansas, Missouri, and the Indian country.[1]

Holmes might have taken heat from the fact that he could command more men than had previously been available in the Trans-Mississippi, but he was pessimistic about the opportunities of his new responsibility. When Hindman suggested a demonstration toward Missouri, Holmes quickly squelched the proposal and cautioned Hindman to concentrate on drill and discipline, on keeping the Indians quiet, and on imparting to northwest Arkansas and the Indian country an air of general tranquility and security.

The Texas troops then arriving would swell his command in Arkansas to thirty-five regiments. Six or seven thousand men were in Indian Territory, and great numbers of refugee Missourians were seeking to enlist. But what impressed Holmes was not the manpower and the challenge of organizing the new department, but the raw and undisciplined state of the troops and the burdens that would be his in training and equipping them. Simply put, Holmes was overwhelmed. Within a month of assuming command he again confessed frankly his own incapacity to President Davis, reminding him

---

1 Harrell, "Arkansas," *Confederate Military History*, x, 120; General Orders No. 5, Hdqrs. Trans-Miss. Department, Little Rock, August 20, 1862, *OR* vol. 9, 731.

of the "very great diffidence" with which he had accepted the Trans Mississippi post, and almost begged to be replaced by Beauregard, Joseph E. Johnston, or Edmund Kirby Smith. Whatever criticism might be made of his future conduct as a department commander, he cannot be accused of concealing his shortcomings. Unfortunately, Davis seemed far less aware of them than Holmes.[2]

General Holmes's problems were real enough. Most of his troops were indeed raw and undisciplined, and most of his officers inexperienced in command. He asked Davis to immediately send six brigadier generals to assist him. The financial situation was desperate. Funds were lacking to buy even basic supplies, the government's credit was no longer good, and $15,000,000 would not cover the government's indebtedness to private citizens in the Department. As if this was not bad enough, the soldiers' pay was in arrears. Small arms were so short that in Arkansas alone it was estimated that at least 5,000 troops were unarmed. Hope for quick resolution of this difficulty had been dashed when the steamer *Fair Play* carrying ammunition and 5,000 muskets destined for Little Rock was captured by the enemy at Milliken's Bend on the Mississippi River. Holmes bitterly reprimanded General Blanchard for a failure of martial spirit in the Louisiana regiment supposed to be guarding the steamer.[3]

Though no activist himself, Holmes was much impressed with what Hindman had accomplished in Arkansas and was ready to defend him staunchly against personal attack. General Pike, who had returned to Little Rock from Texas in the last week of August, almost immediately preferred formal charges against Hindman on grounds of unlawful usurpation of authority in Arkansas and in Indian country. In his defense, Holmes wrote Adjutant General Cooper in Richmond that Hindman's provost marshal system, at which Pike directed much of his criticism, was absolutely essential in Arkansas to preserve order and to collect conscripts, "as the conscripts have to be hunted down, and in some instances have armed themselves and banded together to resist enrollment." To the president, Holmes explained that Hindman had undoubtedly exceeded his powers, but that he had done so in the public interest and in disregard of his own popularity in Arkansas. It might be advisable to legalize Hindman's measures by additional legislation in Congress. He intended to leave Hindman's policies undisturbed, for to alter them would produce ruinous confusion.[4]

2 Holmes to Hindman, August 27, 1862, Holmes to the President, August 28, 1862, both in Correspondence of General T. H. Holmes, 1861-1864, Chapter II, Vol. 358, Record Group 109, National Archives.

3 Holmes to Cooper, October 8, 1862, Holmes to Blanchard, September 7, 1862, ibid.

4 Holmes to Cooper, October 8, 1862, Holmes to the President, August 28, 1862, ibid; Brown, "Pike," 695-700. // See Walter L. Brown, *A Life of Albert Pike* (Fayetteville, 1997), for an overview of this interesting character. Also, see the previously noted recent study Clint Crowe, *Caught in the Maelstrom*, for more on the tensions that existed between the interests of the tribes in the Indian Territory and the Confederacy.

Richard Taylor. *LOC*

Major General Richard Taylor had arrived in Louisiana about the time Holmes reached Little Rock, and had assumed command of the district in accordance with Holmes's orders shortly after they were issued. Before departing Richmond, Taylor had apparently been privately instructed by President Davis to attempt an attack on New Orleans at his own discretion. He found the military situation in Louisiana so deplorable, however, that he made no attempt to carry out the proposed operation. Taylor later described the condition of his district at that time: "Confederate authority had virtually ceased with the fall of New Orleans in the previous April. . . . The Confederate Government had no soldiers, no arms or munitions, and no money within the limits of the district." Taylor did, however, find one or two companies of mounted Louisiana volunteers armed with fowling pieces and a battalion of Texas Partisan Rangers that General Hebert had sent to Louisiana a short time before.[5]

In response to Taylor's report of the critical situation in Louisiana, Holmes promised to forward Henry H. Sibley's brigade, recently returned from New Mexico, once it was reorganized in Texas. Beyond whatever logistical support he could provide, Holmes indicated that he intended to exercise minimal supervision over Louisiana, and he urged Taylor to act with the widest possible discretion. Holmes enunciated the policy that he would continue during his tenure as a department commander. Instead of attempting to weld the Trans-Mississippi Department into a single operating entity, he functioned as a kind of superior district commander over Hindman in Arkansas, and left the district commanders in Louisiana and Texas to act practically independent of one another and of department headquarters in Little Rock.[6]

5 Taylor, *Destruction and Reconstruction*, 120, 130; Archer Jones, *Confederate Strategy from Shiloh to Vicksburg* (Baton Rouge, 1961), 72-73.

6 Holmes to Taylor, September 25, 1862, in Correspondence of General T. H. Holmes, 1861-1864, Chapter II, Vol. 358, Record Group 109, National Archives. // Dr. Geise is pointing out that

General Taylor, fortunately for the Confederacy, was not the type of officer to sit idly by awaiting the help and guidance of his superior. Before long the chaotic District of West Louisiana began exhibiting signs of new vigor. In spite of many handicaps, Taylor's headquarters staff at Alexandria made rapid progress in district administration. The accomplishments of the ordnance department under Major Joseph L. Brent were particularly impressive.

A professional lawyer with little if any previous ordnance experience, Brent displayed extraordinary organizational and improvisational ability. Within five months he was able to report to Colonel Josiah Gorgas, the Confederate chief of ordnance in Richmond, that all outstanding small arms requisitions for General Taylor's district could be cancelled, primarily because hundreds of unserviceable weapons had been repaired in Brent's various workshops at New Iberia, Alexandria, Monroe, and Franklin, Louisiana. Gun carriages could be built at New Iberia. A private foundry at Shreveport cast round and conical shot for artillery, and Brent had also begun preparations to have it cast guns. Using Vicksburg as the principal point of crossing the Mississippi, supply channels were opened from the arsenals at Charleston, South Carolina, and Augusta, Georgia, and from the ordnance depots at Macon, Georgia, and Columbus and Jackson, Mississippi. Ammunition for small arms remained a problem, especially since the variety of weapons in use during the fall of 1862 included the .54 Mississippi rifle, the .577 Enfield rifle, the .58 Minie musket, the .69 Belgian rifle, the .69 smoothbore musket, and the Sharps rifle. An Enfield cartridge manufactured from wallpaper in the New Iberia shops proved unsatisfactory and was soon discontinued, but its production was an example of the ingenuity of this ordnance department. By year's end, Brent had developed his resources sufficiently to begin shipping lead *east* of the Mississippi.[7]

Not long after Taylor's arrival, he received various small reinforcements. This enabled him to employ about 1,700 Confederate troops under Brigadier General Alfred Mouton in an attempt to defend the Bayou La Fourche area, the most exposed part of his district. The attempt failed when Federal troops under Brigadier General Godfrey Weitzel defeated

---

Holmes provided no strategic vision for the department or overarching intent to unify the efforts of the individual district commanders in a common direction.

7 Taylor, *Destruction and Reconstruction*, 13.0-132; Brent to Gorgas, November n.d., 1862, December 15, 1862, February 13, 1863, Brent to A. J. Lindsay, December 14, 1862, January 28, 1863, Brent to Major Bush, December 12, 1862, Brent to Lieutenant T. E. Vick, December 19, 1862, all in Letterbook, 1862-1863, 46-47, 18-22, 71-74, 14-17, 48-50, 6-7, 28-29, A. J. Lindsay to Brent, October 17, 1862, all in J. L. Brent Papers, Louisiana Historical Association Collection, Tulane University Library. // The Trans-Mississippi region had abundant natural resources for war, such as lead and iron. See Anne J. Bailey and Daniel E. Southerland, eds., *Civil War Arkansas: Beyond Battles and Leaders* (Fayetteville, 2000), for excellent essays about the resources available in just the state of Arkansas.

Mouton and his men and pushed them back to Bayou Teche late in October.[8] The Federals stopped at Berwick Bay, leaving Taylor several months to prepare as best he could to defend the Teche.

Because Taylor's district was laced with navigable waterways, river defense—especially of the Mississippi and its many tributaries—was a chief concern. One of his first undertakings was a journey to Vicksburg to consult with Lieutenant General John C. Pemberton. The generals reached the rather obvious conclusion that the Confederates must control the section of the Mississippi between Vicksburg and Port Hudson into which the Red and Ouachita rivers emptied. Elsewhere, Taylor had guns raised that had been abandoned in various rivers after the fall of New Orleans, and began work constructing river defenses.

To hamper the ascent of the Red River by any Federal vessels that might run the batteries at Vicksburg or Port Hudson, two were placed at Fort De Russy on the high south bank of the Red River thirty miles below Alexandria. On the Ouachita, a similar purpose was served by two guns placed at Fort Beauregard at Harrisonburg. To deny or at least to discourage the passage of enemy gunboats concentrated at Berwick Bay through the Atchafalaya River to the Red and Ouachita rivers, Taylor erected Fort Burton on the west bank of the Atchafalaya at Butte a la Rose some eighteen miles east of St. Martinsville. Mostly under the supervision of the capable Major Brent, efforts were made to scrape together naval vessels by converting and arming river and bayou steamboats. Triumphs partly attributable to Brent were scored in the capture of the steam ram *Queen of the West* and then of the ironclad *Indianola*, the first and second Federal vessels, respectively, to run the Vicksburg batteries. Success on the Mississippi and lower Red was only temporary, however. In March of 1863, Farragut would pass Port Hudson with two powerful warships and effective control of the river between Vicksburg and Port Hudson was permanently lost to the Confederates.[9] Even so, Taylor and his growing command had shown during the last months of 1862 that western and northern Louisiana were no longer defenseless.[10]

*   *   *

OVER IN TEXAS, meanwhile, General Hebert had unstintingly forwarded troops to Thomas Hindman for use in Arkansas, though he did unhappily describe himself to

---

8 Barnes F, Lathrop, "The Lafourche District in 1862: Invasion," *Louisiana History*, II (Spring, 1961), 175-201. // See William Arceneaux, *Acadian General Alfred Mouton and the Civil War* (Lafayette, 1981), for more on Mouton's leadership. He was a popular leaders with his Louisiana troops and a favorite of Richard Taylor. He would die in action leading his brigade of Louisiana troops at the battle of Mansfield (Sabine's Crossroads) during the Red River Campaign on April 8, 1864.

9 Discussion of military affairs in Louisiana is based upon Taylor, *Destruction and Reconstruction*, 133-150 and on John D. Winters, *The Civil War in Louisiana* (Baton Rouge, 1963), 187-188.

10 Ibid.

John B. Magruder. LOC

Governor Lubbock as tired of acting as a "recruiting officer" for other commands. Hebert asked General Holmes to give him command of the Texas troops in Arkansas that he had raised in the Lone Star State, but this assignment went instead to General McCulloch.[11]

To add to Hebert's troubles, General Cooper in Richmond rebuked him for "unwarranted assumption of authority." On September 12, the War Department issued a blanket revocation of all proclamations of martial law throughout the South, and a crowning humiliation arrived in the first week of October when Galveston, Texas, was given up without a struggle to a fleet of five small Federal vessels and a landing force of only 260 soldiers. Confederate evacuation of the city was in accordance with Hebert's standing order not to fight if the Confederate batteries were outgunned in a bombardment by an attacking fleet. After Galveston fell, Governor Lubbock urgently requested that Hebert to take personal command of the troops in the immediate vicinity, but Hebert refused to stir from his San Antonio headquarters. Orders had already been issued in Richmond directing Major General John B. Magruder to relieve Hebert in Texas; Hebert was to report to General Holmes for reassignment.[12]

---

11 Hebert to Lubbock, August 28, 1862, *OR* vol. 9, 733-734; "Sketch of H. E. McCulloch," signed "H," apparently from a newspaper and "A Brief of Service of H. E. McCulloch from War Records Office," Washington, August 30, 1866, both photostats in McCulloch Papers.

12 Cooper to Hebert, September 12, 1862 General Orders No. 66, Adj. and Insp. Gen.'s Office, Richmond, September 12, 1862, *OR* vol. 9, 735-736; Report of Brig. Gen. Paul O. Hebert, C.S. Army, commanding First District of Texas, October 15, 1862, Report of Col. X. B. Debray, Debray's Texas Regiment, October 5, 1862, Debray to Capt. S. B. Davis, October 12, 1862, Debray to Col. Joseph J. Cook, October 5, 10, 1862, Report of Col. Joseph J. Cook, Cook's Texas Regiment, October 9, 1862, Special Orders No. 237, Adj. and Insp. General's Office, Richmond, October 10, 1862, ibid., vol. 15, 147-153, 826; Lubbock, *Six Decades*, 415-421. // See Paul D. Casdorph, *Prince John Magruder: His Life and Campaigns* (Hoboken, New Jersey, 1996) and Thomas Settles, *John Bankhead Magruder: A Military Reappraisal* (Baton Rouge, 2009). The second and most recent book by Settles contains a solid reassessment of the career of Magruder. Long dismissed as an ineffectual publicity seeker, Settles paints his subject in a different light—an effective leader for the Confederacy in general, and in the Trans-Mississippi Department in particular.

It was late November before Magruder arrived in Texas and the actual change of command took place. His first general order, issued November 29 from headquarters established at Houston, expanded the name of his command from the District of Texas to the District of Texas, New Mexico, and Arizona. He soon changed the internal organization as well. The former Eastern and Western Districts of Texas were given new boundaries and called "subdistricts" rather than "districts." The "Eastern Sub-District" included everything south and east of a line running roughly from the southeast corner of Panola County west through Marlin to present Killeen, and then south through Austin to the coast in the vicinity of present Palacios. The "Western Sub-District" included roughly that territory west of the "Eastern Sub-District" and northwest of a line extending from Marlin to Fort Belknap at present Graham and then due north to Red River. Later in the spring of 1863, a "Northern Sub-District" was created by dividing the "Eastern Sub-District" along a line roughly from the southeastern corner of Sabine County to Marlin.[13]

Holmes's instructions to the newly arrived John Magruder were reminiscent of those to Richard Taylor in the wide discretion granted. Magruder, advised Holmes, should "consider ... [himself] invested with all the authority I can confer, and use it for the defense of Texas." Holmes did caution Magruder that if it became necessary to exercise extra-legal authority over civil affairs, he should proceed only with the concurrence of the governor of Texas.[14]

Magruder had been concerned for Galveston even before he left Richmond or heard of its fall. On October 16, he had written Secretary of War George W. Randolph (who had replaced Judah Benjamin on March 24, 1862) that he understood General Hebert considered the place indefensible, but that if it held out for two months after his arrival he would defend it indefinitely. The loss had, of course, disappointed Magruder. He was also much distressed to find that under Hebert, the Rio Grande frontier from the mouth of the river all the way up to Ringgold Barracks at present Rio Grande City had been virtually abandoned.

Yet another situation that disturbed him was the shortage of small arms, a chronic issue in the Trans-Mississippi. Magruder reported that only about 6,000 of some 8,000 men present for duty in Texas were armed, and many of them indifferently with shotguns and pistols. He was plagued by successive orders from both Holmes and the War Department to send Henry Sibley's brigade and other troops first to Vicksburg, and then to Louisiana. To do so would seriously deplete his already weak forces at a time when he was convinced (erroneously, though with excellent reason) that a large Union expedition that had sailed

13 General Orders No. 1, Hdqrs. Dist. of Tex., N.M. and Ariz., Houston, November 29, 1862, *OR* vol. 15, 880-881; William F. Amann, ed, *Personnel of the Civil War* (2 vols. in 1, New York, 1968), I, 200-202.

14 Holmes to Magruder, November 28, 1862, Correspondence of General T. H. Holmes, 1861-1864, Chapter II, vol. 358, Record Group 109, National Archives.

from the east coast under Major General Nathaniel P. Banks early in December was destined for Galveston.[15]

Faced with what he considered certain invasion by this force, Magruder nevertheless went ahead with plans he had been formulating for the recapture of Galveston. On Christmas Day 1862, less than one month after his arrival in Texas, he ordered Captain Leon Smith, an experienced seaman and former commodore of the Morgan Line, to prepare two river steamers for a combined land and naval assault on the city.[16]

The successful attack was launched on New Year's Day 1863 by two river steamers "armored" with cotton bales manned by 300 volunteer "marines," supported by two small tenders. Sibley's brigade, delayed in its departure for Louisiana, provided much of the manpower for the action. This victory raised sagging public morale in Texas and yielded several hundred prisoners, fifteen guns, a schooner, two barks, and the revenue cutter *Harriet Lane.* Most important, Galveston would not serve as a Union beach head in Texas.[17]

Even old Sam Houston, lukewarm Confederate that he was, was moved to congratulate Magruder warmly. "You sir, have introduced a new era in Texas by driving from our soil a ruthless enemy." He continued:

> You deserve, sir, not only my thanks, but the thanks of every Texan. Your advent was scarcely known in Texas when we were awakened from our reverie to the realities of your splendid victory. Its planning and execution reflect additional glory on your former fame as well as on the arms of Texas.[18]

---

15 Magruder to Randolph, October 16, 1862, Major General J. B. Magruder, Correspondence, 1861-1865, Papers of Various Confederate Notables, Record Group 109, National Archives; S. S. Anderson to Magruder, November 26, 1862, Magruder to Pemberton, December 1, 1862, Magruder to Cooper, December 1, 1862, Special Orders No. 282, Adj. and Insp. General's Office, Richmond, December 2, 1862, Magruder to Cooper, December 9, 1862, Magruder to S. S. Anderson, December 8, 9, 15, 19, 21, 1862, *OR* vol. 15, 879, 884-885, 894-896, 900-903; Lubbock, *Six Decades,* 425-426.

16 // The Morgan Line refers to the Southern Mail Steamship Company owned by Charles Morgan. This company moved mail throughout the Gulf of Mexico region and received recognition from Congress for its efficiency. Dr. Geise's reference is to the fact that Captain Smith was a boat captain employed by the company in the 1850s. See James M. Day, "Leon Smith: Confederate Mariner," *East Texas Historical Journal* (vol. 3, Issue 1), 34-49, available at https://scholarworks.sfasu.edu/ethj/vol3/iss1/7.

17 Barr, "Texas Coastal Defense," *Southwestern Historical Quarterly,* xlv, 14-18; Lubbock, *Six Decades,* 425-426.

18 Houston to General [Magruder], January 7, 1863, *OR* vol. 15, 933-934; Secretary of War Randolph also warmly congratulated Magruder, remarking that there were circumstances surrounding Magruder's assignment to Texas that would have to remain secret temporarily, but that he had been Magruder's chief advocate for that post. Randolph to My Dear General [Magruder], February 21, 1863, Major General J. B. Magruder, Correspondence, 1861-1865, Papers of Various Confederate Notables, Record Group 109, National Archives.

Immediately after the recapture of Galveston, Magruder turned his attention to protecting the trade across the Rio Grande between Mexico and Texas, a trade that by the fall of 1862 had become important and perhaps vital to the Trans-Mississippi Department. Although small arms were unavailable in quantity in northern Mexico, powder and ammunition were plentiful, as were copper, lead, tin, blankets, coffee, sugar, chalk, and textiles. These items, as well as specie, could be had in exchange for cotton.[19]

To regulate cotton export, General Holmes had continued Hebert's policies of limiting the traffic to government agents and to civilians who agreed to provide some supplies for the army. Sharp operators easily evaded these regulations, however, and corruption flourished. The exemption from conscription of able-bodied teamsters to drive for men who were primarily private speculators soon became an open scandal.[20]

That November, the Confederate government became directly involved in the trade through the appointment of Major Simeon Hart as its purchasing agent in Texas. Conditions were not improved by this appointment. Hart, acting on behalf of the Confederacy, agents acting for both the state and the District of Texas, and private speculators all competed for the same supplies. To halt the confusion, Magruder recommended to Holmes the subordination of all government agents, at least, to Hart.[21]

Some weeks later, however, James Seddon, yet another new secretary of war, directed on January 28, 1863, that all Trans-Mississippi Department orders regulating the cotton trade be revoked as unwarrantable military intrusions on the regulation of commerce and the rights of private property.[22] Either this order was not immediately disseminated within the department, or it was ignored deliberately by Holmes and Magruder. One month later, the latter general issued his own order continuing the District of Texas's control over cotton exports to Mexico and directing the subordination of all military agents to Hart. He also forbid the future exemption from conscription of drivers in the cotton trade.[23]

19 Owsley, *King Cotton Diplomacy*, 92-127.

20 Oldham, "Memoirs," 362-366, Ronnie C, Tyler, "Cotton on the Border, 1861-1865," *Southwestern Historical Quarterly*, lxxiii (April, 1970), 466.

21 Randolph to Hart, November 14, 1862, Magruder to S. S. Anderson, December 15, 1862, *OR* vol. 15, 866, 900-901.

22 James A. Seddon to Holmes, January 28, 1863, *OR* vol. 53, 845-846.

23 General Orders No. 28, Hdqrs. Dist. of Tex., N.M. and Ariz., Houston, February 22, 1863, *OR* vol. 15, 986-988. Senator Oldham was bitter about the military mismanagement of the cotton trade and implied in his "Memoirs," 363-364, that Seddon's directive was suppressed, and its provisions disregarded by Holmes. Robert Garlick Hill Kean, Head of the Bureau of War in Richmond, corroborated Oldham's assertion in his diary, where for stated that Seddon considered the cotton trade orders issued in the Trans-Mississippi beneficial and implied that in April 1863, Seddon was under pressure from Oldham to enforce his own previous revocation of the Trans-Mississippi orders, which he apparently finally did, Edward Younger, ed., *Inside the Confederate Government: The Diary of Robert Garlick Hill Kean, Head of the Bureau of War* (New York, 1957), 51.

Indeed, Magruder did not get around to acknowledging the secretary of war's January order until May. He did so under protest by declaring that without control of the cotton trade, he would require $100,000 in specie every sixty days or he would be forced to evacuate the Rio Grande. Subsequently a board of officers convened by General Kirby Smith to investigate the cotton trade reported that the revocation of Magruder's orders by superior authority had worked to drain the county of its resources without any benefit to the army.[24]

Confusion and corruption notwithstanding, the vital Mexican trade had to be protected, and in January of 1863 Magruder dispatched three battalions and ten additional companies of cavalry to the lower Rio Grande, as well as five companies of infantry and one eight-gun battery of field artillery. Five companies of state troops from the Frontier Regiment were also sent there on temporary duty. To ensure closer command supervision, General Bee removed his headquarters permanently from San Antonio to Brownsville. After these measures were complete Magruder informed Governor Lubbock "that the Rio Grande, that frontier so vital to us is strongly held by men and guns, and . . . I now entertain great hopes that I shall be able to fortify it so as to render it difficult if not impossible for the enemy to take it from us."Considering that not more than 2,500 men in all had been sent to the lower Valley, Magruder was being somewhat boastful. After the steady pessimism of General Hebert, such self-assurance must have been welcome to Governor Lubbock.[25]

*   *   *

LIKE TAYLOR BEFORE him, Magruder had shown himself to be a strong and aggressive district commander. The presence of these energetic officers in the Trans-Mississippi Department resulted in a flurry of renewed Confederate military activity in their districts of Louisiana and Texas. By contrast, General Holmes's presence as the new department commander had little effect on the department as a whole. During more than six months in command, he had made little effort to transform the Trans-Mississippi into a coordinated and fully functioning department. Holmes communicated with Taylor and Magruder infrequently and usually on routine matters only, leaving military operations in their districts almost entirely to their discretion. In addition, he had not altered the provost marshal and other administrative systems established by Hindman and Hebert except as required by Richmond.

In short, Theophilus Holmes seems to have deliberately restricted his interests as a department commander to the District of Arkansas.

---

24 A. W. Terrell to Magruder, March 3, 1864, with enclosure A. W. Terrell and T. J. Devine to S. S. Anderson, n.d., *OR* vol. 34, pt. II, 1017-1019.

25 H. P. Bee to A. G. Dickinson, January 6, 1863, Bee to Edmund P. Turner, January 17, 1863, Magruder to Lubbock, February 11, 1863, *OR* vol. 15, 933, 950-951, 974-975.

Chapter 8

Holmes, Arkansas,
and the Defense of the Lower River
August 1862 — February 1863

In CONTRAST TO Texas and Louisiana, where Theophilus Holmes exercised minimal control, he assumed in Arkansas virtually direct command of the largest concentration of troops in the Trans-Mississippi Department. Thomas Hindman, the nominal district commander in Arkansas, was not permitted to function as such. Instead, Holmes assigned him the immediate command of 7,000 to 8,000 men organized in three brigades in northwest Arkansas and the adjoining Indian country. With these troops Hindman established a defensive line corresponding roughly to the northern boundary of the state.

On his arrival, Holmes had restrained Hindman from making a demonstration toward Missouri even though Holmes professed interest in an invasion of the important border state. His interest was conditional, however, upon having first re-occupied Helena, Arkansas. The difficulty was that Holmes was convinced he could not leave the Arkansas Valley unguarded in his rear while 15,000 Union soldiers under Major General Frederick Steele remained at Helena. His men were also short of arms and of shoes for a project so ambitious as driving the Federals out of Helena.[1]

The strategic situation changed in the first week of September 1862 when the Army of the Frontier under John M. Schofield began moving south from Kansas toward southwestern Missouri and northwestern Arkansas to snuff out Rebel activity, much of it the work of Hindman's pesky patrols. Holmes feared a rumored Union attack on Little Rock

---

1 Holmes to Samuel Cooper, September 27, 1862, Holmes to Lucius B. Northrup, September 28, 1862, both in Correspondence of General T. H. Holmes, 1861-1864, Chapter II, Vol. 358, Record Group 109, National Archives.

from Helena and decided this time to summon Hindman to Little Rock for his advice and assistance. In doing so, he deprived the defensive forces in the northwestern area of their commander at a critical moment. Hindman left Brigadier General James S. Rains, the next senior officer, in charge on September 10. By the time he returned on October 15, he found that the troops of both General Rains and Colonel Douglas H. Cooper in the Indian country had been routed by the Federals and had fallen back many miles to the south. Hindman accused both officers of drunkenness while in the performance of duty and relieved Rains of his brigade command. He was soon persuaded, however, that Cooper had been genuinely ill. Nothing could be done to immediately retrieve the military situation, and by early November Union pressure forced Hindman to withdraw all the way to the Van Buren-Fort Smith area.[2]

In Little Rock, meanwhile, Holmes fretted over his inability to cope with the problems of the Trans-Mississippi. He was bitterly disappointed when a report that General Joseph E. Johnston was coming to replace him proved untrue. He pleaded with Johnston to take the command anyway—one "sufficient to satisfy the highest ambition" so that the service should not suffer from Holmes's own shortcomings.[3]

Richmond went its own mysterious way when it promoted Holmes to lieutenant general and Cooper, whom Hindman and other officers had accused of drunkenness, to brigadier general and Superintendent of Indian Affairs. The letter of October 27, 1862, from the secretary of war announcing these promotions contained startling instructions. Holmes was to assist Lieutenant General John C. Pemberton directly in defending the lower Mississippi:

> Cooperation between General Pemberton and yourself is indispensable to the preservation of our connection with your Department. We regard this as an object of the first importance, and when necessary you can cross the Mississippi with such part of your forces as you may select, and by virtue of your rank direct the combined operations on the eastern bank.[4]

2 Holmes to J. S. Walker, March 5, 1863, ibid. General discussion of military movements in Arkansas is based on Wiley Britton, *The Civil War on the Border*, 2 vols. (New York, 1899), vol. 1, 364-441, and Harrell, "Arkansas," *Confederate Military History*, x, 129-154.

3 Holmes to Johnston, October 15, 1862, Correspondence of General T. H. Holmes, 1861-1864, Chapter II, vol. 358, Record Group 109, National Archives.

4 Randolph to Holmes, October 27, 1862, *OR* vol. 13, 906-907. // The only real way to achieve "cooperation" between commanders is to assign a single commander over both to create a unified command. Thus, the senior commander can issue orders to the two subordinate leaders compelling them to act in concert with each other toward a common objective. A fatal flaw in the strategic design pursued in the western Confederacy was the failure to establish unified command structures in a timely manner when the situation dictated this necessity. As a result, the Union forces were routinely able to exploit the seams between Confederate commands when Rebel commanders failed to cooperate as in the Mississippi Valley. Holmes, meanwhile, had already demonstrated his lack of energy, skill, and interest in holding any responsible field command.

War Secretary Randolph's instructions, which were prompted by the threatened Federal movements down the Mississippi River toward the vital Confederate connecting link at Vicksburg, were highly unorthodox. To confer upon Holmes the authority to command, when necessary, in Pemberton's Department of Mississippi, Tennessee, and East Louisiana ignored departmental integrity. Moreover, Randolph had not secured prior presidential approval for his strange order. Indeed, President Davis had advised Holmes less than a week before, that the retreat of Braxton Bragg from Kentucky and the defeat of Earl Van Dorn at Corinth, Mississippi, on October 3-4 had given the enemy a firmer grip on the Mississippi, meaning that a voluntary Federal abandonment of Helena could hardly be expected. Therefore, the immediate Confederate objectives should be the early recaptures of Helena, Memphis, and Nashville.

To achieve these objectives, Davis suggested that Holmes, Pemberton, and Bragg (then in command of the Army of Tennessee), should exchange "co-intelligence" and even concentrate their troops if necessary, but he did not specifically order concentration and he made it perfectly clear that he did not intend to interfere in the arrangements. "How and when such concentrations should be made can only be determined after the freest communication between the generals," explained Davis, "so that each shall possess exact information in regard to the condition of the others."[5]

Davis was understandably surprised and angry when he learned that his secretary of war had specifically authorized Holmes to cross the river to aid Pemberton. The president rebuked Randolph in a letter dated November 12, 1862, and reiterated the opinions he had previously expressed to Holmes: "The cooperation designed by me was co-intelligent action on both sides of the River, and such detachment of troops as circumstances might require or warrant." Having the Trans-Mississippi commander cross the river and undertake temporary duty outside his department would be a disaster. Instead, Davis expressed again the hope that Holmes would retake Helena. Perhaps the president was remembering the storm of protest that had arisen when General Van Dorn's army had abandoned Arkansas to cross the Mississippi the previous spring. Davis's sharp rebuke off Randolph, who was already dissatisfied with the limited initiative allowed him by the president and ill with tuberculosis, provoked his resignation as secretary of war three days later.[6]

5   Davis to Holmes, October 21, 1862, ibid., vol. 53, 830-831. // In fact, Bragg's army was officiallyt The Army of Mississippi, and would not be renamed the Army of Tennessee until November 20, 1862.

6   Jones, *Confederate Strategy*, 82-96. The quotation of the letter Davis to Randolph, November 12, 1862, is from a copy in the Jefferson Davis Collection, Louisiana Historical Association Collection. The version of this letter in *OR* vol. 13, 917-919, reads as follows: "The cooperation designed by me was co intelligent action on both sides of the River of such detachment of troops as circumstances might require or warrant." In other words, "of such detachment of troops" should read "*and* such detachment of troops." // Yet another issue of regarding Confederate high command were the prerogatives of President Davis. He bristled at any perceived encroachment upon what he

Davis need not have worried about Holmes crossing the river no matter what the authorization. Holmes's replied to the secretary of war that he could not cooperate with the armies east of the river because of the critical situation in Arkansas. He wanted to attack Helena, but would not dare attempt it until he could be sure the enemy in Missouri did not intend to advance on Arkansas. He could not hold Helena anyway, for the enemy's river gunboats had greater weight of metal than his field batteries. Shortly afterward, Holmes informed General Pemberton that because of the importance of defending the Arkansas Valley he could not spare a man east of the river. Then, on December 10, in a curious reversal of opinion, Holmes ordered General McCulloch to move his division from the vicinity of Little Rock to Vicksburg.[7]

Vacillating as Holmes might be about offensive actions anywhere along the Mississippi River, he did authorize Hindman to attempt to drive the Union forces in northwestern Arkansas back into Missouri and Kansas. This endeavor culminated in Hindman being badly defeated at Prairie Grove on December 7 and the withdrawal of his forces to Fort Smith, and then all the way back to Little Rock. The pursuing Federals, deeming it impracticable to sustain operations south of the Boston Mountains without complete control of the Arkansas Valley from Little Rock to Fort Smith, turned back at Fort Smith and withdrew northward to Fayetteville and Springfield. Their success appears to have been sufficient, however, to cause the alarmed Holmes to countermand his orders to McCulloch's division on December 13 and change its destination from Vicksburg to Van Buren, and two days later to Little Rock. Thus ended his modest effort to assist Pemberton.[8]

General Joseph E. Johnston had been appointed to command a new Department of the West on November 24, with jurisdiction over the armies of both Braxton Bragg in Tennessee and John Pemberton in Mississippi. Apparently, Johnston would have preferred for the sake

---

considered his exclusive sphere of action as the president, such as alignment of commands and movement of forces between departments. His insistence on making all decisions of command, regardless of how mundane, caused much friction with his secretaries of war. This inability to delegate some command decisions to his senior executive overseeing the war caused a lack of willingness among the various secretaries to take on responsibility beyond routine bureaucratic responsibilities. In effect, Davis's secretaries were little more than head clerks of the War Department. These men could have relieved Davis of petty details in order to concentrate on the larger strategic picture. Steven E. Woodworth chronicles these issues of high command in his book, including an in-depth discussion of the issues encountered in the defense of Vicksburg. See Steven E. Woodworth, *Jefferson Davis and His Generals: The Failure of Confederate Command in the West* (Lawrence, KS, 1990).

7 Holmes to Secretary of War and to Hindman, both November 15, 1862, *OR* vol. 13, 917-919; Holmes to Pemberton, November 25, 1862, in correspondence of General T. H. Holmes, 1861-1864, Chapter II, vol. 358, Record Group 109, National Archives; J. P. Blessington, *The Campaigns of Walker's Texas Division By a Private Soldier* (New York, NY, 1875), 63.

8 For more on the campaign that resulted in the ferocious battle of Prairie Grove, see William L. Shea, *Fields of Blood: The Prairie Grove Campaign* (Chapel Hill, NC, 2013).

of a better coordinated river defense that his department be composed of Arkansas and Mississippi, instead of Tennessee and Mississippi. As it was, he had no direct authority over the Trans-Mississippi Theater, but he urged the president to give specific orders to Holmes to join Pemberton for a joint campaign against Major General U. S. Grant. In this effort he received considerable support from the new secretary of war, James A. Seddon. Davis's visit to Mississippi in December, accompanied by Johnston, afforded for the general opportunities to press the point.[9]

That Davis had altered substantially his evaluation of strategic priorities appeared in a letter he wrote to Holmes on the eve of his return to Richmond. Retention of the Mississippi was even more important than retention of Richmond, he explained, for Richmond's fall would mean only an unfavorable reaction abroad and the loss of a few factories, whereas the loss of the Mississippi would mean Union use of the length of the river with all its attendant military and commercial advantages—not to mention the severing of the Confederacy. Since Holmes had not managed the recapture of Helena, priority must now be given to holding Vicksburg and Port Hudson. Davis doubted the possibility of a Federal advance on Little Rock from northwestern Arkansas, reasoning much like the Federal commanders that they could not sustain their armies in that desolate region. Since the Confederates could not "hope at all points to meet the enemy with a force equal to his own," they must find security "in the concentration and rapid movement of troops," he continued. "Nothing will so certainly conduce to peace as the conclusive exhibition of our power to hold the Mississippi River."[10]

The president's strong suggestion that Holmes turn his attention to actively supporting Pemberton at Vicksburg fell short of the direct order Johnston had hoped Davis would issue. Holmes's response, as usual, was negative. The department commander reported Hindman's retreat, adding that Hindman's forces were near starvation and riddled with sickness and desertion. Near Little Rock, John G. Walker's Division (formerly McCulloch's) was also reduced by sickness and down to only 5,000 effective men out of some 11,000 on the rolls. If Walker's command was sent to Vicksburg, the entire Arkansas Valley would be

---

9 Johnston to Samuel Cooper, November 24, December 4, 1862, Johnston to the President, December 22, 1862, *OR* vol. 17, pt. II, 758, 780, 800-801; Joseph E. Johnston, *Narrative of Military Operations Directed During the Late War Between the States* (New York, NY, 1874), 490-494; Wigfall to Seddon, December 8, 1862, Johnston to Wigfall, December 3, 15, March 4, 1863, April 30, 1864, all typescripts in Letters of Joseph Eggleston Johnston to Louis T. Wigfall, 1862-1868, Louis T. Wigfall Family Papers, Archives Collection, University of Texas Library. // This is yet another example of flawed command structure and authorities. On paper, Johnston's command encompassed both sides of the river, but in reality he had no actual authority west of the Mississippi, nor could he order Holmes to do anything. Instead, he had to seek the president's approval to facilitate unified action by Confederate forces east and west of the river.s

10 Jones, *Confederate Strategy*, 111-130; Davis to Holmes, December 21, 1862, *OR* vol. 52, pt. II, 397-399.

John G. Walker. *LOC*

unprotected save for Brigadier General Thomas J. Churchill's Division of about 5,000 men now holding Fort Hindman near Arkansas Post. Holmes therefore requested that he be left to his own discretion in deciding upon any movement to reinforce Pemberton. In fact, Holmes had already reached the do-nothing conclusion because of the distance and the bad roads: reinforcements bound for Vicksburg drawn from Arkansas would probably be too late to be effective anyway. The only positive suggestion offered by Holmes was the dubious one that he be permitted to reimpose martial law on Arkansas to combat growing civilian demoralization and unrest.[11]

A clear indication of Holmes's total failure as a department commander was his neglect even to mention Louisiana and Texas, the other two districts of his department. He had failed to integrate the activities of his three districts and was literally incapable of marshaling whatever combined resources the Trans-Mississippi Department might offer to bolster the defense of the lower river. Even in the Arkansas Valley, upon which he had focused his

11 Holmes to the President, December 29, 1862, Correspondence of General T. H. Holmes, 1861-1864, Chapter II, Vol. 358, Record Group 109, National Archives. // John G. Walker served with some distinction in the Army of Northern Virginia before receiving a transfer to the Trans-Mississippi. He is one of the few leaders who moved west having served competently in the Virginia theater of operations. His service in the Trans-Mississippi similarly reflected a steady hand on campaign and in battle. He served in Stonewall Jackson's organization in the Army of Northern Virginia and this service inculcated aggressiveness in Walker. His Texas Division became well-known west of the river as "Walker's Greyhounds" because of its ability to move so rapidly and strike hard upon arrival. Walker's short memoir of his service west of the river, "The War of Secession West of the Mississippi River During the Years 1863-4 & 5" (Mss. Myron Gwinner Collection, United States Army History Institute, Carlisle Barracks, Pennsylvania) provides an interesting account of his thoughts on operations in the Trans-Mississippi after the Union army cut the Confederacy in two following the fall of Vicksburg. It was published with annotations as *Greyhound Commander: Confederate General John G. Walker's History of the Civil War West of the Mississippi*, Richard Lowe, ed. (Baton Rouge, 2013). Lowe is also the author of *Greyhound Commander: Confederate General John G. Walker's History of the Civil War West of the Mississippi* (Baton Rouge, 2004).

attention, Holmes had dispersed his troops so widely under Hindman, Churchill, and Walker that they could not render each other effective mutual support. Concentration of force, the policy that the president had strongly urged on him, was a principle of war General Holmes seems never to have learned.[12]

*   *   *

DISCONTENT INCREASED RAPIDLY in Arkansas in the winter of 1862, with the disgruntled Albert Pike—no longer a Confederate officer—no doubt fanning its flames with public denunciations of Holmes and Hindman. On December 20, Pike wrote a scathing letter accusing his two former superiors of incompetence, dishonesty, and the suppression of civil liberties that was published in the press. Coming hard on the news of Hindman's defeat at Prairie Grove, Pike's intemperate outburst could only have depressed the already low state of public morale.[13]

Real disaster struck in Arkansas the following month on January 9, 1863, when General Churchill was attacked at Arkansas Post by Major General John A. McClernand's 30,000-man Army of the Mississippi, supported by the powerful river fleet of Rear Admiral David Dixon Porter. Holmes ordered Churchill to fight to the last man during the brief siege that followed, but three days later on January 12, Churchill was compelled to surrender his 5,000 men.[14]

Churchill's surrender was a staggering blow to the public morale. A short time before, because of Holmes's reports of the spreading dissatisfaction and indeed outright disloyalty in Arkansas, the president had suspended the writ of habeas corpus in that state and in the Indian country, a measure that served to further increase public hostility to Holmes and Hindman. By February, Holmes admitted frankly to President Davis that the unrest in Arkansas was beyond anything the chief executive could imagine. Pike's letter, a copy of

12 // The Confederacy's only true advantage in the war, since it was severely outnumbered and suffered a paucity of resources and infrastructure, was its interior lines. This enabled the rapid shift of forces to achieve concentration of force that Davis counseled to Holmes. Yet, Holmes seemed incapable of grasping this point.

13 Brown, "Albert Pike," 707-712; A Citizen of Texas to Davis, January 12, 1863, R. W. Loughery to Davis, January 12, 18, February 10, 1863, John M. Chapman to A. H. Garland, January 30, 1863, C. P. Bartmand to A. H. Garland, February 12, 1863, all in Jefferson Davis Collection, Louisiana Historical Association Collection; Holmes to R. W. Johnson and to J. G. Walker, February 16, 18, 1863, both in correspondence of General T. H. Holmes, 1861-1864, Chapter II, vol. 358, Record Group 109, National Archives.

14 // For more on the significance of the loss of Arkansas Post, see Neil P. Chatelain, *Defending the Arteries of Rebellion: Confederate Naval Operations in the Mississippi River Valley, 1861–1865* (El Dorado Hills, CA, 2020), which offers a comprehensive overview of Confederate efforts to defend the Mississippi Valley and its tributaries.

which he forwarded, was merely one of many such examples. Holmes again strongly suggested that another officer be sent to supersede him for the good of the "Holy Cause."[15]

Unknown to Holmes, the Richmond authorities had already decided to reorganize the Trans-Mississippi. Orders of January 14 assigned Lieutenant General Edmund Kirby Smith to command the "Southwestern Army embracing the Department of West Louisiana and Texas." This command, with headquarters at Alexandria, Louisiana, would be distinct from Holmes's Trans-Mississippi Department. Both Davis and Seddon orally instructed Smith that his chief responsibility would be to participate in defense of the lower river. Before he could reach his new headquarters, however, Davis had finally concluded that his old and trusted friend Holmes must be superseded. On February 9, Smith's responsibilities were enlarged to include command of the entire Trans-Mississippi Department. As General Taylor was to write after the war, "Holmes . . . had accomplished nothing except to lose five thousand of his best troops captured at Arkansas Post by General Sherman."[16]

The new commander of the Trans-Mississippi was a West Point graduate of the Class of 1845. Smith distinguished himself in the hand-to-hand fighting at Palo Alto during the Mexican War and afterward taught mathematics at West Point before serving on the Indian frontier. Smith resigned from the United States Army as a major in March of 1861, joined the Confederate service as a colonel, and was soon assigned as chief of staff to Joseph E. Johnston. His rise in rank was rapid. He was promoted to brigadier general in June of 1861 and commanded a brigade of infantry at First Manassas (Bull Run). That October, after promotion to major general, he was given a division. In March of 1862 he became commander of the turbulent Department of East Tennessee. During August and September of 1862, Smith conducted active operations in Kentucky, for which he subsequently received the thanks of Congress and promotion to lieutenant general. The officer was well acquainted with at least a part of his new Trans-Mississippi command from his "Old Army" service on the Texas frontier, where he had acquired a half-interest in a cattle ranch.[17] The assignment promised new vigor in departmental administration for he was, in contrast to the prematurely decaying Holmes, in the prime years of maturity at thirty-nine, and brought with him a reputation as a first rate administrator and a "trouble shooter."

---

15 Samuel Cooper to Holmes, January 29, 1863, *OR* vol. 22, pt. II, 780; Holmes to the President, February 12, 1863, Correspondence of General T. H. Holmes 1861-1864, Chapter II, vol. 358, Record Group 109, National Archives.

16 Jones, *Confederate Strategy*, 206-207; Special Orders No. 11, Adj. and Insp. General's Office, Richmond, January 14, 1863, *OR* vol. 15, 948; Samuel Cooper to Smith, February 9, 1863, ibid., 972; Joseph Howard Parks, *General Edmund Kirby Smith, C. S.A.* (Baton Rouge, 1954), 251-256; Taylor, *Destruction and Reconstruction*, 150.

17 Details of Smith's previous career from Parks, *Kirby Smith*, 22-251. // Joseph H. Parks' biography of Edmund Kirby Smith remains the standard text on the general even though it was published almost seventy years ago.

C hapter 9

The Department Faces Total Isolation
February – July 1863

General KIRBY SMITH had set out for his new assignment in late January, accompanied by his family and staff. The pace was leisurely, and the party separated at Montgomery, with various members of the staff going by different routes to visit families and friends. By March 7 they had reassembled at Alexandria, Louisiana, where Smith established his headquarters.

Smith's personal staff at that time consisted of Captain John G. Meem, Jr., and First Lieutenant Edward Cunningham, aides-de-camp, and one volunteer aid-de-camp. The personal staff was soon increased by two additional volunteer aides-de-camp. Smith's department staff included Brigadier General William R. Boggs, chief of staff; Captains Joseph F. Belton and Henry P. Pratt, assistant adjutants general; Colonel Benjamin Allston, inspector general; Major John F. Minter, chief quartermaster; Major William H. Thomas, chief of subsistence; Lieutenant Colonel John A. Brown, chief of ordnance and artillery, and Surgeon Sol A. Smith, medical director. All of these officers, save Major Minter, appear to have served with the general east of the Mississippi. The surgeon Dr. Smith, a native of Alexandria, was not only a trusted confidential advisor to Smith, but a close family friend as well.[1]

Shortly after Smith's arrival, he and General Richard Taylor conferred on the military situation. Not only were the Federals under U. S. Grant operating against Vicksburg, but General Nathaniel Banks was sure to attempt to clear Taylor's forces from the Teche and lower Atchafalaya and then invest Port Hudson to further isolate the Trans-Mississippi. According to Taylor, Banks had 20,000 men available for use against his 2,700. Taylor

---

1   Parks, *Kirby Smith*, 253-254; General Orders No. 5, Hdqrs. Trans-Miss. Dept., April 20, 1863, *OR* vol. 22, pt. II, 828; William K. Boyd, editor, William R. Boggs, *Military Reminiscences of General William R. Boggs. C.S.A.* (Durham, N.C., 1913), 60.

Edmund Kirby Smith. LOC

requested reinforcement from the District of Arkansas. Smith replied that he was under instructions from President Davis himself to send Walker's Texas Division to Taylor.[2]

Smith set out almost immediately for an inspection of the District of Arkansas. Holmes, at Little Rock, was delighted with the turn of events. "I thank you my Dear Sir, for sending Gen'l. Smith to La. and Texas," he had written President Davis on March 6. "I was unable to do anything there." Holmes was unaware at that time that Smith had completely superseded him, and was pleased to learn that he was now merely district commander of Arkansas.

He urged Smith to establish department headquarters at Little Rock, but Smith had already decided on Shreveport because of its central location, "though a miserable place with a miserable population," thought the new commander. To his wife, Smith confided that conditions in Arkansas were not as bad as they had been painted, and he seems to have told Holmes the same thing, for Holmes happily wrote Davis that Smith had been "agreeably disappointed" at the condition of the army and the country. Smith's visit did confirm, however, that Holmes had devoted most of his attention to Arkansas and very little to the rest of the Department. The new chief of staff, General Boggs, was appalled to find no regular communications between department headquarters and the district headquarters.[3]

While Smith was in Arkansas, Sterling Price recrossed the river with his staff on March 18. Given his choice by Smith of the infantry divisions then in Arkansas, Price on April 1 accepted command of Brigadier General Daniel Frost's division. Price's return climaxed a long campaign by a number of Missouri and Arkansas politicians, the most persistent of

---

2   Taylor, *Destruction and Reconstruction,* 151-152; Boggs, *Reminiscences,* 54.

3   Holmes to Davis, March 6, April 7, 1863, both in Correspondence of General T. H. Holmes, 1861-1864, Chap. II, vol. 358, Record Group 109, National Archives; Smith to his Wife, March 19, 1863, in Edmund Kirby Smith Papers, Ramsdell Microfilms in Archives Collection, University of Texas Library, with the originals in the Southern Historical Collection, University of North Carolina; Boggs, *Reminiscences,* 57.

them being Thomas C. Reynolds, who had assumed the title of governor of Missouri after the death of Governor Claiborne Jackson in December 1862. As far back as February 3, Reynolds had persuaded Davis and Seddon to order Pemberton and Smith to arrange a transfer of an equal number of Trans-Mississippi troops east in exchange for Price and his men, so long as the transfer would not endanger Vicksburg. In spite of these instructions Pemberton did not see fit to release the Missourians for service west of the river, nor did Smith offer substitutes for them, but on February 27 Pemberton released Price and his staff to return to the Trans-Mississippi theater.[4]

Governor Reynolds started for the Trans-Mississippi soon after arranging Price's transfer back west of the river. By May 18, he had set up his temporary capital headquarters at Camden, Arkansas, where he found many Missouri state records and a few state officials. By June 27 Reynolds was in Little Rock, where he planned to establish Missouri's provisional government-in-exile. En route to Arkansas he discussed military affairs with General Smith, who assured him that he was anxious to lead an expedition into Missouri. Reynolds remarked in a letter to a friend that everywhere in Arkansas, people were looking forward to a Missouri invasion for two reasons of equal importance; it would rid them of the enemy, and of Confederate troops.[5]

Even General Holmes had recognized the terrible difficulties of any operations aimed at Missouri through the 150-mile-wide belt of desolation above the Arkansas Valley, however General Smith was necessarily more concerned with Louisiana during the spring of 1863. Upon his return from Arkansas, Smith received word that Federal troops were concentrating at Berwick Bay, apparently in preparation for General Banks's expected sweep of western Louisiana against General Taylor. Smith immediately summoned assistance for Taylor by directing Holmes to send John Walker's Division from Pine Bluff to Monroe, and General John Magruder to dispatch all available troops to Opelousas. On April 20, the Union advance reached Opelousas, obliging Smith to change the destination of the Texan troops to Niblett's Bluff and make a hasty exodus from Alexandria.[6] The

4   Castel, *Price*, 133-136, 139; Davis to the Senators and Representatives from Arkansas, March 30, 1863, *OR* vol. 53, 863-865; General Orders No. I, Hq. Price's Division, April 1, 1863, ibid. vol. 13, pt. II, 811.

5   William R. Geise, "Missouri's Confederate Capital in Marshall, Texas," *Southwestern Historical Quarterly*, lxvi (October, 1962), 199-200; Reynolds to W. P. Johnson, May 26, 1863, Thomas C. Reynolds Papers, Ramsdell Microfilms in Archives Collection, University of Texas Library, originals in Manuscript Division, Library of Congress.

6   Holmes to J. G. Walker, March 5, 1863, in Correspondence of General T, H. Holmes, 1861-1864, Chap. II, vol. 358, Record Group 109, National Archives. The arrival of the Texas troops, who were poorly equipped, strained the meager resources of Major Brent's ordnance department. He had already provided Sibley's brigade, which came half armed, with 500 .69 muskets, 660 bayonet scabbards, 1,100 canteens, and 900 knapsacks, among other things. Lieutenant Colonel James Arthur Lyon Fremantle, the British observer of the conflict, witnessed the departure of a Texas

headquarters staff and all of the moveable supplies were loaded aboard steamboats and moved up the Red River to the comparative safety of Shreveport, where headquarters resumed functioning on April 27.

Fortunately for the Confederates, Banks delayed some two weeks in Opelousas until he learned that Admiral Porter's gunboats had been released from service with Grant below Vicksburg and were steaming up the Red River toward Alexandria. Banks's troops entered the deserted town on May 8.

In the face of a probable powerful Federal thrust up the Red River threatening Shreveport and even portending an invasion of Texas, Smith was prepared to order Holmes's forces to move to Louisiana and abandon the Arkansas Valley. This drastic move proved unnecessary, however, for Banks withdrew from Alexandria across the Mississippi to lay siege to Port Hudson, Louisiana.[7]

Taylor's troops soon moved back into the positions they had previously occupied, but the Union withdrawal had not been forced by Confederate arms, and the local citizens were shocked by the ease of the Yankee occupation. The devastation of their property and the defection to the Federals of hundreds of their slaves had shaken their confidence in the abilities of the Confederate troops to defend them. Taylor now became an "object of misrepresentation and abuse" in many quarters of western Louisiana.[8]

*   *   *

WHILE THESE SIGNIFICANT events were happening in the field, the routine of organizing the new department headquarters continued. One vexing administrative problem had been what to do with the staff officers already serving in the department who held appointments directly from the War Department. The disgruntlement they would have

---

regiment for Niblett's Bluff "armed with every variety of weapon; about sixty had Enfield rifles; the remainder carried shotguns (fowling pieces), carbines, or long rifles of a peculiar and antiquated manufacture. None had swords or bayonets—all had six-shooters and bowie-knives." The sophisticated British officer found their appearance "droll," they being dressed in every variety of costume. He did admit, however, they "were a fine, determined-looking lot." A. J. L. Fremantle, *Three Months in the Southern States: April-June, 1863* (New York, 1864), 74-75; Brent to Lindsay, March 18, 1863, J. L. Brent Papers, Louisiana Historical Association Collection.

7 Discussion of military movements in spring, 1863, is based on Kenneth P. Williams, *Lincoln Finds a General: A Military Study of the Civil War*, 5 vols. (New York, 1959), vol. 5, 25-26; Parks, Smith, 259-266, and Robert L. Kerby, *Kirby Smith's Confederacy: The Trans-Mississippi South, 1863-1865* (New York, 1972), 98-112.

8 Report of Messrs. Pratt and King to his Excellency Henry W. Allen, Governor of the State of Louisiana, n.d., Kirby Smith Papers; Reynolds to Tayler, December 3, 1863, Reynolds Papers; Thomas O. Moore to Davis, December 26, 1863, in Charles L. Dufour, *Nine Men in Gray* (Garden City, N.Y., 1963), 26.

(Right) Benjamin Huger. *LOC*

(Below) William Boggs. *LOC*

felt at being summarily superseded by Kirby Smith's appointees was largely dissipated by assignments to Smith's staff. Colonel Sam S. Anderson, Holmes's adjutant general, assumed the same duties under Smith at Shreveport. Dr. John M. Haden of Holmes's staff was made department medical director, while Smith's medical director, Dr. Sol Smith, became medical director of departmental hospitals. Major Thomas G. Rhett, Holmes's chief of ordnance, was continued in that office, and Smith's appointee Colonel John A. Brown was redesignated chief of artillery. To accommodate Holmes's chief commissary, Major William B. Blair, a new Bureau of Subsistence was created for him to head; Smith kept his own chief commissary, Major Thomas, in that office.

Other new bureaus and staff positions were created as additional officers were ordered to department headquarters in the spring and summer of 1863, either by Smith or by the War Department. The incoming senior officers and their assignments included Major General Benjamin Huger (chief of the Bureau of Ordnance), Brigadier General Elkanah Greer (commandant of conscripts for the Trans-Mississippi Department), and Colonel Thomas Green Clemson (chief of the Nitre and Mining Bureau). Thus began the proliferation of bureaus and staff agencies that moved one later critic to dub Shreveport the "Sacred Benares on the Red River."[9]

According to Chief of Staff William Boggs, Smith's staff functioned quite smoothly. Still, tension existed between Boggs and Dr. Sol Smith, Kirby Smith's close friend and

9 // Colonel Clemson is the namesake for Clemson University. He left the property of his estate to the state of South Carolina for the purpose of establishing an agricultural college. Taylor, *Destruction and Reconstruction*, 188-189.

advisor. Boggs disliked what he considered Dr. Smith's undue influence with the general when it came to military matters. Friction also existed between Colonel Anderson and Major Guy M. Bryan, an assistant adjutant general assigned not to the adjutant general's office, but to headquarters as Smith's personal advisor on affairs in Texas.

Other working relationships in the department staff seem to have been less tense. Among the aides-de-camp, Captain Meem acted as signal officer as well as chief aide. Of the assistant adjutants general, Captain Belton worked in Smith's private office as a kind of confidential clerk, while the other, Captain Pratt, supervised the adjutant general's clerks. In the chief of staff's office were Captain P. H. Thompson, an acting assistant adjutant general, and Boggs's brother Robert, who served as aide-de-camp to Boggs. The inspector general, Colonel Benjamin Allston, had two assistants: Major Wright Schaumburg, who had accompanied him west of the river, and Captain B. W. Marston. A captain named William Freret acted as chief engineer until the arrival of Major Henry T. Douglas in July. Two quartermaster officers, Major Charles E. Carr and Major William H. Haynes, served as, respectively, chief of the Pay Bureau and chief of the Clothing Bureau.

A few headquarters staff officers performed important duties without official titles. One of these was Dr. David W. Yandell, who owed his presence in the Trans-Mississippi Department to President Davis's personal disfavor. Yandell was serving in the Army of Mississippi when he was accused of writing derogatory statements about the president that were published in the press; not long after, he was transferred west of the river. Yandell served as Smith's physician in the field. Later, when Smith attempted to promote him to the position of department medical director, Richmond flatly rejected the recommendation.[10]

Although the Trans-Mississippi Department was often used by the War Department as a dumping ground for officers unwanted east of the river, the bureau chiefs and staff officers at Shreveport and Marshall in Texas possessed, in the aggregate, a considerable amount of quality military experience. General Huger had served on the staff of Winfield Scott during the Mexican War and at the outbreak of the Civil War was a respected ordnance inspector at foundries for the United States Army. General Boggs was also a career officer. After he graduated from West Point in 1849, Boggs spent twelve years in staff assignments and was thus crafted by experience for his position as chief of staff. Many of the less senior officers

---

10 The wording of the letter forbidding Yandell's appointment as medical director approaches official admission of the use of the Trans-Mississippi Department as a sort of "Devil's Island" by the War Department. The intention behind the transfer of Yandell to the Trans-Mississippi was to remove him from his former position "to one in which he could have less opportunity for exercising undue influence upon the Army and the community." H. L. Clay to Smith, July 9, 1864, in Jefferson Davis Collection, Louisiana Historical Association Collection. Discussion of staff assignments and functions is based on Boggs, *Reminiscences*, 59-68, and General Orders Nos. 3, 5, 15, and 37, Hdqrs. Trans-Miss. Dept., March 10, April 20, June 3, August 17, 1863, *OR* vol. 22, pt. II, 799, 828, 853, 969; Boggs to Bryan, Bryan to Boggs, both December 14, 1863, Bryan to Smith, December 15, 1863, all in Bryan Papers.

had also followed the military profession. Lieutenant Colonel Lawrence W. O'Bannon, who became chief of the Quartermaster Bureau in the fall of 1863, was originally commissioned from the ranks for bravery in the Mexican War. Colonel Sam Anderson was a Regular Army artillery officer. Colonels William Blair and John Brown and Major Thomas Rhett had served in the United States Army. Major Minter, the chief quartermaster, had many years of quartermaster officer experience before the Civil War, and Dr. John M. Haden, the medical director, became a medical officer in 1847 and served in the Mexican War as well as on several expeditions against the Indians.[11]

One of Boggs's first cares as chief of staff was to establish a courier service. Six companies of teen-aged boys age fifteen and younger were recruited, given the same pay and allowances as cavalrymen, and put under the command of appropriate unattached officers. At any given time, three of these companies were on actual courier duty, the other and the other three in camp for rest and instruction. According to Boggs, this system worked well for the remainder of the war. Indeed, a cursory examination of the sending and receiving dates of later departmental correspondence indicates quite satisfactory communications for that time and place. For example, on average, a dozen separate items sent from Alexandria were received at Shreveport 200 miles distant and two and one-half days later. This suggests that correspondence was carried, at least to the more accessible places, at a rate of about seventy-five miles a day.[12]

Of course, this courier service was not the only mode of communication. Correspondence between Shreveport and Louisiana district headquarters at Alexandria could and doubtless did go by steamboat on thje Red River when vessels were available. A telegraph line existed between Shreveport and Camden, soon to become the site of district headquarters in Arkansas, and instructions were given that June to string wire between Shreveport and Marshall or Tyler, Texas.[13]

A stage line connected Shreveport with Marshall, which after General Smith's arrival began developing as a kind of auxiliary headquarters to Shreveport. A small amount of usable railroad track existed between Shreveport and Marshall, and in the spring of 1863, the journey between those two places by rail and stage took about eight hours. Subsequently, on Smith's orders, more railroad track was laid so that by the spring of 1864, the line extended from about one mile east of Marshall to a point about fourteen miles west of Shreveport. Although circuitous, the fastest route between Texas district headquarters, at Houston, and Shreveport was probably by way of Navasota on the Houston and Central Texas Railroad. The run to Navasota, some seventy miles to the northwest of Houston, took six hours

11   Boggs, *Reminiscences*, x-xii, 61-67; William S. Speer, ed., *The Encyclopedia of the New West*, 2 vols. (Marshall, Texas, 1881), vol. 1, 317-318, 366-368.

12   Boggs, *Reminiscences*, 68-69.

13   Special Orders No. 56, Hdqrs. Trans-Miss. Dept., June 11, 1863, in Civil War Papers, Louisiana Historical Association Collection, Tulane University Library.

including a stop at Hempstead, where stage connections could be had for Austin. At Navasota, stages departed three times weekly for Shreveport.[14]

At the same time communications were improving west of the river in the spring of 1863, communications and supply lines to the east bank of the river were collapsing. Although occasional supplies might find their way westward across the river—an agent of the indefatigable Major Brent brought 2,000 friction primers across in the first week of June— the Yankee gunboats roaming freely between Vicksburg and Port Hudson made large shipments impossible. Even individuals or very small parties were forced to use extreme caution in crossing. The favored place seemed to be between Natchez and Vidalia, Louisiana. Governor Reynolds, on his passage there, experienced the excitement of sighting a Federal gunboat.[15]

This breakdown of communications across the Mississippi naturally meant the end of resupply for the Trans-Mississippi from eastern arsenals and depots. It also meant that corn, sugar, and Texas beef that might otherwise have reached the Armies of Tennessee and Mississippi were cut off. Officers commanding Trans-Mississippi troops east of the river told Governor Reynolds that the principal reason for desertion among them was the "difficulty of communicating with their families." The final severing of the vital Confederate supply and communications chain across the river would not occur until the surrenders of Vicksburg and Port Hudson in July of 1863, but it was already truly broken by early spring. The loss of the last two Confederate fortresses on the river meant that the break would be permanent. As Joseph E. Johnston lamented after the war, "the river had been captured by the Federal fleets, and the 'severance of the Confederacy' accomplished" *before* General Grant's army even landed below Vicksburg.[16]

Because of the ominous possibility that the "severance" would be permanent, steps were taken in the Trans-Mississippi Department to cope with that eventuality. In the District of Louisiana, Major Brent, whose problems had increased with the arrival of the badly armed Texas units, intensified his efforts to render his ordnance department self-sustaining. As early as May 13, he ordered the ordnance workshops to prepare to support the district without help from the east bank of the river, and he directed Captain A. J. Lindsay at Shreveport to buy or to seize the J. W. Jones Foundry there. Lindsay was given $30,000 with which to hire civilians and was authorized to request details of men from post commanders,

14 Fremantle, *Three Months in the Southern States*, 65; Andrew Forest Muir, "The Thirty-Second Parallel Pacific Railroad in Texas to 1872," unpublished Ph.D. dissertation, University of Texas, 1949, 163-164.

15 Brent to Rhett, June 16, 1863, J. L. Brent Papers, Louisiana Historical Association Collection; Fremantle, *Three Months in the Southern States*, 99-100; Reynolds to W. P. Johnson, May 26, 1863, Reynolds Papers.

16 M. Jeff Thompson to W. K. Handy, February 24, 1864, General M. Jeff Thompson Collection, Tulane University Library; Reynolds to J. H. Reagan, May 20, 1863, Reynolds Papers, Johnston, *Narrative*, 224.

from the commander of state troops, and from hospitals having patients who were suffering only from fatigue.

The manufacturing priorities assigned in Brent's directive give an interesting picture both of the ordnance shortages in Louisiana and of the weapons in principal use. First, Lindsay was to make 50,000 rounds of shotgun ammunition with caps, mainly for use by the cavalry. Next, he was to prepare 6,000 cartridges for the .69 Belgian rifled musket, primarily an infantry weapon. Thereafter, he was to make as much ammunition as possible—six-pounder round shot and spherical case—for the field artillery. A month later, because "of the critical condition of our communications with the east of the Mississippi," Brent appealed for help from General Magruder's chief of ordnance in Texas. Brent wanted particularly to borrow shotgun caps and enough ammunition for the twelve field batteries of light artillery he had to supply. Brent also persisted in his attempts to get supplies across the river. On June 24, he wrote his agent in Natchez, Captain Henry F. Springer, to send over immediately everything possible from Mississippi arsenals without waiting for supplies to come in from more distant sources. Brent was particularly anxious for good friction primers, an item frequently defective, and he hoped to receive artillery harnesses and three-inch rifled shell. He even mentioned the great opportunities for employing several Parrott guns along Louisiana's broad waterways, but he had to content himself with one thirty-pound 4.2 Parrott gun he had already set his men to salvaging from the wreck of the steamer *De Soto*.[17]

Colonel Brown, at department headquarters, helped Brent in his mad scramble for ordnance. In the first week of May, Brown ordered Little Rock to supply Louisiana with 1,500 rounds of field artillery ammunition. He had already sent special agents east of the river to attempt to procure 10,000 stand of small arms—evidently at Vicksburg—as well as artillery ammunition, harnesses, and accouterments. In all likelihood, none of this got across to the Trans-Mississippi. Brown also put Captain Lindsay in charge of both the Shreveport arsenal and the Jones Foundry at Shreveport. Soon thereafter, Lindsay was able to report to Brent that he was rapidly turning out round shot and six- and twelve-pounder spherical case. Lindsay promised to supply the cartridges for shotguns and Belgian rifles Brent wanted as soon as Brent provided him with the caps.[18]

If the river was permanently lost to the Confederacy, the chief munition of war, i.e., currency, would be in short supply. On June 4, General Smith suggested to Secretary of the Treasury Christopher Memminger that in order to provide funds the notes held by Confederate receivers and collectors in the Trans-Mississippi should be reissued. Smith had already ordered local depositories to retain collected notes without cancellation subject to

17 Brent to Lindsay, May 13, 1863, Brent to Chief of Ordnance, District of Texas, June 16, 1863, Brent to Rhett, June 18, 1863, Brent to Springer, June 24, 1863, all in J. L. Brent Papers, Louisiana Historical Association Collection.

18 John A. Brown to Brent, May 7, 1863, Brent to John A. Brown, May 28, 1863, Lindsay to Brent, May 17, 1863, all ibid.

the secretary's approval. He also urged that tax collectors and a Treasury agent with full power to conduct Treasury affairs should be sent to the Trans-Mississippi Department at once. Smith painted a grim picture: "All communication between this point and Richmond is now attended with great hazard, and owing to the superior naval force of the enemy on the Mississippi, it is liable at any time to interruption, and possibly may be entirely suspended."[19]

*   *   *

EVENTS ALONG THE Mississippi River had little visible effect in Texas. General Magruder pointed out to Governor Lubbock in early June that the failure of the Federals to secure a foothold on the Texas coast had given Texans a false sense of security. The people of the state, explained Magruder, seemed "to have lost all apprehension for the future." Recent events in Louisiana provided sufficient warning of the enemy's intention to subjugate Texas whether the Union was successful in controlling the Mississippi or not. Magruder asked Governor Lubbock to call up 10,000 state militia for six months of active training. The general also expressed eagerness to meet the enemy beyond Texas "even at sea"—a reference to Magruder's having at his disposal a small coastal fleet composed of vessels used in the retaking of Galveston and the Federal vessels captured there. He had placed this small fleet under command of Leon Smith, who bore the title of Superintendent of Vessels.[20]

Magruder's apprehensions notwithstanding, Texas remained relatively peaceful, though rumors of a secret movement to overthrow the Confederacy did circulate. They were strong enough to impel Guy M. Bryan to warn President Davis confidentially that Sam Houston had publicly referred to him as "Jeffy Davis," and that Houston was ready at any moment to take advantage of the undercurrent of unrest, perhaps by restoring the Lone Star flag to Texas. The only actual violence, however, was on the Indian frontier, where Indians were raiding from the Red River and had forced the abandonment of Clay County to within forty miles of Austin. Reports of Indian forays southwest of Austin in Gillespie, Bandera, and Kerr counties, caused the adjutant general of Texas to request Confederate troops from Magruder to augment the state's Frontier Regiment. A good deal of grumbling could be heard among frontier people about whether it was really necessary "to take off . . . men to protect the cows and calves of the people of the lower country against a prospective or threatened invasion from the abolitionists and leave their own women and children

19 Smith to C. G. Memminger, June 4, 1863, Civil War Papers, Louisiana Historical Association Collection.

20 Magruder to Lubbock, June 4, 1863, Guy M. Bryan Papers; S. R. Mallory to Magruder, March 31, 1863, Seddon to Magruder, April 2, 18, Leon Smith to Assistant Adjutant; General District of Texas, June 6, 1863, all in District of Texas, New Mexico, and Arizona, Trans-Mississippi Department, Military Departments, Chap. II, vol. 252, Record Group 109, National Archives.

exposed to a real and positive inroad of murderous savages who respect neither age nor sex."[21]

Up in Arkansas, meanwhile, General Holmes still procrastinated and his operations continued to evidence his characteristic arbitrary nature. At a time when he should have been concentrating his forces, probably for a movement against Helena, he instead authorized John S. Marmaduke to take his cavalry division on what proved to be an abortive raid into Missouri. Even Holmes did not expect any worthwhile results from Marmaduke, who counted "too much on the promises of Missouri people." Holmes's only real explanation for having personally authorized the raid was that Marmaduke had no forage for his horses at his base near Pocahontas.

Holmes's indecision over Helena is understandable. About the time of Marmaduke's departure, Holmes was directed by Kirby Smith to send John Walker's division to Louisiana. Smith, he feared, had "gone off half-cocked" because Holmes was sure Walker would be needed in Arkansas. Nevertheless, Holmes seemed to be contemplating offensive action at this time. On May 22, 1863, he observed that if he was not required to send more troops south, he would shortly concentrate his forces at Jacksonport, which in relation to Little Rock lay toward Missouri rather than toward Helena.[22] Five days later Holmes ordered Sterling Price's division to move to Jacksonport and placed the hero of Confederate Missourians in command of all the troops in northern Arkansas. More orders arrived for Holmes to disperse his troops. On June 1, Smith directed him to send Brigadier General James C. Tappan's Arkansas brigade, part of Price's division, south to reinforce General Taylor. This directive and his inspector general's report that Marmaduke's division, just returned from Missouri, was "in perfectly dilipidated [sic] condition" seems to have shattered these plans. That same day Holmes wrote to General Boggs that he had hoped to strike Helena and then Missouri, but he now felt incapable of doing so. His complaint to Boggs was a curious one in the light of his concentration of Price's forces in the direction of Missouri, rather than Helena.[23]

By June, dissatisfaction with Holmes had reached epidemic proportions in Arkansas. Although his acquaintance with Holmes was brief, the astute Governor Reynolds had already suggested to General Smith that, in view of the old man's despondency, a close

21 Bryan to Davis, March 9, 1863, Jefferson Davis Collection, Louisiana Historical Association Collection; J. Y. Dashiel to Magruder, March 7, 1863, District of Texas, New Mexico, and Arizona, Trans Mississippi Department, Military Departments, Chap. II, vol. 252, Record Group 109, National Archives; Shreveport, *South-Western*, April 1, 1863.

22 Holmes to Davis, April 7, 1863, Holmes to J. G. Walker, April 22, 1863, Holmes to Marmaduke, May 22, 1863, all in Correspondence of General T. H. Holmes, 1861-1864, Chap. II, vol. 358, Record Group 109, National Archives.

23 General Orders No. 5, Hq. Price's Division, June 6, 1863, *OR* vol. 22, pt. II, 860; Holmes to Boggs, June 1, 1893, Correspondence of General T. H. Holmes, 1861-1864, Chap. II, vol. 358, Record Group 109, National Archives.

supervision be maintained over his decisions—particularly regarding the Arkansas Valley.[24] But this was not the case. On June 8, apparently seething with indecision, Holmes set out accompanied by Reynolds to confer with Price at Jacksonport. The ambulance in which they were riding soon broke down, forcing their return to Little Rock. During the abortive journey Holmes revealed to Reynolds his reluctance to mount an attack on Helena. Failure, he insisted, would mean loss of the Arkansas Valley. Both Price and Reynolds urged such an attack, however, and within a week of his interrupted journey Holmes had reluctantly adopted their opinions. On June 15, he telegraphed Smith for permission to attack Helena and immediately set out for Jacksonport to take personal charge of the operation without waiting for Smith's reply.[25]

Smith's approval was soon received, and on June 22 Price's troops began the march to Helena, joined at Cotton Plant by Marmaduke's division of cavalry. The men had a miserable time struggling slowly through the rain-drenched land between the Mississippi and White rivers. On July 3, they finally joined forces some five miles from Helena with General Fagan's infantry brigade (which had marched from Little Rock) and Brigadier General Lucius Marsh Walker's cavalry division (which had been reconnoitering the Helena area). In total, the Confederate forces now under Holmes's personal command numbered between 7,000 and 8,000 men, perhaps double the number of the Union defenders at Helena. More than counterbalancing their numerical superiority, however, were the strongly fortified Union positions, the high ground held by the defense, and the more than adequate Federal artillery support, including cannons belonging to the gunboats *Hastings* and *Tyler*.

Holmes's poorly coordinated attack began early on the morning of July 4. By mid-morning, the broken terrain, fatigue, poor discipline, inept battlefield leadership, and the well-prepared Union defenses had played a part in shattering the Confederate effort. Holmes realized the attack had ground to a standstill (no units except a few of Price's had taken their objectives) and at 10:30 a.m. ordered a general withdrawal. The short battle of Helena was over. About the same hour downriver some two hundred miles, General Pemberton was surrendering the fortress of Vicksburg to General Grant. Holmes's attack had not merely failed, but his procrastination had rendered it totally irrelevant to the relief of Vicksburg.[26]

The repulse at Helena was followed by a wave of recriminations. Holmes, embittered no doubt by Price's part in persuading him to make the attack in the first place, wrote to

---

24 Brown, "Pike," 713-714; Reynolds to Smith, May 13, 23, 25, 1863, in Reynolds Papers.

25 Reynolds to E. C. Cabell, July 4, 1863, ibid.

26 Military movements connected with the battle of Helena are based on Williams, *Lincoln Finds a General*, vol. V, 8-17; Castel, *Price*, 143-145; and Kerby, Kirby Smith's *Confederacy*, 131-132. // See Mark K. Christ, *Civil War Arkansas, 1863: The Battle for a State* (Norman, OK, 2010), and Mark K. Christ, *Rugged and Sublime: The Civil War in Arkansas* (Fayetteville, NC, 1994), for more information about the abortive battle of Helena.

President Davis that the Missourian was "utterly and entirely worthless in the field, an imbecile in the cabinet without resource and everywhere thinking of nothing and caring for nothing but some sound that will echo and re-echo Sterling Price." In justification of himself Holmes explained to Davis that the attack was made "against my own judgment" on the advice of the other generals. He even reminded the president that Davis himself had wanted Helena taken and had expressed surprise that it had not already been done. Holmes preferred charges of "misbehavior before the enemy" against Dandridge McRae, one of Price's brigade commanders. (The accusation was later found to be groundless by a court of inquiry.) The censure did not stop with mere words. General Marmaduke insisted that Lucius M. Walker, the newly assigned division commander, had, by the inactivity of his command, exposed the left flank of Marmaduke's division. Walker hotly denied this. Subsequent events at the Battle of Reed's Bridge on August 26 further strained relations between the two men, and Walker charged Marmaduke to a duel. A series of unfortunate events thereafter transpired, and Marmaduke fatally wounded Walker with his second shot and he died on September 7.[27]

No amount of bravado, self-justification, or excuses could alter the failure of Confederate arms in Arkansas, nor could they lift the gloom that descended ther following the repulse at Helena. Though Governor Reynolds might congratulate both Holmes and Price on their undoubted personal bravery and maintain the necessity of the attempt on Helena, however risky, the fact still remained that Holmes's record was one of unbroken failure. Clamor for his removal became insistent.

Pleading illness, Holmes on July 23 turned command of the District of Arkansas over to General Price. The arrangement was only temporary, for Holmes would return that September to preside over another six months of futile inactivity before his final removal.[28]

27 Holmes to the President, July 14, 1863, in Correspondence of General T. H. Holmes, 1861-1864, Chap. II, vol. 35 Record Group 109, National Archives; General Orders No. 100, Hdqrs. Trans-Miss. Dept., December 29, 1864, *OR* vol. 41, pt. IV, 1132-1133; Leo E. Huff, "The Last Duel in Arkansas: The Marmaduke-Walker Duel," *Arkansas Historical Quarterly* (Spring, 1964), 36-49.

28 Reynolds to Price and to Holmes, both July 9, 1863, both in Reynolds Papers.

Chapter 10

Isolation

July – December, 1863

While GENERAL HOLMES HAD remained mired in indecision as the drama of Vicksburg unfolded, General Taylor had striven to relieve the Union pressures on both Vicksburg and Port Hudson. After John Walker's Division and James Tappan's Brigade arrived in Louisiana, Kirby Smith ordered Taylor to take personal command of them and operate directly across the river from Vicksburg. Hampered by flood waters and unable to reinforce the eastern bank bastion directly because the western approaches to the city were under the guns of the Union fleet, Taylor from the start apparently realized the futility of these operations.

In the second week of June, having achieved no results opposite Vicksburg, Taylor proposed the removal of Walker's and Tappan's commands south of the Red River for operations in lower Louisiana, where he reasoned that threats to both Banks's communications and to New Orleans might compel the Union general to lift the siege of Port Hudson, freeing the bulk of its defenders to go to the aid of Vicksburg. Taylor's propositions, which were probably overly optimistic, were flatly rejected by Smith, although he did authorize Taylor to relinquish immediate command of the troops from Arkansas to General Walker and to go south himself. While he was angered by Smith's decision and considered it a serious strategic blunder, Taylor remained a loyal subordinate and later in the year strongly defended his commanding general against attacks in the Louisiana press. After the war, however, he commented sarcastically on the retention of Walker's and Tappan's troops opposite Vicksburg, remarking that "the pressure on General Kirby Smith to do something for Vicksburg was too strong to be resisted."[1]

---

1 Reynolds to Taylor, December 3, 1863, Reynolds Papers; Taylor, *Destruction and Reconstruction,* 166.

As a result of Smith's determination "to do something for Vicksburg," Walker's reinforced division remained opposite the city until a week after the surrender and was then withdrawn, having accomplished nothing. Taylor, meanwhile, reached his Alexandria headquarters on June 10, en route to take command of his three brigades below Opelousas. For the next two months he conducted a vigorous campaign in lower Louisiana with his tiny force during which he captured Berwick Bay in late June, bagging there 1,700 prisoners and much equipment, and at one time his scouts reached Kenner just sixteen miles above New Orleans. Taylor's brigades were too weak, however, and their accomplishments too transitory to draw Banks from Port Hudson, which surrendered five days after Vicksburg on July 9. This surrender releasing Banks's army from siege duty, which forced Taylor to fall back from his advanced positions or risk being cut off. In mid-July, Taylor withdrew his men to the comparative safety of the Bayou Teche.[2]

The twin surrenders of Vicksburg and of Port Hudson, coming so abruptly after the shock of Gettysburg, were generally considered major calamities throughout the South. Both before and after those events, however, a certain ambiguity persisted in the opinions of many Southerners, including some highly placed ones, of the value of Vicksburg and Port Hudson—especially as connecting links with the Trans-Mississippi West. Some viewed the losses realistically as confirming the grim fact of the severance of the Confederacy. Many others, however, seemed not to comprehend that the fall of Vicksburg and of Port Hudson sealed the permanent cleavage of the Confederacy. Colonel Josiah Gorgas of the Ordnance Bureau noted in his diary that the loss would probably prolong the war, but mentioned no other possible consequences. Colonel Arthur Fremantle found that people in the Trans-Mississippi deplored the loss of Vicksburg "more on account of the effects its conquest may have in prolonging the war than for any other reason." Fremantle continued: "No one seems to fear that its possession, together with Port Hudson, will really enable the Yankees to navigate the Mississippi. Nor do they fear that the latter will be able to prevent communications with the Trans Mississippi country."[3]

This relatively optimistic attitude could only be accounted for by continued Confederate possession of the west bank, which seemed to offer great possibility of interfering with Federals on the river. President Davis certainly hoped as much, arguing that, "by use of cavalry accompanied by light batteries . . . [Smith would] be able to prevent the enemy from using the Mississippi for commercial purposes." He fully recognized, however, that with their fall, Smith's "difficulties must be materially enhanced."[4]

---

2 Discussion of military movements in summer, 1863, is based on John D. Winters, *The Civil War in Louisiana* (Baton Rouge, LA, 1963), 198-204, 284-292; Kerby, *Kirby Smith's Confederacy*, 112-120, and Taylor, *Destruction and Reconstruction*, 164-176.

3 Fremantle, *Three Months in the Southern States*, 220; Frank E. Vandiver, ed., *The Civil War Diary of General Josiah Gorgas* (Birmingham, AL, 1947), 41.

4 Davis to Smith, July 14, 1863, *OR* vol. 22, pt. II, 925-927.

In recognition of these "enhanced" difficulties, especially the fact that communications with Richmond were now more uncertain than ever, all officers and government agents operating in The Trans-Mississippi Department under direct orders from Richmond were instructed to report in the future by letter to General Smith and to take their orders from him. Department staff agencies that had submitted reports directly to bureaus of the War Department were now to deliver them to the appropriate bureaus of Smith's department.[5]

President Davis, Secretary of War Seddon, and Kirby Smith himself all perceived that Smith's problems would extend well beyond strictly military matters. The war secretary suggested that Smith might have to assume civil powers. The president hinted as much in his letter to Smith of July 14: "You now have not merely a military but a political problem involved in your command." Davis feared especially that loss of the river would encourage a resurgence of separatist feelings west of the Mississippi, and he suggested a conference between Smith and the Trans Mississippi governors.[6]

Smith had anticipated the president's suggestion by writing to the four governors on July 13, inviting them and a number of the supreme court justices of their states to a conference at Marshall, Texas, on August 15.[7] Smith hoped the justices would advise him what powers he could legally assume, and the governors about how far he would be supported by the civil authorities. The men who actually came together included those from Texas (Governor Lubbock, Governor-Elect Pendleton Murrah, Senator Williamson S. Oldham, and Major Bryan); Louisiana (Governor Moore, his aide Colonel Thomas C. Manning, and Chief Justice Edwin Merrick and Associate Justice Albert Voorhies of the state supreme court); Arkansas (Senators Robert W. Johnson and Charles B. Mitchell, representing Governor Harris Flanagin, accompanied by Judge W. K. Patterson); and Missouri (Governor Reynolds). Governor Lubbock was elected chairman of the conference and committees were formed to consider a number of subjects suggested by General Smith.

The reports and recommendations of the various committees were heard by the conference on August 18. Since Richmond could no longer directly contact officials in Mexico without great difficulty, it was recommended that Smith appoint commissioners to the French and Mexican officials there. The committee considering public morale reported little active disloyalty, but warned that continued Confederate reverses or apparent abandonment of the Trans-Mississippi by the Confederate Government could fan disloyal

---

5   General Orders no. 31 and 37, Hdqrs. Trans-Miss. Dept., July 25, August 17, 1863, *OR* vol. 22, pt. II, 948, 969.

6   Davis to Smith, July 14, 1863, *OR* vol. 22, pt. II, 925-927.

7   Discussion of 1863 Governors' Conference is based on Smith to Davis, September 11, 1863, with enclosures dated August 15, 18, 1863, *OR* vol. 22, pt. II, 1003-1010; Reynolds to Cabell, to Smith, to William Preston Johnston, and to John B. Clark, July 23, 25, August 27, December 12, 1863, all in Reynolds Papers; Lubbock, *Six Decades*, 493-502; and Report of the Conference at Marshall, Texas, by Representatives from Tex., Ark., La., copy in Jefferson Davis Collection, Louisiana Historical Association Collection.

fires. Voluntary organization of the public in "Confederate Associations," dedicated to the war effort, was to be encouraged. The committee reviewing the difficult currency and cotton questions upheld Smith's right under the Confederate "Impressment Act" to buy or impress cotton in any amounts necessary to procure supplies for the army. Realizing that department procurement officers held too few Confederate Treasury notes to carry out this program, and that payment in notes would only further depreciate the Confederate currency, the committee recommended that certificates pledging the government to issue 6 percent coupon bonds to the planters for their cotton be issued by the Department. The interest on these certificates for the first two years would be paid in specie from the proceeds of government cotton sales. To provide disbursing officers with funds to pay the department's outstanding debts, non-interest-bearing Confederate notes already collected in Confederate depositories should be reissued to disbursing officers and a pledge made to refund these notes in interest-bearing bonds.

Perhaps to be expected, the extent to which Smith might exercise civil power was not clearly delineated. While one committee suggested that he could only assume the administrative powers of other branches of the central government during emergencies, another recommended that in departmental matters he assume at once the powers and prerogatives of the president. He must not, however, encroach on the authority of existing state governments.

The conference endorsed all the reports and recommendations save only the plan for issuing specie certificates for cotton. Before adjournment a resolution proposed by Senator Mitchell expressing the members' "implicit confidence" in General Smith and pledging him "united and vigorous" support was adopted, as well as a public address by Governor Reynolds that promised a "San Jacinto defeat" for "every invading army" that polluted the soil of the department.[8]

General Smith had begun to deal with the troublesome problem of regulating the cotton trade even before the conference. In addition to a Cotton Bureau at Shreveport under Lieutenant Colonel William A. Broadwell, Smith decided to establish a bureau in Texas and selected for the job Major Guy M. Bryan, the member of his staff most conversant with Texas affairs. Major Bryan found organization of the Texas bureau difficult because the aura of corruption and mismanagement already surrounding the cotton trade made Texans of standing reluctant to have their names associated with it. Colonel Alexander W. Terrill, after considerable backing and filling, declined to head this bureau not only for his reputation's sake but also because he disliked Colonel Broadwell. Judge Thomas J. Devine, to whom Terrill suggested the position, was also not interested. In the first week of October, Congressman Peter W. Gray reluctantly consented to accept the post, but he too disliked Broadwell and declined to serve after an arrangement for Terrill to replace Broadwell at

---

8 Report of the Conference at Marshall, Texas, by Representatives from Tex., Ark., La., copy in Jefferson Davis Collection, Louisiana Historical Association Collection.

Shreveport fell through. Bryan next approached William Pitt Ballinger, and thereafter B. A. Shepherd. Both men declined the offer, though Ballinger did assist Bryan with solving the problem by persuading William J. Hutchins, George Ball, James Sorley, B. A. Shepherd, and W. J. Kyle to serve in the bureau. Hutchins would be chief; Ballinger agreed to serve as legal counsel.[9]

On November 22, Hutchins was appointed chief of the bureau with the rank and pay of lieutenant colonel. His primary duty was to acquire by sale, agreement, or impressment the cotton necessary to procure army supplies. All government officers, agents, and contractors engaged in cotton trading in or through Texas were to report immediately to him the details of their transactions. All future applications for making cotton contracts or requesting exemptions from regulations were to be directed to him for approval, and all contracts and exemptions already in effect were to be reviewed by him. Although the Texas Cotton Bureau was not required to obtain approval from Colonel Broadwell for its transactions, all reports to the department commander were to be forwarded through Broadwell's cotton bureau at Shreveport.[10]

By the time the Texas Cotton Bureau was opened, a routine procedure existed for dealing with civilians agreeing to exchange army supplies for cotton. After approval of the initial application a standard contract between the commanding general and the contractor was prepared by a procurement officer of the interested supply service. This contract stipulated that the commanding general would pay the contractor an amount of cotton equivalent to the sum of the invoice and transportation costs of the supplies plus an additional 50 percent of the invoice cost as an allowance. To arrive at the money value of the cotton, the standard in mid-1863 was set at five pence sterling per pound of New Orleans "middling grade" cotton. Adjustments of value for superior or inferior grades would be made by referees. A certificate was then prepared in which the contractor guaranteed to deliver the required supplies to any post designated within the Trans-Mississippi Department. The commanding general guaranteed in return that the military would deliver the necessary number of bales of cotton to any point the contractor desired in the Trans-Mississippi Department, so long as it was within ten miles of a railroad or a navigable stream. It was further guaranteed that the cotton would be protected from impressment or other injury to its point of export from the department. Although the contractor held a copy of the contract, he would not be furnished a copy of the certificate until he could show that he had bought and received the required supplies. Upon delivery of the goods to a

---

9 Terrill to Bryan, September 16, 1863, Gray to Bryan, September 28, 1863, Smith to Gray, October 13, 1863, Smith to Bryan, November 1, 1863, Devine to Terrill, November 2, 1863, Bryan to West, November 17, 1863, all in General Correspondence, 1862-1863, Bryan Papers.

10 Special Orders No. 198, Hdqrs. Trans-Miss. Dept., November 22, 1863, *OR* vol. 26, pt. II, 437-438.

Confederate post, his certificate would be redeemed by delivery of the government cotton to the place he designated.[11]

This simple but efficient procedure was the normal routine for acquiring supplies with cotton, but there must have been frequent breakdowns. One was reported by Major Rhett to Colonel Anderson in November 1863, when Rhett's representative was not promptly furnished with cotton to pay a contractor for ordnance stores delivered at Marshall. Rhett's frantic complaints to Anderson that he might thereby lose an old and trusted supplier must have been echoed many times by the other staff officers at Shreveport.[12]

To ensure that a plentiful supply of cotton for army procurement would be available and to prevent such breakdowns, Hutchins announced in December that the Texas Cotton Bureau would in the future purchase one-half of all available cotton. Planters delivering one-half of their cotton crop to the bureau's agents would be reimbursed at specie value in certificates redeemable at some future date in as yet unissued interest-bearing Confederate cotton bonds. The other half of the planter's cotton and his transportation would be exempt from impressment. Any planter who refused to cooperate, however, was threatened with the confiscation of all of his cotton and his transportation. This policy was essentially that adopted at Marshall, although there, Army purchase or impressment of all cotton had been urged. As would be expected, the planters were bitterly resentful of these new arrangements. The small operator, in particular, saw himself transporting half of his crop at his own expense to a government warehouse, only to receive payment in doubtful paper at specie prices and being left in many cases, after the 10 percent tax-in-kind had been exacted, with little cotton with which to meet his own growing expenses.[13]

Since almost all of the supplies imported into the vast department, whether by sea or by land, now necessarily came through Texas, regulations were published to ensure their equitable distribution both within and beyond that state. Regardless of the port of entry, four-tenths of each incoming quartermaster shipment was to be divided between the depots at Bonham and Jefferson, Texas, for the use of the District of Arkansas, Indian Territory, and the northern subdistrict of Texas. Two-tenths of each shipment was to be divided between the depots at San Antonio and Houston for the remainder of the District of Texas, New Mexico, and Arizona. Three-tenths was directed to the depot at Shreveport, serving the District of West Louisiana, and one-tenth was reserved for the quartermaster at department headquarters.[14]

11 Cotton Certificate issued to D. W. Bouldin and D. K. Newell, Shreveport, October 24, 1863, Contract between Lt. Gen'l. E. Kirby Smith and D. W. Bouldin and D. K. Newell, October 24, 1863, both in General Correspondence, 1862-1863, Bryan Papers.

12 Rhett to Anderson, November 20, 1863, ibid. 296-297.

13 Kerby, *Kirby Smith's Confederacy*, 177; Parks, *Kirby Smith*, 296-297.

14 General Orders No. 56, Hdqrs. Trans-Miss. Dept., November 16, 1863, *OR* vol. 22, pt. II, 1071.

*   *   *

AS WITH COTTON, problems of foreign relations had a history long antedating the Marshall Conference. In the spring of 1863, Brigadier General Hamilton P. Bee, who commanded the southern subdistrict of Texas, had attempted unsuccessfully to induce the French to occupy Matamoros.[15] A French expedition to Matamoros not having materialized, Smith took the extraordinary step for a department commander of writing directly to John Slidell, Confederate commissioner in Paris, to urge him to get Napoleon III to intervene in Trans-Mississippi affairs. Smith wanted the French to occupy a part of his own jurisdiction, "the east bank of the Rio Grande," in the hope of forestalling an invasion of the Rio Grande Valley while keeping his supply lines open. Smith pointed out to Slidell that if the French did so, they would enjoy the entire benefits of the Trans-Mississippi cotton trade as well as avoid the presence of United States troops, unfriendly to their regime in Mexico, on the border.[16]

A month later Major John Tyler, son of President John Tyler and an aide to Price, proposed to Texas authorities that they request French intervention on the basis that Texas was part of the Louisiana Purchase, and that the United States had violated the rights of the citizens of that former French territory under the treaty of 1803.[17] Neither Tyler's suggestion nor Smith's produced any results. Instead, the French were less than cooperative during the last six months of 1863, seizing the cargoes of at least two ships off the coast of Mexico that were loaded with arms and ammunition bound for the Trans-Mississippi Department.[18]

Both the depreciation of Confederate currency and the Army's lack of funds to pay outstanding debts had plagued Trans-Mississippi district and department commanders since 1861. The Marshall Conference had offered as a solution to the problems only the suggestion that notes in the Confederate depositories be reissued with a pledge to redeem them eventually in interest-bearing bonds. Smith himself had, of course, made similar suggestions

15   A. Superville to Bryan, March 5, 1865, in General Correspondence, 1865, Bryan Papers; Owsley, *King Cotton Diplomacy*, 135. // Hamilton was the older brother of Barnard Elliott Bee, the brigadier general mortally wounded in Virginia at First Manassas on July 21, 1861, who is credited with providing Thomas J. Jackson with his immortal nickname "Stonewall."

16   Smith to Slidell, September 2, 1863, *OR* vol. 22, pt. II, 993-994; Kerby, *Kirby Smith's Confederacy*, 144-145; Parks, *Kirby Smith*, 281. // In essence, Smith was requesting a violation of Confederate States sovereignty as a means of staving off what he considered the greater threat of a Federal incursion in Texas.

17   Charles W. Ramsdell, "The Last Hope of the Confederacy: John Tyler to the Governor and Authorities of Texas," *Quarterly of the Texas State Historical Association*, XIV (July, 1910), 129-145; Lubbock, *Six Decades*, 513-514; Kean, *Inside the Confederate Government*, 87.

18   Smith to President Davis, September 5, 1863, *OR* vol. 22, pt. II, 992-993; Slidell to Benjamin and inclosures, September 22, October 9, 1863, in Richardson, ed., *The Messages and Papers of Jefferson Davis and the Confederacy including Diplomatic Correspondence, 1864 – 1865*, vol. 2, 563-569, 584-587; Parks, *Kirby Smith*, 301-302.

to President Davis before the conference convened, and he had also repeatedly requested the appointment of Treasury agents and tax collectors in the Trans-Mississippi. Were such officials not appointed soon, he explained, he would be forced to name his own to provide funds. Smith suggested an issue of certificates redeemable in Confederate interest-bearing bonds, or the issuance of Treasury warrants redeemable in either bonds or currency; or, should these measures be insufficient, a reissue to the Army of the Confederate notes held without cancellation in the depositories. To soak up the surplus currency in the hands of the public, and to curb depreciation, Smith asked for an immediate shipment from Richmond of fifty or one hundred million dollars worth of government bonds. What Smith emphatically did not want from the Confederate Treasury was a large shipment of Confederate notes to depreciate the currency further.[19] Meanwhile, he issued stern warnings to the citizens, reminding them that they must accept Confederate money, and that anyone who failed to do so might be declared an enemy alien and sent beyond the lines.[20]

What the Treasury actually did in response to Smith's plans was send a courier, Clarence T. Thayer, by way of Mexico with $16,000,000 in new Confederate bills. Because Brownsville was temporarily in Union hands, Thayer hired the Mexican firm of Milmo and Co. to haul his crates of money from Matamoros to Piedras Negras, to be ferried across the river to Eagle Pass. Major Hart already owed a large amount of cotton to Milmo and other Mexican firms for supplies already delivered, and Patricio Milmo seized Thayer's money to hold against delivery. Appeals to Governor Santiago Vidaurri of Nuevo Leon and Coahuila, the father-in-law of Milmo, were in vain, and the money was not released until February of 1864—after General Smith had applied strong pressure by closing down the border trade.[21]

By the end of 1863, all the various the measures undertaken to strengthen the department proposed at Marshall in August had produced no tangible results. Overtures to the French had failed, and negotiations over French and Mexican seizures of Confederate property and money were still in the air. Planters in the Trans-Mississippi remained thoroughly disgruntled over the cotton policies presided over by the military and actively evaded them whenever and wherever possible. The Army's paymasters and disbursing officers remained short of both funds and cotton to pay the troops and to purchase equipment, and hundreds of soldiers remained unarmed. Extra troops from Missouri, which Governor Reynolds had predicted at the Marshall Conference would be forthcoming, had not materialized; even his own recruiter, M. Jeff Thompson, had been captured in northern

---

19 Smith to C. G. Memminger, June 4, August 31, September 1, 1863, Smith to Davis, September 8, 1863, all in Civil War Papers, Louisiana Historical Association Collection, Manuscripts Division, Tulane University Library; Reynolds to William Preston Johnston and to Davis, August 27, November 16, 1863, both in Reynolds Papers.

20 General Orders No. 45, Hdqrs. Trans-Miss. Dept., September 16, 1863, *OR* vol. 22, pt. II, 1018.

21 Tyler "Cotton on the Border, 1861-1865," *Southwestern Historical Quarterly*, LXXIII, 471-472; Kerby, *Kirby Smith's Confederacy*, 196-198; Parks, *Kirby Smith*, 303-305.

Arkansas without having enticed a single Missouri recruit to the colors. Southern currency continued its slide and stood at about ten cents on the gold dollar. The Confederate Associations had failed to fan patriotic spirit, no more than six of them having been formed. Most important of all, perhaps, the exact extent to which Kirby Smith would be supported by the state officials in exercising civil powers remained undefined.

*   *   *

THE MILITARY RECORD of the Trans-Mississippi Confederates after the Marshall Conference was also discouraging. The one success in the last half of 1863 was Lieutenant Richard Dowling's spectacular defense of Sabine Pass in September against Major General William B. Franklin's invasion force. Elsewhere, losses in territory, supplies, and manpower more than offset any meager gains. By September, Brigadier General William Steele, who had replaced Colonel Cooper in command of Indian Territory in January, had been forced back to Boggy Depot, losing Fort Smith and the rest of the Territory to General James G. Blunt. Little Rock was taken on September 10 by Major General Frederick Steele after a two-month campaign against Price, whose defense was singularly inept.

The loss of Little Rock worried General Smith greatly. He feared the enemy would now overrun the greater part of his department, for it seemed likely that Steele would continue his advance through Arkansas to the Red River, while at the same time Nathaniel Banks advanced up the Teche for another invasion of the Red River Valley, this time coordinating his movements with those of Steele.

It was during this crisis, on September 25, that the aging General Theophilus Holmes resumed command of the District of Arkansas. Still scornful of Sterling Price, Holmes seems to have actively encouraged Governor Reynolds to appoint Price to fill a Missouri vacancy in the Confederate Senate, thus gracefully ridding Arkansas of his presence. Reynolds did not fall in with the idea and declined to act. Because of Holmes's obvious physical and mental degeneration and demonstrated lack of enthusiasm for his job, his own days as district commander were numbered. Reynolds spoke of the 59-year-old general at this time as alternating between being "active, decided" and "even brilliant," to "irritable, dull, oblivious, and feeble." As early as August of 1863, Reynolds had reported to President Davis's aide, Colonel William Preston Johnston, that at least three physicians, including Holmes's own surgeon, had diagnosed him as suffering from progressive mental deterioration. Reynolds hoped that Johnston could persuade the president to replace Holmes with someone younger and with more vigor like Major General Simon B. Buckner, who (it was reported) was willing to come west and accept the post.[22]

22 Reynolds to William P. Johnston, August 27, 1863, Reynolds to Davis, Nov. 16, 1863, Memoranda Relative to the Appointments of Confederate Senators from Missouri, n.p., N.d., Reynolds Papers.

Fortunately for Smith, what he most feared—simultaneous advances on the Red River Valley by both Generals Banks and Steele—were not carried out. Having taken Little Rock, Steele did not press the offensive in Arkansas, contenting himself for the time being with the occupation of Pine Bluff and Arkadelphia. In Louisiana, part of Banks's command, under General Franklin, advanced as far as Opelousas, but by mid-November was back in New Iberia taking up winter quarters.

The lack of expected aggression was because Banks's real objective was not in Louisiana, but in Texas, where he hoped to raise the United States flag once again. For months he had been under pressure from Washington to accomplish this. Consequently, on November 2, 1863, some 5,000 of Bank's soldiers under Major General Napoleon Dana went ashore near the mouth of the Rio Grande and a few days later occupied Brownsville, General Bee's meager force having quietly withdrawn inland. From there, Federal detachments moved out to occupy various coastal points while others moved northwest up the Rio Grande Valley as far as Rio Grande City, a move that seriously disrupted the vital Mexican trade and ended all dreams of French intervention for the year.[23]

As the last days of the year passed, and as an early and severe winter slowed the pace of military activity, the future of the isolated Trans-Mississippi Department seemed bleak indeed. Most of Arkansas and the Indian Territory had been lost, with the Confederates clinging only to the most southern parts of both those regions. Louisiana was now in Union hands as far north as New Iberia. Union gunboats could freely roam the Mississippi, the Arkansas, and many lesser rivers. Only Texas, among the department's several states, was relatively intact, and even there the most accessible routes for foreign trade through the lower Rio Grande Valley were plugged by General Dana's enemy soldiers.

Where only two years before hopes had been high that the Missouri River would be the northern frontier of the Trans-Mississippi, now the Arkansas was gone and of the east-west rivers, only the Red remained in Confederate hands.[24]

23 Discussion of military movements after the fall of Vicksburg is based on Winters, *The Civil War in Louisiana*, 294-300; Williams, *Lincoln Finds a General*, vol. V, 81-89, 103-107, 112-116; Ludwell H. Johnson, *Red River Campaign: Politics and Cotton in the Civil War* (Baltimore, MD, 1958), 31-41, and Kerby, *Kirby Smith's Confederacy*, 220-225.

24 // This chapter of Dr. Geise's dissertation is truly groundbreaking. Note that the majority of his sources in this chapter are firsthand accounts or other primary documents. Robert L. Kerby, Joseph H. Parks, and Ludwell Johnson also conducted research into the intricacies of the economics of cotton and the administrative responsibilities of the Trans-Mississippi Department. However, none did so in the depth of Dr. Geise, nor with the singular focus on the responsibilities of the military command. The desperate situation created by the region's isolation convinced the state governors west of the Mississippi River that vesting the Trans-Mississippi military department and Kirby Smith with extraordinary powers was the only way by which the idea of the Confederacy could survive there. Thus, Smith and the military department he commanded became a virtual principality governed by a viceroy in the absence of the Confederate government.

Chapter 11

Kirby Smith's War Department, 1864

Unlike THEOPHILUS HOLMES, General E. Kirby Smith had shown himself determined to command his vast department, both in the field and from his headquarters, from the moment of his arrival. One Confederate military failure had followed another in the Trans Mississippi Department during the last half of 1863, but department organization had continued to progress at a steady pace. Smith had not hesitated to create new bureaus and staff agencies to administer the department more effectively.

By mid-1864, the Confederate Congress had authorized the establishment of bureaus west of the Mississippi corresponding to the War Department bureaus in Richmond, and had authorized Smith to staff them. Well before these formal authorizations arrived, Smith already had most of them operating at Marshall.

The chiefs of these many bureaus—quartermaster, ordnance, subsistence, conscription, and medical—although appointed by General Smith and thus subordinate to him, were not members of his department staff. Instead, they were comparable to bureau chiefs in the War Department in Richmond and thus performed duties that would normally have been performed in the distant Southern capital. These men included: Lieutenant Colonel O'Bannon, quartermaster; Major General Benjamin Huger, ordnance; Major William B. Blair, subsistence; Surgeon Haden, medical; and Brigadier General Elkanah Greer, conscription. Each had to be supplied with the necessary officers, clerks, teamsters, guards, and the like to carry out his respective duties. In addition, several operating agencies more or less under the supervision of Lieutenant Colonel William O'Bannon carried out quartermaster procurement and maintenance functions. Among these were the Clothing Bureau, the Pay Bureau, and the Office of the Chief Inspector of Field Transportation. A Bureau of the Engineer Department was added during the war's final months in 1865, located in Shreveport, Louisiana, instead of Marshall, Texas. This new bureau was headed by

Lieutenant Colonel Henry T. Douglas, who also continued his duties as Department Chief Engineer.[1]

The Clothing Bureau, directed by the dedicated Major William H. Haynes, was located in early 1864 at Shreveport. Under Holmes in 1863 it had been at Little Rock, its issues confined almost entirely to the District of Arkansas. At Shreveport, troops in Louisiana as well as Arkansas were supplied directly by the bureau during 1864. Probably because of the distances involved, troops in Texas and Indian Territory continued to draw their clothing from depots at San Antonio, Houston, Tyler, and Jefferson.

Although raw cotton and wool were abundant in the Trans-Mississippi Department, the only large manufactory of textiles and clothing was the Texas State penitentiary at Huntsville. All other cloth had to come either from Major Hart, whom Haynes described as "having failed entirely in supplying the requisitions on him," or from one or two civilian contractors, or from home looms often operated by the soldiers' own families. The dearth of manufacturing, coupled with the losses of Vicksburg and Brownsville and the heavy depreciation of Confederate currency, were blamed by Haynes on June 10 for "paralyzation of the operations of this bureau."[2]

"Paralyzation" was perhaps too strong a word to describe the Clothing Bureau's condition during 1864, as issues to Walker's division serve to show. From February 1864 to February 1865, this division received 3,069 hats, 915 jackets, 1,101 pairs of pants, 2,622 shirts, 1,950 pairs of drawers, 5,643 pairs of shoes, 1,000 blankets, 1,227 yards of gray cloth, 1,156 yards of brown cloth, 916 yards of osnaburg, and various other items.[3] In all likelihood, the establishment by late 1864 of additional textile and clothing manufacturing facilities, most of them in east Texas, had contributed to the totals. Still, these quantities were inadequate

---

1 "Circular: To Officers of, and Others Having Business with the Treasury in Trans-Mississippi Department," Houston, May 29, 1864, copy in Civil War Papers, Louisiana Historical Association Collection; General Orders No. 33, Hdqrs. Trans-Miss. Dept., May 30, 1864, *OR* vol. 34, pt. IV, 635-636; General Orders-No. 18, Hdqrs. Trans-Miss. Dept., March 6, 1865, ibid., vol. 48, pt. 1 1411. // This chapter chronicles how the Trans-Mississippi Department oversaw all of the administration and logistic planning and management for the region, including taking on responsibilities of the Confederate War Department following the fall of Vicksburg. In modern parlance, this is the function of a theater army. As complex as it is for a modern theater army to provide what is known as "common user logistic support" and personnel administration for today's joint forces, it was an even greater challenge in 1864 because of problems with communications and transportation. Dr. Geise illustrates in detail the efforts of every staff section and bureau to keep the Trans-Mississippi army in the field. Though at times the effort seems inadequate, Dr. Geise demonstrates that the various staff agencies did a reasonably competent job in establishing some order and regularity to what had been a chaotic operation. His descriptions illustrate the true challenge of high command: sustainment of the force.

2 Haynes to W. R. Boggs, June 10, 1864, ibid., vol. 34, pt. IV, 656-657.

3 // Osnaburg is a coarse heavy linen or cotton used to make such items as sacks.

for a division with perhaps as many as 8,000 men still on the rolls; Haynes remained dissatisfied.[4]

After December 1864, Haynes made few issues direct to units such as Walker's division. By then, procedures for handling clothing as well as other quartermaster supplies had been more or less standardized. General depots controlled by the department's chief quartermaster, had been established at Shreveport, Houston, and Bonham, Texas. Requisitions from units in each district were consolidated by their district quartermasters and submitted to the department's chief quartermaster, who filled them from the nearest general depot having available the necessary supplies. The general depots, in turn, were replenished from two sources. Quartermaster goods coming from abroad were funneled directly to the depots. Domestic supplies, on the other hand, were obtained by requisition of the chief quartermaster or Colonel O'Bannon, chief of the quartermaster bureau at Marshall. Haynes was responsible to O'Bannon alone, his Clothing Bureau supplying O'Bannon's Marshall bureau with clothing from domestic sources.[5] Some representative prices the Clothing Bureau paid in the fall of 1864 for this clothing were $25.00 for overcoats, $10.00 for blankets, $15.00 for jackets, $4.50 for woolen shirts, $3.00 for cotton drawers, and $6.00 a pair for shoes.[6]

The Pay Bureau at Shreveport was directed by Major Charles E. Carr. Since in the usual pay procedure the district paymasters drew funds from the several Confederate depositories and then delivered them directly to the brigade and regimental quartermasters for payment to the troops, Carr's function must have been mostly that of bookkeeping. Unfortunately, most of his accounts show the soldiers' pay sadly in arrears. In June 1864, for example, Carr reported to General Smith that all the troops in his department had been paid up to August 31 of the previous year, i.e., 1863, and a few regiments in Louisiana had been paid through a later date. He recommended that the available funds, in old issue currency, not be used to reduce the back pay. The Confederate Congress, by the Currency Act of February 1864, had authorized a new issue of currency to replace the old at a rate of two new dollars for three old, but this new currency was not yet available in the Trans-Mississippi. Carr recommended that the "old issue" still available not be used because it would, in effect, be subject to a 33 and 1/3 percent tax come July 1. A shipment of "new issue" finally arrived at the Treasury agency in Marshall in the fall of 1864, and by that November some troops had been paid with the latest currency up to December 31, 1863. The pay of many others continued well over a

4 Haynes to Guy M. Bryan, February 10, 1865, in Bryan papers.

5 General Orders No. 94, Hdqrs. Trans Miss. Dept., December 3, 1864, *OR* vol. 41, pt. IV, 1093-1094.

6 Circulars, Hdqrs. Trans-Miss. Dept. Clothing Bureau, September 11, 1863, September 24, 1864, both in General Orders, Department of the Trans-Mississippi, 1863 1865, Military Departments, Chap. II, vol. 74, Record Group 109, National Archives.

year in arrears. It is hardly necessary to add that the persistent failure to provide the Trans-Mississippi Confederate soldier his pay lowered morale.[7]

Problems, perhaps even more vexing and persistent than those of clothing and pay, were faced by the Chief Inspector of Field Transportation, another officer responsible to Colonel O'Bannon. The first appointee to that post, Major Horace J. Lacy, had scarcely time to set himself up at Shreveport and to select subordinate inspectors for each of the districts before Major Clement D. Hill arrived from Richmond to replace him. Even before assuming his new duties on March 3, Hill dispatched to the Inspector General of Field Transportation in Richmond a report remarking on the shortage of iron in the department and making immediate requisition of $5,000,00 to purchase animals and materials and to establish manufacturing and repair shops in Texas.[8] Hill did not receive the money requested, but he had brought $1,000,000 with him. In the next seven months he received an additional $357,000 in quartermaster funds. By all appearances, he seems to have made good use of the funds.[9]

About the time of Hill's arrival, district inspectors of field transportation were appointed with offices at Paris, Texas, Washington, Arkansas, Doaksville, Choctaw Nation, and Natchitoches. They were directly under Major Hill rather than under their respective district commanders. District chief quartermasters were to make requisitions for field

---

7   Carr to Smith, June 10, 1864, *OR* vol. 34, pt. IV, 659; J. C. Clarke to Allen Thomas, June 3, 1864, Jefferson Davis Collection, Louisiana Historical Association Collection; Kerby, *Kirby Smith's Confederacy*, 388-389; Harry N. Scheiber, "The Pay of Troops and Confederate Morale in the Trans-Mississippi West," *Arkansas Historical Quarterly*, XVIII (Winter, 1959), 359, states that Carr erred in reporting all troops paid up to August 1863, that in Louisiana many were not paid to that date until some months after June 1864.

8   General Orders No. 3, Hdqrs. Trans-Miss, Dept., January 13, 1864, Hill to A. H. Cole, February 24, 1864, *OR* vol. 34, pt. II, 864, 986-987. Artillery horses were in particularly short supply in Louisiana. "Long marches, short forage and defective harnesses" in the hard campaigning there of late 1863 had crippled the available horses, threatening many field batteries with breakdown. In September, the district was short 261 artillery horses and 337 sets of harnesses. In October, Major Brent sourly observed, "the Chief QM of the Trans-Mississippi Depart. at his Head Qtrs. cannot furnish you a train of ten wagons." That December, an outbreak of glanders and distemper in the government stables at Shreveport threatened catastrophe; fortunately, no epidemic materialized. Brent to Rhett, August 7, September 7, October 28, 1863, Brent to R. W. Sanders, to Taylor, and to G. L. Hall, December 1, 1863, January 28, February 29, 1864, "Payroll of Wagon Masters & Teamsters employed in Ord Train of Dist. W. La.," December 26, 1863, with endorsements by Post Quartermaster, Alexandria, February 10, 1864, and Chief of Artillery and Ordnance, District of West Louisiana, February 10, 1864, all in J. L. Brent Papers, Louisiana Historical Association Collection.

9   "Consolidated Report of the Means of Transportation in the Trans-Miss. Dept., July 1, August 10, 1864," in Letters and Telegrams Sent, 1862-1865, Letters and Telegrams Received and Sent, Trans Mississippi Department, 1861-1865, Departmental Records, Trans Mississippi Department, Record Group 109, National Archives.

transportation to Major Hill, upon whose approval their requests would be filled by the inspectors of field transportation.[10] The duties of Hill and his subordinates comprised the purchase or impressment and the issue and inspection of all animals and all equipment used for field transportation. This included artillery horses, which at that time were in critically short supply, and other draft animals (but not cavalry mounts). In addition, they were responsible for the rehabilitation of broken-down draft animals and the manufacture and repair of all items of transportation equipment.[11]

In August, a consolidated report of the field transportation available in the department showed 2,106 horses, 14,637 mules, 2,879 wagons, 189 ambulances, and 1,590 oxen. West Louisiana had more horses and mules than did either Arkansas or Texas, both of which employed large numbers of oxen. Indian Territory, comparatively smaller, had rather less than half as much transportation as any of the others. Hill reported that both the transport shops and the animal infirmaries were generally giving good service, the latter at that time treating about 1,500 animals.[12]

On October 31, Hill reported more precisely the amount of work done by his repair and rehabilitation facilities in the half year preceding that date. The figures support the optimism of his earlier report. Five hundred and fourteen wagons had been built, 548 were under construction, thirty ambulances had been completed, twenty-five were in the works; 3,339 harnesses had been made, 738 were being completed; 989 wagons and 143 ambulances had been repaired, 3,053 animals had been restored to service by the infirmaries, 577 artillery horses and 1,068 mules purchased or impressed, and 159 oxen bought. By far the greatest amount of this activity had occurred in Texas, just as Hill had planned. Workshops had not yet been built in Indian Territory.[13]

An inspection made in June 1864 by one of Hill's subordinate officers revealed considerable information about Hill's Texas workshops. At Rusk, where abundant oak, ash, and hickory were available, timbers were being soaked for the construction of forty to sixty wagons. Supplies of iron were on hand, as were suitable tools including a twenty-four horsepower engine with spoke-turning, planing, and mortising attachments. The shop was manned by twenty-four experienced white mechanics and forty-two black teamsters and

10   General Orders No. 7, Hdqrs. Trans-Miss. Dept., March 3, 1864, *OR* vol. 34, pt. II, 1014.

11   General Orders No. 45, Hdqrs. Trans-Miss. Dept., June 15, 1864, ibid., pt. IV, 674-675.

12   Consolidated Report of the Means of Transportation in the Trans-Miss. Dept., July 1, August 10, 1864, in Letters and Telegrams Sent, 1862-1865, Letters and Telegrams Received and Sent, Trans Mississippi Department, 1861-1865, Departmental Records, Trans Mississippi Department, Record Group 109, National Archives.

13   "Statement of Public Funds Received by Major C. D. Hill, Chief Inspr. Fd. Transpn. TMD for Account of the Fd. Transpn. Dept. 4th District from March 1st, 1864 to November 15th, 1864," and "Report of Means of Transportation Fabricated, Repaired, etc. in the Field Transportation Department, 4th District from March 1, 1864 to October 31, 1864," both ibid.

laborers. Its manufacturing capacity, however, was limited by the constant demands for repairs on the equipment of passing commands. Hill requested that sixteen blacksmiths, sixteen black strikers, and twenty-five wagon makers be added to the work force.[14]

The shop at Tyler, even larger than that at Rusk, employed some seventy-seven whites, mostly men detailed from other commands; 123 blacks, of whom thirteen were listed as qualified mechanics, and sixteen black women to weave and spin cloth for the black workmen. Supplies of iron and of wood—white oak, ash, hickory, and water oak—were reported to be sufficient. This shop was burdened not only by the demands for repairs to passing commands, but also by heavy work for the large and important post at Tyler. Consequently, it was recommended that six more harness-makers and six more blacksmiths be assigned there.

Slightly smaller shops were located at Mount Pleasant, Paris, and Dallas. In addition, a transport repair shop maintained by the Cotton Bureau at Jefferson might be called upon, if necessary. According to Major Hill's inspector, the wagons manufactured at Mount Pleasant and Paris were "unsurpassed in materials and workmanship." Both places were plagued with iron shortages, and the inspector called attention to an unused cage of bar iron in a local county jail, weight 10,000 pounds, which might be acquired at General Smith's request. Iron might also be obtained from the government cannon foundry at Jefferson or from the Marion County Ironworks, also located there. Outside Texas Hill had other shops at Washington and at Camden in Arkansas, and at Shreveport, Keatchie, and Alexandria in Louisiana.[15]

The efforts of Hill and his subordinates appear to have been admirable, but the best they could do was keep abreast of the situation during 1864. Complaints about transportation did not disappear, but they do not seem to have increased greatly either; in Louisiana, at least, there was actually some improvement.

One of the major problems faced by Hill was the great lack of discipline in the treatment of government transportation. As an example, hundreds of the 5,000 Yankee mules captured during the Red River and Camden campaigns of spring 1864 were driven off without accountability by both civilians and soldiers.[16] At unit level, it was difficult to keep individuals from burdening already overworked horses and mules by loading caissons and other transport with personal baggage. Officers often illegally appropriated wagons and

---

14 // Mortising means to join together securely. In woodworking, it is the creation of a mortise and tenon joint to connect two pieces of wood.

15 "Inspection Report, Feild [Field] Transportation Department by Major D. N. Spear, Inspr. Fd. Transpn.," Tyler, June 2, 1864, ibid.; James L. Nichols, *The Confederate Quartermaster in the Trans Mississippi* (Austin, TX, 1964) 89.

16 A. S. Morgan to Hill, May 2, 1864, with Hill's indorsement, May 7, 1864, *OR* vol. 34, pt. III, 801-802; Hill to A. H. Cole, June 5, 1864, ibid, pt. IV, 645; Reynolds to W. P. Johnston July 14, 1864, in Reynolds Papers.

ambulances for their personal use or drew excessive amounts of scarce government forage for their private mounts.[17]

A particularly flagrant abuse occurred in September 1864, when General Hindman, relieved from duty with the Army of Tennessee, arrived back across the Mississippi with four to six wagons loaded with tobacco he had purchased in Selma, Alabama, and hoped to sell in San Antonio. Before he was apprehended, Hindman had moved this tobacco a considerable distance through Louisiana and Arkansas by government wagons hauled by government teams, which drew forage from the the depots en route. General Magruder, then commanding in Arkansas, reported to General Smith that the parties to "this outrage . . . be arrested, and brought in irons if necessary to Camden for trial." No charges against Hindman were ever filed, however. Instead, Smith quietly ordered that he pay for the transportation and forage at government rates.[18]

The hordes of ill-disciplined cavalry that afflicted the Trans-Mississippi contributed to the chronic shortages of horses and forage. A general order dated January 1, 1864, threatened to dismount misbehaving cavalrymen, and in March Magruder dismounted an entire company for looting. The men were assigned *en masse* to the artillery, and their horses turned over to the quartermaster. So determined were the authorities to reduce the cavalry and put their horses to more productive uses that an order made retroactive to August 31 forbade the acceptance of volunteers for the cavalry or assignment of recruits to that arm without special permission of department headquarters. All cavalrymen recruited after August 31 were to be reassigned to the infantry and their horses, if suitable for artillery use, turned over to Major Hill.[19]

An agency related to the Quartermaster Bureau, but apparently not reporting thereto, was the office of the Inspector of the Tax-in-Kind. The bureau was established at Marshall in 1864 under Major Benjamin A. Botts, who had been sent from Richmond by the Confederate assistant quartermaster general. Botts was assigned because the War Department had never

17   Artillery General Orders No. 5, Bayou Robert, May 24, 1864, J. L. Brent to Lieutenant Colonel Fontaine, May 24, 1864, both in J. L. Brent Papers, Louisiana Historical Association Collection.

18   Hindman to M. M. Parsons, September 21, 1864, with indorsement, Parsons to Assistant Adjutant General, District of Arkansas, November 18, 1864, W. A. Alston to N. S. Hill, October 17, 1864, David Provence to W. A. Alston, November 12, 1864, John B. Burton to W. A. Alston, November 13, 1864, E. P. Turner to W, H. Parsons, October 17, 1864, Magruder to Boggs, October 14, 1864, Magruder to William Steele, November 6, 1864, J. K. P. Pritchard to W. A. Alston, November 12, 1864, with enclosure, Receipt for Twenty-Five Bushels of Corn signed by B. J. Duncan, October 23, 1864, all in Letters Received 1862-1864, Letters and Telegrams Received and Sent, 1861-1865, Departmental Records, Trans-Mississippi Department, Record Group 109, National Archives; Hindman to Smith, November 22, 1864 with indorsement, Smith to Hindman, n.d., in Major General T. c. Hindman, Papers of Various Confederate Notables, ibid.

19   General Orders No. 1, Hdqrs. Trans-Miss. Dept., January 9, 1864, *OR* vol. 34, pt. II, 849; General Orders No. 90, Hdqrs. Trans-Miss. Dept., November 25, 1864, ibid. vol. 41, pt. IV, 1077; General Orders No. 74, Hdqrs. Dist. of Tex., N. Mex., and Ariz., March 24, 1864, vol. 34, pt. II, 1079-1081.

received tax-in-kind reports from the Trans-Mississippi Department. Inasmuch as the tax-in-kind was a principal supply source for the quartermaster and commissary services, both of which were authorized to collect it from producers, the assistant quartermaster general was anxious to have a representative subject only to his and the departmental commander's orders operating in the Trans-Mississippi.[20]

When Botts reported to Shreveport in early spring, the department adjutant general refused to assign him to duty without subordinating him to Colonel O'Bannon. Botts protested that he had orders from higher authority to report only to General Smith and to Richmond. This difficulty seems not to have been resolved until September, when departmental orders placed Major Botts in charge of the Tax-in-Kind Bureau in Marshall without reference to Colonel O'Bannon. Since tax-in-kind supplies were collected, stored, and distributed by post quartermasters directly subordinate to the state quartermaster, Botts's duties, independent of O'Bannon's, must have been confined chiefly to processing reports of tax collections for forwarding to Richmond.[21]

The Ordnance Bureau, also located at Marshall, was directed by General Huger, who received all reports that Colonel Gorgas in Richmond would normally have received from the Trans-Mississippi. In addition, Huger's office processed reports of survey of damaged and lost ordnance property and verified the accounts of ordnance disbursing officers, as well as performing other purely administrative tasks in connection with ordnance.[22] Since the only arsenal Huger actually controlled was that at San Antonio, the procurement, manufacture, and supply of ordnance materials, along with artillery operations, were mainly in the hands of Major Rhett, the chief of ordnance and artillery at department headquarters.[23] Major Rhett was directly subordinate to General Smith rather than to Huger, while the district chiefs, who were primarily responsible to their individual district commanders, also reported to Major Rhett. During actual field operations, the district chiefs usually served as chiefs of artillery.

In addition to arms and ammunition captured from the Yankees, ordnance supplies came from several sources: east of the Mississippi River, local manufacture, state arsenals, and from abroad. Surprisingly, even as late as 1864 considerable amounts of arms and

20 Botts to E. K. Smith and to Major [Bryan], April 24, 1864, unnumbered order headed "Assistant Quartermaster General's Office 'Tax in Kind,'" February 6, 1864, both in Bryan Papers.

21 General Orders No. 67, Hdqrs. Trans-Miss. Dept., September 1, 1864, *OR* vol. 41, pt. III, 904; Richard D. Goff, *Confederate Supply* (Durham, NC, 1969), 86; Nichols, *Confederate Quartermaster*, 104.

22 Brent to Rhett, Rhett to Brent, September 8, 22, 1863, both in J. L. Brent Papers, Louisiana Historical Association Collection; General Orders No. 76, Hdqrs. Trans-Miss. Dept., September 27, 1864, *OR* vol. 41, pt. III, 960; General Orders No. 2, Hdqrs. Trans-Miss. Dept., January 3, 1865, ibid., vol. 48, pt. I, 1314-1315. // A report of survey is an investigation conducted to determine accountability and monetary adjustments to government property.

23 Benjamin Huger to J. P, Johnson, January 15, 1864, ibid., vol. 22, pt. II, 1139-1140.

munitions from depots and arsenals east of the Mississippi arrived in the Trans-Mississippi. Because of the continuing importance of this source of supply, Brigadier General Alfred Mouton's infantry division was moved late in 1863 to the northern subdistrict of Louisiana, headquartered in Monroe, for the purpose of convoying arms across the river. Mouton reported in December that some 1,400 arms had been brought over. In January 1864, Major Springer ferried across 5,000 friction primers sent out by Colonel Gorgas, and in that same month another ordnance officer reported that he had personally supervised the bringing across of 1,000 stand of arms on the two days of January 9 and 10. In February, General Leonidas Polk suggested to Smith and the War Department that he would equip cavalry to protect the shipments of arms in Mississippi, and furnish amphibious wagons to get the shipments across the river if Smith would send over 100 men with officers to form the cavalry escorts and drivers for the wagons. This plan was apparently never implemented, and thereafter Polk adamantly refused to escort arms for the Trans-Mississippi. In fact, over the course of several months in 1864, his forces appropriated 2,869 weapons sent by Major Thomas H. Price, the representative of the Trans Mississippi at the Selma Arsenal, on the grounds that it was impossible to get them across the river.[24]

Internal resources continued to provide some ordnance supplies, mostly in the form of ammunition. In late 1863, the arsenals west of the river capable of manufacturing cartridges were those at Shreveport, San Antonio, and Houston. After the campaigns of 1863, small arms ammunition was in seriously short supply throughout the department. This was in large part because of poor fire discipline in many Trans-Mississippi units. According to Brent, in Louisiana alone, 3,000 or 4,000 rounds per day were used up in the most insignificant skirmishes, and large quantities of ammunition were wasted by picket fire at the enemy when he was out of range. "The carelessness of our Soldiers in the use of arms and ammunition has no parallel," complained Major Joseph L. Robards, the ordnance officer for Brigadier General Tom Green's division of Texans.[25]

By mid-1864, following the removal of men and equipment from the Little Rock Arsenal and from Arkadelphia to new arsenals at Tyler and Marshall, Rhett happily reported that he

24 Brent to Rhett, January 29, 1864, in J. L. Brent Papers, Louisiana Historical Association Collection; R. C. Crow to Allen Thomas, June 12, 1864, in Civil War Papers, Louisiana Historical Association Collection; R. A. Duncan to Adj. Gen. Dept. of Mississippi and Eastern Louisiana, January 1, 1864, OR vol. 34, pt. II, 810-811; Smith to Polk, January 14, 1864, ibid., 865; E. Cunningham to Taylor, January 18, 1864, ibid., 885; Polk to Smith, February 7, 1864, ibid., 947-948; Polk to Cooper, March 5, 1864, with four endorsements, March 17, 31, April 5, 8, 1864, ibid., 1020-1021; Thomas H. Price to Gorgas, April 11, 1864, with three endorsements, April 21, 21, 23, 1864, and two enclosures, one dated April 7, 1864, the other, "Statement of Arms in transit to Trans-Mississippi Department, and taken by order of Lieutenant General Polk, and by officers under his command as follows," n.d., ibid., pt. III, 757-758.

25 Brent to Taylor, October 20, 1863, Robards quoted in Brent to Taylor, December 4, 1863, in J. L. Brent Papers, Louisiana Historical Association Collection.

had a "very fair" supply of Enfield cartridges at these locations. Even so it became necessary in January of 1865 to issue stringent regulations controlling the use of cartridges. Except in combat, unit issues of cartridges would be on the basis of three rounds per man per month, and when expenditures exceeded this limit the cost of the excess was to be charged to the unit ordnance officer's pay.[26]

In addition to ammunition, other ordnance items were manufactured within the Trans-Mississippi theater, although production was usually limited by shortages of men and materials. Most of the pig iron for ordnance purposes was probably provided by Nash, Perry, and Company, a private iron works near Jefferson, Texas. In June 1864, attempts were made to establish a government cannon factory at Jefferson. Construction continued into 1865, and the few field pieces fabricated in the Trans-Mississippi seem to have been mostly the work of the T. W. Jones Foundry at Shreveport and the state foundry at Austin. In addition, there were foundries at Waco and a few other places that supplied some materials to the army. There were facilities for making percussion caps at Houston, and at Austin the state percussion cap factory provided caps for the department as well as for state troops. In addition to the arsenal at Marshall, which was a major repair center for small arms, there was a large gunpowder mill. Probably most ordnance installations suffered shortages of skilled workers, as did the arsenal at Marshall. The commander there, worried over the lack of trained gunsmiths, for example, reported that his two best workmen were a cabinetmaker and a wagonmaker and that most of the remainder of his men were cabinetmakers, carpenters, and filers.[27]

A fraction of the ordnance material used by the Trans-Mississippi Department was borrowed from the states or issued by them directly to the Confederate Army. In January of 1864, for example, 50,000 cartridges were transferred from the "Louisiana Army," as that state's militia was styled, to the Confederate Army. Earlier, the District of West Louisiana had borrowed 300 Enfield rifles and 300 sets of cavalry accouterments from the state. When Governor Moore requested their return in February 1864, the items were no longer available. The best that could be managed was caliber .54 Austrian rifles (these also had

---

26 Rhett to Brent, November 30, 1863, June 24, 1864, ibid.; Special Orders Nos. 169 and 172, Headquarters District of Arkansas, September 28, October 1, 1863, in Special Orders, 1863-1864, District of Arkansas, Trans-Mississippi Department, Departmental Records, Record Group 109, National Archives; General Orders No. 2, Hdqrs. Trans Miss. Dept., January 3, 1865, *OR* vol. 48, pt. 1 1314-1315; Rhett to J. P. Johnson, October 22, 1863, ibid., vol. 22, pt. II, 1141-1142.

27 Brent to E. Surget, December 20, 1862, Brent to Rhett, June 8, 21, 1864, Rhett to Brent January 4, 1863, June 15, 1864, all in J. L. Brent Papers, Louisiana Historical Association Collection; J. B. Early to Guy M. Bryan, January 12, 1865, Bryan Papers; message of Governor Lubbock quoted in Houston *Weekly Telegraph*, November 10, 1863; Kerby, *Kirby Smith's Confederacy*, 70-71, 73-77; F. J. Herron to J. J. Reynolds, May 11, 1865, with inclosure, Report of C. S. Bell, Scout, *OR* vol. 48, pt. II, 397-403.

originally come from the state) and infantry cartridge boxes in place of the cavalry accouterments.[28]

Ordnance supplies continued to be brought in through the Union blockade. By 1864, Colonel Charles J. Helm, stationed at Havana, was responsible for the purchase of supplies and the loading of cargoes destined for Confederate ports. He was the only Confederate agent stationed at a neutral port reasonably convenient to the Trans-Mississippi Department, there being none at Vera Cruz. Helm, therefore, was charged by Colonel Gorgas in Richmond to pay particular attention to the arms supply of the Trans-Mississippi, especially the purchase of 10,000 stand of arms.[29]

On February 3, 1864, Helm wrote Magruder that a schooner had sailed from Havana for the mouth of the Brazos with 600 Belgian rifles, another was due to sail with about 1,000 rifles, and that a steamer would depart shortly with muskets and powder and about 2,000 Enfield rifles. On April 2, Helm happily informed Magruder that he had on hand several thousand stand of small arms, a ship would depart the following day with 100 Enfield rifles and 120 English Tower muskets, and he would take advantage of every ship sailing for Texas to send 200 or 300. Again on April 30 he reported that the steamer *Susannah* was departing Havana with 300 Enfield rifles and 320 muskets purchased in Havana, and 500 Enfield rifles from Nassau. At that time, he added, he had on hand some 6,000 Enfield rifles for which he had not yet paid because he lacked the necessary cotton. Helm assured Magruder, however, that so anxious was Gorgas to protect future supplies for the Trans-Mississippi that Magruder could help by having cotton shipped from Mobile to Havana for use in payment. Still, Helm added wistfully, "a few cargoes or parts of cargoes from Texas would be of infinite service" in the future.[30]

Anxious as they must have been for arms, it was unfortunate that General Magruder and his subordinates in Texas were apparently unaware until mid-summer of 1864 of the Confederate law that had been passed several months earlier on February 6 requiring every vessel leaving a Confederate port to carry one-half of her cargo for the account of the Confederate government, and that every vessel returning had to bring in one-half of her cargo in Confederate supplies. Secretary of War Seddon informed Kirby Smith of this law that June, perhaps for the first time, saying he had learned of the recent arrival at Havana of at least five vessels from Texas with "cargoes of cotton exclusively on private account." Because the law exempted from compliance vessels carrying cotton in payment of Confederate debts, unless they were not fully laden, Texas at first benefitted only slightly from it. When in September, however, the Texas Cotton Office began requiring all vessels to

28 Adjutant General, Louisiana Army to Brent, January 26, 1864, Brent to John M. Sandige, February 24, 1864, both in J. L. Brent Papers, Louisiana Historical Association Collection.

29 Seddon to Smith, June 11, 1864, *OR* vol. 34, pt. IV, 666.

30 Helm to Magruder, February 3, April 2, 30, 1864, ibid., II, 941, pt. III, 727-728, 798.

provide one-fourth of their carrying capacity for the government, shipments of supplies to Texas increased.[31]

Blockade runners continued to arrive on the Texas coast with ordnance supplies until the end of the war, and apparently in the last year an increasing number of large steamers were employed in this enterprise. Perhaps these operations became even more efficient late in 1864 and 1865 when Leon Smith, erstwhile head of Magruder's "Marine Bureau," took to piloting blockade runners between Havana and the Texas coast and to advising captains and pilots of heavy draft steamers on the best approaches.[32]

Supervision over the procurement and distribution of subsistence supplies was largely the province of Major William H. Thomas, chief commissary of subsistence at Shreveport.[33] When it came to matters of subsistence the Trans-Mississippi was more self-sufficient than most other Confederate military departments because beef, pork, and bacon were generally plentiful in Texas, wheat and corn were grown in quantity along Red River, salt was available, and sorghum, beans, potatoes, sugar, and other crops were all produced within the limits of the department. While the department on the whole was comparatively well supplied, various districts and subdistricts suffered at one time or another critical shortages of important foodstuffs. These shortages were often the result of procurement failures, sometimes attributable to farmers who were alienated by impressment and the tithe and reluctant to sell their produce at fixed prices for depreciated currency. Food prices were fixed in Confederate currency by local or state appraisers. Representative prices set by the state appraisers in Texas in January 1864 were $5.00 per bushel for wheat, $3.00 per bushel for flour, $2.50 per gallon for molasses, $40.00 per head or 10 cents per pound for beef cattle four years or older, and mutton $8.00 per head or 12-1/2 cents per pound.[34]

If the legal requirements were not enough to annoy the average farmer, there were also illegal impressments and unauthorized tithe collections. These were the subject of numerous complaints and attempted remedies. A general order of January 1865 directed that illegal tax gatherers be arrested and reiterated earlier orders that the tax could be

31 Seddon to Smith, June 11, 1864, ibid., pt. IV, 666; L. Tuffly Ellis, "Maritime Commerce on the Far Western Gulf, 1861-1865," *Southwestern Historical Quarterly*, LXXVII (October,1973), 215-217.

32 Helm to Leon Smith, January 31, 1865, Leon Smith to Magruder, March 31, 1865, both in Major General J. B. Magruder, Correspondence, 1861-1865, Papers of Various Confederate Notables, Record Group 109, National Archives; Ellis, "Maritime Commerce," *Southwestern Historical Quarterly*, LXXVII, 217-222.

33 A Bureau of Subsistence had been established at Marshall under Major W. B. Blair, but the scanty surviving records pertaining to it seem to indicate a brief existence or minimal functions.

34 "Schedule of Prices," Rusk, Texas, January 1, 1864, signed by W. R. D. Ward and Frank E. Williams, *OR* vol. 34, pt. II, 811-814. // The availability of food in the Trans-Mississippi stands in marked contrast to the state of affairs east of the Mississippi River at the same time in the war. Nevertheless, the lack of an adequate transportation infrastructure in the Trans-Mississippi often meant the troops in the field were still short of rations, as Dr. Geise points out later in this chapter.

collected only by officers and agents of the Tax-in-Kind Bureau, bonded quartermasters and commissaries, authorized agents of the state controlling quartermasters, and quartermasters and commissaries serving with troops and especially authorized to do so by district chief quartermasters or commissaries.[35]

Farmers showed their ire by selling their products commercially, by holding back as much as they could from the military, or by not producing to full capacity. In January 1864, Brigadier General Henry McCulloch wrote Kirby Smith that the people of his northern subdistrict of Texas, the principal larder of the whole department, had only partially harvested their crops. Smith feared with good reason that this might be the result of "utter indifference or disaffection." About the same time, General Taylor reported similar dissatisfaction among Louisiana farmers. Corn, which sold for $3.00 a barrel on the open market, was fixed at only half that amount on the government price lists. As a consequence, farmers were hiding their corn from government agents and falsely declaring they had only enough for their own use. Taylor complained that a lively private trade in corn along the Red River between Alexandria and Shreveport was hurting military supply. Moreover a beef shortage had forced him to impress cattle, and impressment convinced many citizens of his district to simply drive their herds to the enemy.[36]

At least as serious as shortages induced by the farmers were those caused by lack of quartermaster transportation, which prevented equitable distribution of the usually ample foodstuffs throughout the department. In January of 1864, Taylor complained that in spite of an abundant harvest in Texas the previous autumn, only enough flour for ten days' rations had reached his troops in seven months, and during approximately the same period they had received no salted meat at all. Both Louisiana and Arkansas suffered shortages of flour and bacon in May, while the Chief Purchasing Commissary of Subsistence of the fourth commissary district at Paris, Texas, had on hand some 200,000 pounds of flour and bacon he was anxious to ship to those districts. General McCulloch, in whose subdistrict the Paris depot lay, was also anxious to move these supplies, but he could not furnish the commissary "with one single wagon to aid you in pushing supplies forward to our suffering friends in Arkansas and Louisiana." McCulloch did, however, authorize the commissary to impress, for one trip only, such wagons and hands as the farmers of the district could spare, though he rightly feared this would increase the farmers' problems.[37]

35 General Orders No. 1, Hdqrs. Trans-Miss. Dept., January 2, 1865, ibid., vol. 48, pt. I, 1311.

36 Smith to H. E. McCulloch, January 4, 1864, photostat in McCulloch Collection; Taylor to Boggs, January 21, 1864, OR vol. 34, pt. II, 902-903; Taylor to Boggs, March 5, 1864, Trans-Mississippi Department, Letters Received and Sent (Incomplete), 1861-1865, Departmental Records, Record Group 109, National Archives.

37 H. E. McCulloch to Boggs, May 9, 1864, with Enclosure No. 1, Thos. Lanigan to General [McCulloch], n.d., sub-enclosure, Wm. H. Thomas to Lanigan, April 30, 1864, and Enclosure No. 2,

Under the circumstances there was occasional stiff competition between district commanders for available foodstuffs. Early in 1864, General Taylor complained that agents working under Generals Holmes and Price from Arkansas were stripping the northern subdistrict of Louisiana of food supplies to the extent that his small force there under Brigadier General St. John R. Liddell might be forced to abandon the region. This sort of wasteful competition was presumably stopped by the establishment under orders from Richmond of commissary districts, wherein one officer had sole responsibility for procuring subsistence. The Trans-Mississippi Department was divided into four such districts, their boundaries corresponding roughly to the areas of southeast Texas, the Indian Territory and the remainder of Texas, Arkansas, and Louisiana.[38]

The Bureau of Conscription at Marshall was directed by Brigadier General Elkanah Greer during most of Kirby Smith's tenure west of the Mississippi.[39] Under Greer's supervision, the state chief enrolling officers and their subordinates carried out conscription. They also operated several camps of instruction for conscripts in each district. Field commanders complained frequently about exemptions from conscription granted by the enrolling officers, especially to skilled craftsmen, as well as the practice of detailing conscripts directly to the various bureaus and workshops. General Magruder hinted darkly in May of 1864 that bribery might be involved in some of the exemptions and details. He also disliked the practice of sending conscripts home on thirty-day furloughs as soon as they were enrolled. He suggested they be immediately assigned to depleted regiments, which would provide them with better training than they received in camps of instruction.[40] Various changes relative to camps of instruction, exemptions, details, and assignments of conscripts were eventually made under War Department instructions, but they came too near the end of the war to have any real effect.[41]

A Medical Bureau was established in March of 1864, and Surgeon John M. Haden, the department's medical director, was designated to head it. All reports, returns, and other matters that would normally have been referred to the Confederate Surgeon General in Richmond were to be sent to him. Dr. Haden, a regular medical officer in the old Army, had

---

McCulloch to Lanigan, May 8, 1864, *OR* vol. 34, pt. III, 813-815; W. H. Thomas to Boggs, June 10, 1864, with Enclosures A, B, and C, ibid., pt. IV, 659-661.

38 Goff, *Confederate Supply*, 83-85; Taylor to Boggs, February 24, 1864, St. John R. Liddell to E. Surget, February 19, 1864, both in Trans-Mississippi Department, Letters Received 1862-1864, Letters and Telegrams Received and Sent (Incomplete), 1861-1865, Departmental Records, Record Group 109, National Archives.

39 General Orders No. 26, Hdqrs. Trans-Miss. Dept., March 27, 1865, *OR* vol. 48, pt. 1 1446-1447. 833-834.

40 Magruder to Boggs, May 20, 1864, ibid., vol. 34, pt. III.

41 General Orders No. 78, Hdqrs. Trans-Miss. Dept., October 4, 1864, ibid., vol. 41, pt. III, 981; General Orders No. 27, Hdqrs. Trans-Miss. Dept., March 28, 1865, ibid., vol. 48, pt. 1 1448-1450.

begun his Confederate service on the staff of Major General David E. Twiggs in Louisiana. General Holmes, one of Dr. Haden's old friends, appointed him Medical Director of the Trans-Mississippi Department, and Smith continued him in that duty until he was appointed bureau chief. Haden's assistant in the medical bureau, Dr. E. K. Du Val, had graduated in medicine from Pennsylvania College in 1858, served one year as a Regular Army surgeon, and then resigned to enter private practice in Fort Smith. Having begun the war as an assistant surgeon, in March 1863 he was appointed by General Hindman to be medical director of the District of Arkansas. He went thence to be Haden's assistant at Marshall, remaining in that role until the end of the war. Haden and Du Val appear to have been competent professionals. The levels of medical experience and training of the medical officers under them in the Trans-Mississippi Department also seem to have been quite respectable. Cursory examination of the qualifications of a small sample of medical officers from regimental level up reveals not only much practical experience in medicine, but academic and medical training in such schools as the University of Pennsylvania, the University of Edinburgh, the University of Paris, the University of Louisiana (now Tulane), the University of New York, Philadelphia College of Medicine, and Transylvania College.[42]

Among minor agencies in the Trans-Mississippi that corresponded to offices in Richmond was the "Army Intelligence Office." Established at Shreveport in November 1863 under supervision of R. S. Thomas, this agency was tasked with performing duties comparable to those of a similarly named office in the Confederate War Department, i.e., "to inform the friends and relatives of sick and wounded soldiers of their whereabouts and condition; to facilitate communication with the army; and to receive a correct list of the deaths which have occurred . . . whether within our lines or those of the enemy." Surgeons were instructed to submit lists of the sick, wounded, and dead to Thomas through normal channels, and commanding officers were directed to report casualties to him immediately after any engagement. Thomas was given clerical assistance and quartermaster and subsistence support, but his task in gathering accurate information must have been formidable and frustrating.[43]

Oddly enough for a Confederate general, Kirby Smith possessed a navy department, or at least a "Marine Bureau," under the immediate command of his subordinate John Magruder. It was Magruder who established the Marine Bureau at Houston sometime after the recapture of Galveston. Leon Smith, who had been the water-borne commander in that action, was placed in charge. Subsequently, three substations of the Marine Bureau were

---

42 Speer, *Encyclopedia of the New West*, vol. I, 366-368, vol. II, 40-42; General Orders No. 9, Hdqrs. Trans-Miss. Dept., March 25, 1864, *OR* vol. 34, pt. II, 1082; Special Orders No. 102, Hdqrs. Trans-Miss. Dept., August 3, 1863, in Special Orders, Trans-Mississippi Department, Lt. Gen. E. K. Smith, 1863-1864-1865, Departmental Records, Record Group 109, National Archives.

43 General Orders No. 53, Hdqrs. Trans-Miss. Dept., November 12, 1863, *OR* vol. 22, pt. II, 1067 1068.

established, one at Galveston under Captain Henry S. Lubbock, one at Sabine Pass under Captain L. C. Irwin, and one at Matagorda Bay under Captain S. K. Brown. By 1864, "Commodore Smith," as Magruder usually referred to him, commanded thirty-five vessels, twelve of them armed steamers, two armed schooners, and the rest transports, dispatch and police boats, and miscellaneous craft, all located on the bays and bayous of the coast of Texas. The Marine Bureau can hardly be said to have performed any outstanding service despite the undoubted abilities of its chief. The failure evidently resulted from lack of opportunity, the poor seagoing ability of many of the vessels, and the shortage of trained seamen. Many of the crews were composed mostly of soldiers, a fact which rankled some Army officers from whom men had been taken.[44]

Taken together, the bureaus and other agencies under Kirby Smith amounted to a kind of War Department for the Trans-Mississippi. The need for a subordinate secretary of war to preside over this war department suggested itself to various prominent citizens, particularly Governor Reynolds, whose choice for the position was Simon Bolivar Buckner.[45] For reasons that Secretary of War Seddon explained carefully to General Smith, Richmond was not in favor of such an arrangement. "I advised against the appointment of an Assistant Secretary of War for the Trans-Mississippi Department," explained Seddon to Smith,

> because though even intended to be subordinate to you, the very name might engender suspicions or give color of a disturbing authority, which in doubtful circumstances might prove mischievous. My own judgment was and is that you should in your capacity as commander of the department combine with your strictly military duties somewhat of that relation (as far as our Constitution allows) to the Department and the President.[46]

Smith would continue to be his own secretary of war, attending to both the multiple and complex administrative problems of the vast department and the overall conduct of its military operations.

---

44 William Steele to J. E. Slaughter, March 23, 1864, L. G. Aldrich to William Steele, March 25, 1864, Leon Smith to L. G. Aldrich, March 30, 1864, J. B. Cleveland to Magruder, June 15, 1864, *OR* vol. 34, pt. II, 1075-1076, 1083, 1000-1001, pt. IV, 675-676; James M. Day, "Leon Smith: Confederate Mariner," *East Texas Historical Journal*, III (March, 1965), 43; Unnumbered Special Orders, Hdqrs. Dist. of Texas, N.M., and Ariz., August 16, 1864, J. E. Slaughter to Robert B. Scott, August 16, 1864, Magruder to s. R. Mallory and to C. McRae, both August 16, 1864, Charles J. Helm to Leon Smith, January 31, 1865, Leon Smith to Magruder, March 3, 1865, all in Major General J. B. Magruder, Correspondence 1861-1865, Papers of Various Confederate Notables, Record Group 109, National Archives.

45 Reynolds to Buckner, to Waldo P. Johnson, and to E. K. Smith, June 25, July 14, 25, 1864, all in Reynolds Papers.

46 Seddon to Smith, June 15, 1864, *OR* vol. 34, pt. IV, 671-674.

Chapter 12

Kirby Smithdom, 1864

With BURGEONING ORGANIZATION under General Smith came administrative improvement. By late 1863 and early 1864, official correspondence moved with considerable (or at least more) celerity from one level of command to another and from one staff agency to another. Most correspondence moved through what might then be considered "normal" channels. A letter of late 1863 concerning a routine ordnance problem offers what is probably a fair example.

This matter was referred to the department commander by the chief of ordnance and artillery, District of West Louisiana, in a basic letter headed Alexandria and dated October 5, 1863. Four days later October 9, the chief of ordnance and artillery at Shreveport endorsed it to the department commander. The department commander's answer, signed by an assistant adjutant general, and the forwarding endorsement by the department chief of ordnance and artillery to the district ordnance officer were dated Shreveport, October 10 and 12, respectively. The date of receipt back at district is not indicated, but the total time consumed in transmission, staff work, and other necessary handling of this correspondence was probably about ten days from start to finish. A routine request for furlough from a private soldier stationed at Alexandria moved with equal speed. Initiated on January 27, 1864, it passed successively through the soldier's battery commander, district chief of artillery and ordnance, department chief of artillery and ordnance, and reached the department adjutant general's office by February 2, whence it was returned with the endorsement that it should be sent to the district commander's office for action.[1]

---

1 Brent to Rhett, October 5, 1863, 1st Endorsement, Department Chief of Artillery and Ordnance, October 9, 1863, 2nd Endorsement, Department Chief of Artillery and Ordnance, October 12, 1863, Robert Nelson to E. Surget, January 27, 1864, 1st Endorsement, Maunsel Bennett, n.p., n.d., 2nd Endorsement, Office Chief of Artillery and Ordnance, Dist. West La., January 28, 1864, 3rd

Lest the impression be gained from these two examples that only department headquarters and the nearby military district headquarters in Louisiana were closely administered, it is apparent that even on the frontiers of Texas and the Indian Territory administration had been greatly strengthened by 1864—although longer distances made transmittal times correspondingly longer. A routine letter from headquarters of the Border Regiment at Gainesville, Texas, reached northern subdistrict headquarters at Bonham, forty-five miles away, the next day, and district headquarters at Houston, almost 300 miles away, one week later. Dispatches from Brigadier General Samuel Maxey's District of Indian Territory headquarters at Fort Towson to Shreveport, a distance of about 130 miles, normally required from two to four days. Thus, by 1864 routine correspondence moved at a rate comparable to modern routine military correspondence.[2]

Administrative errors also received close attention by 1864 and often drew sharp criticism from higher headquarters. When the inspector general of Douglas Cooper's Division of Indian troops attempted to defend the practice of reporting directly to department headquarters rather than through Maxey's headquarters, Colonel E. E. Portlock, Jr., Maxey's inspector general, silenced him by replying curtly, "I am compelled for the future to decline any discussion [of proper military channels] with my military inferiors as incompatible with and subversive of good order, military discipline and system, etc." Portlock added that General Maxey himself had directed Cooper to report through district headquarters.[3]

By 1864, under the direction of Colonel Benjamin Allston, department inspector general at Shreveport, a reasonably thorough inspection system had been established throughout the department. All basic personnel reports such as muster rolls, payrolls, and other returns were normally forwarded through the district inspectors general who monitored them carefully. These officers were occasionally given to acidity in commenting on the weaknesses of reporting officers, for example, "You will also give your attention to the neatness of your report as well as its correctness. We have as much as we can attend to in this Office—Exclusive of deciphering hierogliphics [sic]."[4] In instances of inadequate

---

Endorsement, Office Chief of Ordnance and Artillery, Department of Trans-Mississippi, February 2, 1864, all in J. L. Brent Papers, Louisiana Historical Association Collection.

2   // For Dr. Geise, "modern" would mean that military correspondence moving by the standards of the early 1970s before electronic communications via the Internet.

3   James A. Bourland to McCulloch, April 25, 1864, 1st Indorsement, Headquarters Northern Subdistrict of Texas, April 25, 1864, 2nd Indorsement, Headquarters District of Texas, Etc., May 3, 1864, Boggs to Maxey, April 2, 1864, both in *OR* vol. 34, pt. III, 792-793, 725; Portlock to Matthews, June 8, 1864, Portlock to Marston, August 10, 1864, both in Inspector General's Office, District of Indian Territory, Chap. II, Vol. 260, Record Group 109, National Archives.

4   Portlock to Allston, June 1, July 18, August 27, 1864, Boggs to Maxey, June 14, 1864, and 1st Indorsement, Headquarters District Indian Territory, July 20, 1864: Portlock to E. G. Gurley,

reporting by units in the field or where special one-time reports were required, assistant inspectors general were sometimes dispatched to the field units to supervise preparation.

Inspection schedules were established in accordance with Confederate Army regulations. Inspectors general at brigade level were to inspect at least one regiment weekly, at division at least one brigade every two weeks, and at corps or district level at least one division every month. Inspection results were in each case to be forwarded to the inspector general at the next higher level. The department inspector general was to inspect all corps or districts every six months and report to General Smith. This must have been a difficult schedule to live up to, and doubtless active campaigning and distance sometimes precluded compliance. The unit inspector was expected to keep a complete file of regulations and general orders of all headquarters from the Adjutant General's Office in Richmond down to his own level. Considering the state of communications with the capital after 1863, this must have been another difficult task for Trans-Mississippi inspectors.

Inspectors spent a good deal of time conducting investigations. Partly these concerned alleged misconduct, especially by officers, some of whom were apparently given to the most unbecoming conduct. One officer was accused of borrowing a lady's carriage and subsequently selling it to a fellow officer. Another was accused of kidnapping a slave girl. More important were such investigations as that assigned to Captain B. W. Marston, an assistant inspector general in Indian Territory. Because white deserters illegally enlisted in the comparatively inactive Indian regiments to avoid arrest, Marston was directed "to ascertain the status and military history of every white man in the Indian Territory," a task Marston admitted was impossible to oversee. In any case, attempts to tighten administration and discipline in a frontier army must have been frustrating. Governor Thomas Reynolds on one occasion remarked wearily that his efforts to disseminate information through posters and official circulars had been "more successful in furnishing pipe lighters than in defusing information."[5]

In spite of increasingly tight administrative procedures and a strengthening of discipline, the total number of men actually present for duty in all units of the Trans-Mississippi was disappointingly low in 1864, and indeed remained so throughout the war. In January 1864, the aggregate strength, both officers and men, was reported to be 73,289, but the effective total present was only 34,845. The aggregate present was 40,987, which meant that some 6,142 of those present in their units were not available for duty because they were

---

November 7, 1864, James Patterson to L. C. Gillett, December 9, 1864, all ibid.; General Orders No. 16, Hdqrs. Trans-Miss. Dept., June 5, 1863, in Confederate States Army, *General Orders. Headquarters Trans-Miss. Department from March 6. 1863 to January 1. 1865, in Two Series* (Houston, 1865), 6.

5 N.W. Battle. to W, C. Schaumburg, December 10, 1864, Portlock to Captain Miller, May 18, 1864, N. W. Battle to Maxey, January 5, 1865, B. W. Marston to T. M. Scott, April 11, 1865, all in Inspector General's Office, District of Indian Territory, Chap. II, Vol. 260, Record Group 109, National Archives; Reynolds to Kerr, February 24, 1864, Reynolds Papers.

sick, in local arrest or confinement, or in some other local temporary non-duty status. Most astonishing, however, is the great difference between aggregate strength and aggregate present. In January of 1864, 32,302 men, or close to one-half of the enrolled troops of the department, were absent from their units on detached service, authorized leave or furlough, in distant sick status, in distant arrest or confinement, absent without leave, or in desertion.

A comparison of the causes of absences by districts possibly provides a clue to troop morale and discipline in the various districts for excessive absences for whatever reasons are frequently linked with low morale and poor discipline. The districts in descending order of percentages of absences was as follows:

DISTRICT	AGGREGATE STRENGTH	AGGREGATE ABSENT	PERCENT ABSENT
Indian Territory	8, 885	2,241	74.8
Arkansas	25,623	13,905	46.0
West Louisiana	21,829	13,441	38.4
Texas	16,952	11,400	32.0

Even Texas, the district with the lowest percentage of men absent, had an abnormally high rate. Unfortunately, neither the departmental nor the district returns break down absences by cause. The return of a Louisiana battalion about the same time suggests the various major causes of absence, though it would be dangerous to assume that this battalion was typical. In February 1864, for example, the aggregate strength of Brent's Battalion of Reserve Artillery, District of West Louisiana, was 675. The total absent numbered 109—a far better record than those of the district or department as a whole. In this apparently superior unit the numbers and causes of absences in descending order of importance were listed as twenty-nine sick, twenty-five away on leave, twenty-four without leave, twenty on detached service, and eleven under arrest or held in confinement. The proportion of men absent without leave was probably much higher than this in many other Trans-Mississippi Department units.[6]

---

6 Abstract from return of the Trans-Mississippi Department, General E. Kirby Smith commanding, for January 1, 1864, *OR* vol. 34, pt. II, 814; Return of Major J. L. Brent's Battalion of Reserve Arty., D. W. La., Army of the Confederate States of America for the month of February, 1864, February 29, 1864, in J. L. Brent Papers, Louisiana Historical Association Collection.

Sickness and absence without leave are not surprising, given the field conditions of some units by late 1863 and early 1864. One Texas regiment serving in Louisiana at that time had large numbers of men without shoes, and for the numerous sick there were not even tents, much less houses to shelter them. In some cases of absence without leave men on authorized leave had been conscripted into other units. In other cases, the absentees were seriously ill at home in rural areas where means of communication with the Army were nonexistent.

Of course, large numbers of those absent without leave, probably most of them, had no intention of returning to their units. Almost every section of the Trans- Mississippi was plagued by such men, and they often banded together for protection and plunder. General McCulloch's northern subdistrict of Texas, a frontier region, was a special hideout for them. Magruder's advice to McCulloch on the subject was brutally direct: "These men should be shot without hesitation or mercy, and should be hunted down with the forces you have, operating all the time, day and night, until the work is done." In spite of the "utmost exertions" to arrest all such persons "found in the brush," McCulloch's subdistrict continued to be plagued with them until the war's end.[7]

To some extent absences from sickness and without leave could not be controlled, but the number of men on authorized leave, which could be controlled, was also excessive. In 1864, stringent leave policies were adopted in the conviction that many officers had been too lenient. Except for the hospitalized sick, only department or district headquarters could approve leaves. Any officer who authorized a leave contrary to these orders was subject to court martial, and any absent enlisted man without department or a district approval on his furlough papers, was subject to immediate arrest.

In November 1864, after the hard campaigning of the year had ended, these policies were relaxed somewhat and the authority to grant leaves was delegated in some cases to division commanders. District commanders, however, were still required to pass upon sick leaves and all leaves for general officers and their staffs, field grade officers, staff noncommissioned officers, band members, and those on post duty. Moreover, by the end of 1864, every soldier's request for furlough had to be accompanied by his company commander's certificate that the soldier still had all the arms and accouterments issued to him. A stiff price schedule was to be followed when a soldier's equipment was missing: $400

---

7 J. E. Harrison to Colonel Moncure, October 20, 1863, Bryan Papers; F. C. Cornay to Brent, February 21, 1864, J. L. Brent Papers, Louisiana Historical Association Collection; Magruder to McCulloch., January 20, 1864, *OR*, vol. 34, pt. II, 925926; H. E. McCulloch to J. E. Slaughter, March 13, 1864, *OR* vol. 53, 970-971; General Orders No. 30, Hdqrs. Northern Subdistrict of Texas, December 29, 1864, ibid., vol. 48, pt. I, 1310-1311; Magruder to Boggs, April 8, 1865, ibid., pt. II, 1271; H. E. McCulloch to James A. Bourland, April 5, May 23, 1865, both in James A. Bourland Papers, 1837-1876 (Ramsdell Microfilms in Archives Collection, University of Texas Library, originals in Manuscript Division, Library of Congress).

for a Navy revolver, $500 for an Army revolver, and $200 each for a musket, carbine, or rifle.[8]

Another serious cause of absence was the ever-increasing number of men assigned to special duty as the bureaus and staffs of the department and of the districts proliferated. Complaints from field commanders kept pace with the special details. At least one regimental commander blamed low morale in his regiment on "the facility with which men seeking it can procure detailed service at Hospital Posts, Qr. Master's Dept.—thereby reducing the ranks very much and producing restlessness and dissatisfaction with those remaining."[9]

Perhaps significantly, most complaints about details seem to have originated in the District of West Louisiana. No one was more persistent in criticizing the system nor stubborn in refusing to fill details than the commander of that district, Richard Taylor. The proximity of his headquarters to the department headquarters at Shreveport presumably made his troops an easy target for such service, increasing his resentment. An example of this was the creation of a headquarters guard at Shreveport. This guard was taken from the manpower of Taylor's district rather than equally from all the districts.

When Taylor requested relief of one of his noncommissioned officers from this guard, he was told there could be no reduction in the guard's strength. He was further informed that the guard as constituted was unstable, being made up of convalescents and soldiers pending trial for being AWOL, and that he should prepare to send a weak regiment to replace it. This was one of several occasions upon which Taylor either formally protested a departmental detail, or ordered his subordinates not to fill it. After the war, in his influential memoir *Destruction and Reconstruction*, Taylor continued to insist that the Shreveport headquarters had swarmed with special duty men, to the detriment of active operations:

> The commander of the Trans-Mississippi Department displayed much ardor in the establishment of bureaux, and on a scale proportional rather to the extent of his territory than to the smallness of his force. His staff surpassed in numbers that of Von Moltke during the war with France and to supply the demands of bureau and staff, constant details from the infantry were called for, to the great discontent of the officers in the field. Hydrocephalus at Shreveport produced atrophy elsewhere.[10]

---

8 General Orders No. 58, Hdqrs. Trans-Miss. Dept., November 27, 1863, *OR* vol. 32, pt. II, 1078-1079; General Orders No. 93, Hdqrs. Trans. Miss. Dept., December 1, 1864, Confederate States Army, *General Orders, Trans-Miss. Department*, 82-83; General Orders No. 81, Hq. Dist. Ark., November 22, 1864, in Maj. Gen. J. B. Magruder, General Orders, 1864-1865, District of Arkansas, Trans-Mississippi Dept., Departmental Records, Record Group 109, National Archives.

9 J. E. S, Harrison to Colonel Moncure, October 20, 1863, Bryan Papers.

10 Boggs to Taylor, January 12, 1864, *OR* vol. 34, pt. II, 855-856; endorsement to preceding letter Hd. Qrs. D. T. M. Shreveport, n.d., in Smith Papers; Brent to Faries, December 7, 1863, Brent to Rhett, February 2, 1864, Taylor to Boggs, February 2, 1864, Rhett to Brent, May 28, 1864, all in J. L.

Taylor's diagnosis of "Hydrocephalus at Shreveport" is not supported by the available data. In December 1864, thirty-two officers in all were assigned to the staff and the bureaus at Shreveport.[11] Unfortunately, the returns do not show the numbers of enlisted men employed there because they were not considered staff members. The number of officers does not seem excessive, however, when compared with the numbers of officers assigned to similar Union headquarters. In December 1864, for example, the Federal Department of the Gulf had seventy-nine officers assigned at headquarters, the Department of Missouri sixty-one, the Department of Arkansas forty, and the Department of Mississippi eighteen. It must be remembered, moreover, that Smith's bureaus were charged with some of the functions performed for other departments by the Confederate War Department, and in any case he had been ordered to establish them by the secretary of war and presumably had no choice in this matter. Taylor's comments in that regard seem to be more bitter than accurate.[12]

On the other hand, the complaints of Taylor and others about excessive details of enlisted men to various special assignments throughout the Department are at least partially justified. In March of 1865, Smith commented (obviously using round numbers) that 10,000 of the 50,000 enlisted men in the Trans-Mississippi Department were on details away from their units.[13] About the same time, returns of the Federal Department of the Gulf show 38,758 present out of 48,220 assigned enlisted men.[14] Total enlisted absentees for all causes in this numerically similar Union command were only seventeen percent as against roughly twenty percent absent on detail alone in Kirby Smith's department. A report of the Superintendent of the Bureau of Conscription in Richmond also supports the conclusion that numbers of detailed men in the Trans-Mississippi were high compared to other commands. Although only approximately correct, this report shows that of 154,285 men enlisted or conscripted east of the Mississippi River between April 1862 and February 1864, 20,809 or 13.4 percent were placed on special details. This did not include details to post quartermasters and commissaries, and were they included, the total percentage would be

---

Brent Papers, Louisiana Historical Association Collection; Taylor, *Destruction and Reconstruction*, 183.

11   Abstract from return of the Army of the Trans-Mississippi Department, General E. Kirby Smith commanding, for the month of December, 1864, *OR* vol. 41, pt. IV, 1140-1141. // See Jeffery S. Prushankin, *A Crisis in Confederate Command: Edmund Kirby Smith, Richard Taylor, and the Army of the Trans-Mississippi* (Baton Rouge, 2005). This book traces the contentious relationship between Smith and Taylor and emphasizes how the poor tenor of the working relationship between these men negatively affected military operations, much to the detriment of the department's effort to defend the region.

12   Abstract from return of the Military Division of West Mississippi, Maj. Gen. Edward R. S. Canby, U.S. Army, Commanding, for the month of December 1864, ibid., 972.

13   E. K. Smith to Jefferson Davis, March 7, 1865, ibid., vol. 48, pt. I, 1411-1412.

14   Abstract from return of the Military Division of West Mississippi, Maj. Gen. Edward R. S. Canby, U.S. Army, commanding, for the month of January 1865, ibid., 701-702.

slightly higher, but probably not as high as the Trans-Mississippi's twenty percent. It can once again be asserted in mitigation that the Trans-Mississippi was charged with more functions than other departments, but there is no doubt that more opportunities also existed there for "empire building" and other abuses of that kind. In any case, the one sure conclusion that can be drawn is that details were a constant drain on the combat strength of the Department.[15]

Men absent in arrest or confinement constituted another serious loss of manpower, though guardhouse sentences normally included hard labor. Probably the most common reasons for such arrests and confinement were absence without leave and desertions. Sentences for these familiar military crimes varied widely, ranging from death in some cases to almost trivial punishments in others. In at least one such case, thirty lashes was adjudged by a court that must have been poorly instructed because the reviewing authority at district headquarters promptly threw out the punishment as illegal. The ominous words "to be shot to death with musketry at such time and place as the Commanding General shall direct" appears frequently in sentences in 1864, although a cursory examination of a limited number of case records of that year leaves the impression that district commanders, as reviewing authorities, tended to reduce these sentences except where men had been found behind the enemy lines.

In one such case the reviewing authority remitted the death sentence of an Arkansas private because of the "excellent conduct of his Regiment and Brigade." In another case, the reviewing authority reprimanded the general court martial attached to Major General John H. Forney's Division:

> Again has this Court given evidence of their disregard of law and the discipline of the service. This Court has condemned a private soldier to be shot to death (for desertion), whilst in two instances, it has shrunk from inflicting that punishment upon Sergeants. Further comment is unnecessary.[16]

It would be easy to attribute the deplorably high absentee record in the Trans-Mississippi to a peculiarly western lack of discipline and disaffection from the Confederate cause. Comparison with the much admired Army of Northern Virginia shows, however, that the proportions between present and absent were almost the same there as in the Trans-Mississippi during roughly the same period. Soon after Gettysburg in 1863, for example, the aggregate present and absent in General Lee's army was 109,915, while present

15 John S. Preston to J. C. Breckinridge, February n.d., 1865, with Inclosures A and L, ibid., ser. IV, vol. 3, 1099-1101, 1109-1110.

16 General Orders No. 61, Hdqrs. Dist. Ark., December 3, 1863, General Orders Nos. 7, 8, 9, 14, 20, and 82, Hdqrs. Dist. Ark., February 9, 12, 13, 22, March 14, November 22, 1864, all in Lt. Gen. T. H. Holmes, General Orders, 1863-1864, District of Arkansas, Trans Mississippi Department, Departmental Records, Record Group 109, National Archives.

for duty was 50,184. Just before the Wilderness in early May of 1864, aggregate present and absent was 98,346, the present for duty 62,925. Absenteeism was a Confederate curse not confined to the lands west of the Mississippi.[17]

White manpower in the Trans-Mississippi was augmented frequently by black slave labor. In December of 1863, Magruder directed that Texas slaveholders provide their male slaves between sixteen and fifty years with entrenching tools and send all of them, excepting one per owner, to various depots throughout the state. Needless to say this decree aroused widespread resentment in Texas, and shortly thereafter department headquarters notified Magruder that he had violated War Department orders allowing only one fifth of the male slave population to be called, except in the most extreme emergency. In April of 1864, Magruder declared that an emergency did exist and again violated the standing orders by calling out one-fourth of the slaves in four south Texas counties to work on coastal fortifications. That July, in accordance with an act of Congress signed the previous February, department headquarters ordered that all free black men between eighteen and fifty years of age, except those freed by the Treaty of Paris of 1803 and the Transcontinental Treaty of 1819, be enrolled immediately by the Bureau of Conscription, and that one-fifth of all male slaves between eighteen and fifty be enrolled for labor. District commandants for slave labor were appointed, from whom commanding officers could requisition black labor as required. Finally, in 1865, much too late to have any real effect, district commandants of slave labor were ordered to turn their slaves over to their district engineers to be organized into gangs of 100 and employed under the general supervision of the engineers.[18]

Military bureaus proliferated and staff agencies multiplied and expanded under Kirby Smith's command. As previously noted, however, Smith had problems and responsibilities that no other Confederate department commander faced, and it was necessary for him to man agencies, both military and nonmilitary, for which Confederate tables of organization provided no replacements. In addition to bureaus of the war department type, a number of civilian governmental agencies, with Smith's support, were established in the Trans-Mississippi. The two principal civilian agencies were those of the Post Office Agent and of the Treasury Agent.

The position of Post Office Agent, created by Congress in February of 1864, was filled by James H. Starr, who established his office at Marshall, Texas. In this post, Starr was the supervisor of all postmasters and all mail contractors operating within the department. How

---

17 Randolph H. McKim, *The Numerical Strength of the Confederate Army: An Examination of the Argument of the Hon. Charles Francis Adams and Others* (New York, 1912), 44.

18 Edmund P. Turner to the Planters and Farmers of Texas, December 7, 1863, C. S. West to Magruder, January 7, 1864, *OR* vol. 34, pt. II, 838-839; Magruder to B, April 22, 1864, ibid., pt. III, 784-785; General Orders No. 55, Hdqrs. Trans-Miss. Dept. July 20, 1864, ibid., vol. 41, pt. II, 1014; General Orders No. 29, Hdqrs. Trans-Miss Dept., March 30, 1865, ibid., vol. 48, pt. I, 1451-1452.

much this agency actually improved Trans-Mississippi mail service would be difficult to ascertain.[19]

The office of the Treasury Agent was supplemented by two other bureaus, one of the Auditor and one of the Comptroller, both subordinate to the Treasury Agent. For the treasury agent, Congress authorized powers comparable to those of the secretary of the treasury, with all reports and returns normally made to the secretary to be made to him. The new treasury agent, Congressman Peter W. Gray of Texas, apparently arrived in May of 1864. Shortly thereafter, General Smith recommended to President Davis that all cotton operations be placed under Gray, since the raising of funds and the payment of debts in cotton belonged more properly to the civilian treasury agency than to the Confederate Army. Orders to that effect were not issued until October, and even then officers of the military Cotton Bureau were required to continue at their duties until Treasury officers could replace them.[20]

The establishment of these civilian facilities was long overdue. By January 1864, the outstanding government debt in the department was $30,000,000, and some military agencies had resorted to highly unorthodox sources of funds for survival. Governor Moore of Louisiana made a direct personal loan of $30,000 to the Ordnance Department of the District of West Louisiana in January 1864 for the purchase of critical supplies. Earlier, after the fall of Little Rock in 1863, when much of the cavalry in Arkansas was demoralized by being defeated, dismounted, and unpaid, Governor Reynolds had advanced without interest all of the funds of the exiled Missouri government, an amount $170,000, to the Confederate depository in Arkansas to pay the cavalrymen.[21]

Congressman Gray directed that his office as well as those of the Comptroller, Thomas H. Curry, and the Auditor, D. F. Shall, be established in Marshall as of July 1, but operations were slow in getting started. Apparently Shall and some of the clerical personnel had not arrived by that time, and these bureaus did not begin functioning until September. After that time a more orderly system of funding and accounting for receipts and disbursements was possible, although responsibility for the cotton trade was not assumed by the Treasury agency until sometime after February 1865. This new agency could do nothing to alleviate the extensive problems created by the generally slipshod financing of the Confederacy, nor

19 John Nathan Cravens, *James Harper Starr, Financier of the Republic of Texas* (Austin, 1950), 136-145.

20 "Circular: To Officers of and Others Having Business with the Treasury in Trans-Mississippi Department," Houston, May 29, 1864, copy in Civil War Papers, Louisiana Historical Association Collection; Smith to Davis, May 12, 1864, *OR* vol. 34, pt. III, 821-822; General Orders No 77, Hdqrs. Trans-Miss. Dept., October 3, 1864, in Confederate States Army, General Orders. Head Quarters Trans-Miss. Department, 68-73.

21 Smith to Davis, January 28, 1864, *OR* vol. 34, pt. II, 920; J. L. Brent to Thomas o. Moore, Receipt for $30,000, January 8, 1864, in J, L. Brent Papers, Louisiana Historical Association Collection; Reynolds to H. J. G. Battle, June 4, 1864, in Reynolds Papers.

could it do anything about the physical difficulties of providing funds for the Trans-Mississippi region.[22]

Yet another civilian agency in Marshall for which Smith provided military support was the exiled government of Missouri. After brief sojourns in Camden, Little Rock, Arkadelphia, and Shreveport, Louisiana, Thomas Reynolds and his quasi-government had moved to Marshall in November 1863. To conserve dwindling state funds, Reynolds had, upon arrival in Marshall, reduced his staff to seven Missouri State Guard officers who performed both military and civil functions. These officers, plus a civilian combination teamster-carpenter exempted from conscription, constituted the permanent staff of the exiled government. In addition, Reynolds managed to obtain five conscripts from the Trans-Mississippi Bureau of Conscription to serve as teamsters and guards.

The modest support rendered this establishment by the military was adequately compensated by the services Reynolds and his staff provided. "The State government of Missouri is kept up," explained Reynolds to General Elkanah Greer in December 1863, ". . . mainly for the purpose of paying off claims arising out of the services of the old Missouri State Guard, and recruiting in Missouri for the Confederate Army."[23] Both of these tasks would have meant long hours of work and many headaches for one or more of Smith's staff agencies or bureaus had not the tiny exiled government constantly sought to cope with them.

Reynolds's attempts to settle old claims from Missouri State Guard veterans against both the state and the Confederacy were never ending. Most of these claims were extremely difficult and some impossible to adjust because of the chronically poor record-keeping of the Missouri State Guard during its short active life span. Even when a claim could be substantiated, money for payment proved scarce. Reynolds did receive $2,000,000 in Confederate currency to satisfy the claims of those guard veterans who had subsequently enlisted in the Confederate Army, but this was not nearly enough money to satisfy outstanding claims. Many veterans, including some serving in the Confederate Army, had to be content with receiving Missouri Defense Bonds in settlement of their claims.[24]

Reynolds adamantly turned down persistent requests from disgruntled exiles for reactivation of the Missouri State Guard. The state treasury, he explained, could not support the Guard, and its reactivation would hurt Confederate recruiting. His comments on these requests were sometimes scathing. "I cannot admire the patriotism which is too proud or too

---

22 "Circular: To Officers and Others Having Business with the Treasury in Trans-Mississippi Department," Houston, May 29, 1864, copy in Civil War Papers, Louisiana Historical Association Collection; Kerby, *Kirby Smith's Confederacy*, 146-147; Reynolds to C. S. Stone, May 24, June 30, 1864, both in Reynolds Papers.

23 Reynolds to Greer, December 16, 1863, April 25, 1864, to H. W. Allen, July 11, 1863, all ibid.

24 Reynolds to H. Jennings and to P. W. Gray, March 4, June 25, 1864, Henry A. Bragg to Reynolds, May 17, 1864, all ibid.

sectional to join an army led by General Price." The only active Guard commissions he would grant, besides those to his own staff, were to officers such as M. Jeff Thompson and Jo Shelby and two or three others he counted upon to recruit short-term Missouri troops for transfer into the Confederate State Army.[25]

Governor Reynolds was especially disturbed by the recruiting practices then prevalent in northern Arkansas, which he sought to remedy. His vivid description of these procedures warrants quotation at some length:

> The usual career of one of these recruiting officers is this. He procures an "authority" or "permission" to recruit, from anybody who will give him one, without much regard to law or regulations, or sometimes he contents himself with a mere letter of recommendation, especially if he can procure one from General Price. With this he goes to the frontier, establishes a 'camp' and collects his recruits. To acquire popularity he relaxes every rule of discipline; to subsist his band he issues 'scrip' to the unsuspecting, impresses supplies from the reluctant, scents a Unionist in every owner of a good horse & in plain English plays the petty tyrant generally.

> If orders are sent him he disregards them, for he is either not yet an officer as he takes care not to muster his men into service, or he claims to be his own master as an officer "on special service under authority from the War Department" or from somebody else. If by any favorable circumstances he raises a company, his ambition excites him to continue recruiting in order to raise a regiment; that raised, he would try to increase it to a brigade, and successful in that, would probably attempt to get up a division and ask to be made a major general.

> In any event, he avoids bringing his men to the army, demagogues about an advance into Missouri, and plays the hero on the strength of some safe raid upon the farmers outside of our lines. Though not an officer he obtains assistance from facile ordnance officers in our advanced posts.

> Occasionally the enemy or winter or the better sense of his own men forces him to bring to our army his "command" which usually then for the first time organizes itself regularly & elects some private or subaltern to command it, while its "played out" ex-leader curses the fickleness & ingratitude of mankind, is condoled with by his friends, struts about headquarters for a while (usually in a Federal uniform) bores for promotion or an assignment to command until his money . . . is exhausted, and then returns to the frontier to begin again his old game of military loafing & lawless plunder.[26]

25 Reynolds to Warner Lewis, to James A. Thompson, to L. C. Bohannon, February 20, 23, March 4, 1864, to Smith, March 17, May 19, 1864, all ibid.

26 Reynolds to Smith, March 26, 1864, ibid.

Missouri's governor in exile, Thomas C. Reynolds.

Missouri State Capitol

Reynolds was much too modest in telling General Greer that the exiled government existed solely to settle claims and carry on Missouri recruiting. The governor constantly worked to soothe the difficulties that arose between the Confederate authorities and some of the more irregular regiments of Missourians. On the one hand, he asked General Smith to assign William Quantrill and his men to an independent field of activity suitable to their peculiar circumstances. On the other, he urged Quantrill to live up to the pledges he had made General McCulloch and wisely suggested, "Strive to organize a regular command and enter the regular Confederate service. All authority over undisciplined bands is short lived."[27]

The exiled government also performed an extremely useful political function for the Confederacy in general, and in particular for the Trans-Mississippi Department. So long as Reynolds's tiny establishment continued to exist, it was possible to maintain the fiction of a "Confederate Missouri" and justify raids for its recovery. The same fiction helped the voice of the Trans-Mississippi in Confederate national affairs, for the Missouri delegation in the Confederate Congress was large. Indeed, the two Missouri senators and seven representatives amounted to about one-third of the Congressional representation from the Trans-Mississippi states as a whole. During his tenure Reynolds appointed two senators friendly to both President Davis and General Smith, and sought to use his influence in such a way that Missouri voters in the Army would elect men of like mind to the lower house when Congressional elections were held for Missouri in May of 1864.[28]

Reynolds's cooperative attitude toward Smith was not always characteristic of the Trans-Mississippi governors, especially in 1864. Henry W. Allen of Louisiana informed Reynolds in March that he wanted a meeting of the Trans-Mississippi governors to consider grave questions. As chairman of the governors' Committee of Public Safety, Reynolds notified Governor Pendleton Murrah of Texas that any meeting time would be convenient for him and Allen, and that he supposed the same was true of Governor Harris Flanagin, who

27 Reynolds to Quantrill, March 5, 10, 1864, ibid.

28 Reynolds to Smith, February 27, May 21, 1864, to Davis, May 10, 1864, to Snead, May 19, 1864, all ibid.

Texas Governor Pendleton Murrah.

Texas State Library and Archives Commission

was in Washington, Arkansas, within ninety miles of Shreveport. Perhaps General Smith would be invited, perhaps not. According to Reynolds, the subjects to be discussed much concerned Texas, thereby implying that the cotton trade and the use of state troops, matters of open disagreement between General Smith and Governor Murrah, would be high on the agenda. On April 23, when Murrah's representative Judge Thomas J. Devine arrived in Shreveport, Reynolds invited Governor Flanagin to meet with them. Reynolds informed Flanagin that the cotton trade and the supply of the Army would be principal topics at the meeting.[29]

Allen, Reynolds, and Devine held a series of meetings in the last two weeks of April and in early May; Governor Flanagin did not attend. The main topic was state rights—especially in relation to suspension of the writ of habeas corpus, exemptions of men liable to conscription, control of the state militia, and regulation of the cotton trade. Devine worked up a "state rights" declaration, but Allen, who believed that the governors of Georgia and North Carolina had already moved in a similar direction with no good result, was reluctant to sign and publish it. As a consequence, the document was never published and the meetings served only to show the private dissatisfaction of these important men with Confederate policies. Afterwards, Reynolds wrote privately to Murrah to express his support for Murrah's position on the cotton trade and on conscription.[30]

Murrah's confrontation with the Confederate authorities on these two questions actually dated from December 1863. At that time, the Texas legislature (at his urging) passed a series of acts that reorganized the state troops and exempted the eligible men in fifty-four western counties from Confederate conscription. The exempted men were to provide the frontier protection of the state in place of the Texas Frontier Regiment, which was to be transferred to Confederate service. These acts tended to encourage desertion by men who had already been inducted from the exempted counties, and to deprive the Confederate

29 Reynolds to Murrah, to Flanagin, March 12, April 23, 1864, both ibid.

30 Reynolds to Murrah, May 24, 30, 1864, to Flanagin, May 24, 1864, to Devine, August 6, 1864, all ibid.

Army of a large number of Texas conscripts. Moreover, state troops were now to be raised and organized as brigades, which meant that they could not be accepted into the Confederate Army under existing law, which required they be raised as regiments. Controversy over this question continued from January to April 1864 between Murrah, on the one hand, and Kirby Smith and John Magruder on the other. Only in the face of Nathaniel Banks's dangerous Red River invasion did Murrah gave up his stubborn resistance to Confederate law and agree to the further reorganization of Texas troops in accordance with the national law.[31]

Kirby Smith, however, was unsuccessful in persuading the Texas authorities that they were nullifying Confederate law by exempting men in the western counties from conscription. In February 1865, he submitted the matter to President Davis, noting that the Texas senators proposed laying it before Congress. No decision seems to have been forthcoming from Richmond. In any case, Texas continued to maintain its frontier defense force in this way until the end of the war.[32]

An equally bitter quarrel had erupted in December 1863 between Murrah and the military authorities over Texas cotton policies enacted by the state legislature. Texas law permitted a vendor to protect his cotton from impressment or Confederate purchase by consigning all of it to the state for shipment to the Rio Grande at his expense. Across the border, the vendor recovered half the cotton and received seven percent state bonds, payable in land warrants, for the other half. These state bonds were far more attractive than depreciated Confederate currency or doubtful Cotton Bureau certificates, and the Texas agents offered better prices than the agents of the Cotton Bureau. The policy was making it very difficult for the Cotton Bureau to obtain Texas cotton.

Alarmed, Colonel William A. Broadwell, the Cotton Bureau officer in Shreveport, suggested to Smith that all Texas cotton be impressed or that Texas be abandoned militarily by the Confederates. In March 1864 Smith sent Major Guy M. Bryan, his staff officer with the best grasp on thorny Texas issues, to try to get Murrah to alter his plans. Bryan conferred in Houston with E. B. Nichols, the head of the Texas cotton operation, before laying Smith's objections before Murrah. On April 2, Murrah agreed to suspend the state's cotton purchases, but insisted that until a final settlement could be reached, contracts already made would be honored. Controversy over this issue continued to simmer until July of 1864, when in a conference near Hempstead Smith seems finally to have convinced Murrah that the military needed at least one-half of the Texas cotton. Once convinced, Murrah cooperated immediately by urging Texas citizens to relinquish one-half of their cotton to the military

31 Kerby, *Kirby Smith's Confederacy*, 218-220; Florence E. Holladay, "The Powers of the Commander of the Confederate Trans Mississippi Department, 1863-1865," *Southwestern Historical Quarterly*, XXI (1918), 354-355; W. F. Mastin to R. H. Chilton, February 6, 1865, *OR* vol. 48, pt. I, 1369-1370.

32 E. K. Smith to Jefferson Davis, February 10, 1865, with Inclosures Nos. 1, 2, 3, and 5, ibid., 1373-1377.

and by declaring all cotton contracts with the state void, except in those cases where the contracted cotton was already below San Antonio.[33]

Cotton was used to furnish supplies for other states as well as Texas. Governor Allen of Louisiana was particularly successful in its use, probably because the Confederate government owed Louisiana a good deal of money and Allen used this debt to begin his operations. He prevailed upon General Smith to transfer tax-in-kind cotton collected in Louisiana to the state until the debt was liquidated. Later, Allen maintained purchasing agents in Texas. The proceeds of the cotton sales were used strictly for the purchase of medicines, dry goods, wool cards, machinery, and other necessities, part of which was sold to the public in state stores, the rest going to supply foundries and other manufactories. Murrah was jealous of Allen's success. In March 1865, the Texas governor plaintively asked Colonel Bryan why Allen had been so successful in state cotton operations when he had not. Bryan's reply was rather blunt: "Governor Allen is a cordial and warmhearted generous man in his associations which with his good deeds makes him popular." Bryan also pointed out that bobtailed Confederate Louisiana was a great deal easier to administer than sprawling Texas.[34]

Even Governor Reynolds of Missouri hoped to get into the cotton business. As early as the summer of 1863, he had decided to try to export cotton to obtain supplies for the Missouri Confederate troops. Enemy operations prevented this in 1863, but in the spring of 1864, impressed with Governor Allen's success, Reynolds tried once again. His plan was to export from 1,000 to 2,000 bales for the account of the state by means of agents, preferably Missourians, who would furnish capital to buy the cotton, pay transportation and duties to Mexico, assume liability for all losses, and guarantee the state a certain amount per bale in gold. Reynolds expected the amount to be $12.00 to $15.00 per cotton bale, which was the current value of the export permit that he, as a state executive, could furnish. After a few weeks Reynolds again temporarily dropped his cotton project because a talk with Colonel Broadwell convinced him that cotton operations by the states were interfering with military supply efforts. Later in the year, Reynolds's preoccupation with Sterling Price's campaign into Missouri distracted his attention from his cotton scheme. Reynolds resurrected his plan again in January of 1865. This time he was able to make over the next three months a number

33 Agnes Louise Lambie, "Confederate Control of Cotton in the Trans-Mississippi Department" (unpublished Master's thesis, University of Texas, 1915), 71-77; Kerby, *Kirby Smith's Confederacy*, 199-202; Smith to Murrah, July 5, 1864, in Letters and Telegrams Received and Sent, 1861-1865, Departmental Records, Trans-Mississippi Department, Record Group 109, National Archives; Smith to Murrah, July 4, 1864, Bryan to W. J. Hutchins, March 16, 1864, E. B. Nichols to Murrah, March 19, 1864, Murrah to Bryan, April 2, 1864, all in Bryan Papers; Sholars, "Life and Services of Guy M. Bryan," 126-133.

34 Dorsey, Allen, 239; Murrah to Bryan, March 29, 1865, [Bryan] to Governor [Murrah], April 15, 1865, both in Bryan Papers.

of contracts with cotton exporters. The war's end probably prevented the consummation of any of them.[35]

State schemes like the one implemented by Reynolds did not go uncriticized, Peter W. Gray, the Treasury agent, was particularly upset by the interpretations the states placed upon President Davis's regulations for the cotton trade (promulgated in February 1864, but not published in the Trans-Mississippi Department until October). Allen and Murrah assumed the right of the state under these regulations to ship entire cargoes of cotton to Mexico without reserving one-half for the Confederate Government as required of other shippers. Gray maintained that the states were only exempted from giving bond to meet the one-half requirement, not from the requirement itself. He saw as a potential evil under the governors' interpretation the very scheme which Reynolds had already attempted to implement. "If the states are to be at liberty to export entire cargoes without restriction," he argued, "they can and will make bargains with private parties to take out cotton for them, in a joint account in the name of the state." Gray felt strongly that such practices would absorb the resources of the country and leave the army unsupplied.[36]

Another aspect of the cotton trade that evoked often bitter criticism was the trading of cotton through the enemy lines in Louisiana and Arkansas. The ostensible purpose of this trade was to obtain needed supplies, particularly medicine. These activities, however, often led to private speculation and petty graft. Perhaps the most common form of this trade was for a private individual to bring supplies to the Confederates through the lines and receive cotton for them, usually at a price quite favorable to the government. Holding a pass from the Confederate authorities, the trader then conveyed his cotton through the lines to the Federals and made most of his profit on it.[37]

Aging General Holmes much disapproved of the trade, considering it "villainy" even in cases of grave necessity. Generals Smith and Taylor apparently had fewer scruples in the matter, for the chief quartermasters of both the Trans-Mississippi Department and the District of West Louisiana were authorized to make cotton contracts for supplies. On January 6, 1864, Taylor submitted to Smith a proposal from agents of the Metropolitan Bank of New York who offered gold or sterling for all the government cotton the Trans-Mississippi officials could produce. These same bank agents had, Taylor understood, been paying as much as fifteen cents per pound in the Plaquemine area. This offer was the most

35 Reynolds to J. T. Thornton, May 26, 30, 1864, to John McMerty, May 24, 1864, to C. B. Alexander, June 25, 1864, to Boggs, January 31, February 7, March 29, 1865, to Broadwell, February 28, March 4, 1865, to J. Q. Burbridge, February 13, 1864, to E. C. Cabell, February 28, 1864, to J. T. Thornton, March 1, 1864, to Thomas Monroe, March 8, 1864, to G. A. Gallegher, April 13, 1865, all in Reynolds Papers.

36 General Orders No. 77, Hdqrs. Trans-Miss. Dept., October 3, 1864, in Confederate States Army, *General Orders, Head Quarters Trans Miss. Department*, 68-73; P. W. Gray to Bryan, to My Dear Sir [Bryan], January 12, 14, 1865, both in Bryan Papers.

37 Taylor to Boggs, January 11, 1864, *OR* vol. 34, pt. II, 852-853.

advantageous to the government of any he had ever heard, and he was anxious to proceed. The same month, January 1864, Smith was actively attempting to negotiate an agreement with the Federal authorities at New Orleans whereby cotton could be exchanged for gold, sterling, or supplies through certain foreign exchange houses.[38]

Perhaps it was the failure of these two enterprises that soured Taylor on trading with the enemy. In any case, he had become skeptical of the possible benefits by mid-February 1864. "After fully testing the practicability of getting supplies from the enemy for the use of our army, and exchanging cotton therefore," explained Taylor, "I am satisfied that the policy of the enemy is so decidedly opposed to such arrangements that nothing can be procured from them with the consent of their authorities." A short time later he remarked, "The rage for cotton speculation has reached all classes of the people. . . . Notwithstanding our warm sympathies with the sufferings of our people, I am now convinced of the necessity for destroying every pound of cotton likely to reach the enemy."[39]

A year later in January of 1865, however, cotton trading through the lines was still brisk in Arkansas and Louisiana, both with and without permission of General Smith, and bitter complaints about the trade were still being heard. The important issue remained one of the sources of deep contention until the end of the war.[40]

The control of the state militia, the regulation of the cotton trade, and the problems connected with an ever-increasing Trans-Mississippi bureaucracy, although of great importance, by no means commanded the whole attention of the military and civil leaders of the Trans-Mississippi in 1864. The year was one filled with important military activity, beginning with a resounding Confederate military success in the spring and terminating with a crashing Confederate defeat in the fall.

All told, 1864 was a year of many important changes in the military command structure of the Trans-Mississippi, some of them long overdue.

---

38 Holmes to Boggs, February n.d., 1864. in Correspondence of General T. H. Holmes, 1861-1864, Chap. II, Vol. 358, Record Group 109, National Archives; Taylor to Smith, January 6, 1864, in Letters and Telegrams Received and Sent, 1861-1865, Departmental Records, Trans Mississippi Department, Record Group 109, National Archives; Smith to Taylor, January 15, 17, 1864, *OR* vol. 34, pt. II, 871, 883.

39 Taylor to Boggs, February 16, 21, 1864, ibid., 971-972, 977-978.

40 Robert W. McHenry to President Davis, January 5, 1865, J. F. Belton to Lieutenant General Buckner, January 6, 1865, both quoted in Boggs, *Reminiscences*, 109-111.

Chapter 13

Military Command
and the Campaigns of 1864

In JANUARY OF 1864, General Kirby Smith wrote a letter to Senator Robert W, Johnson of Arkansas that evaluated rather harshly his chief subordinates. "Taylor is the only district commander in whom I can rely; he is a good soldier and a man of ability, and could he only forget his habits and training as a politician would be all that could be asked," explained the department commander. "General Holmes is a true patriot," Smith continued,

> faithful and devoted; time, his troubles and responsibilities have preyed upon him, his memory is failing, he has no confidence in himself, and is without fixity of purpose, I love him for his virtues, but a younger man should command the District of Arkansas, where boldness, energy and activity with prudence are essential to success. Price is not equal to the command, and I would regard it unfortunate were he to succeed to it. Magruder has ability and great energy; he acts by impulse, commits follies, and has an utter disregard for law; he has no faculty for drawing around him good men, and his selection of agents is almost always unfortunate; he has no administrative abilities, though he is active and can do a large amount of work; he would be a better commander of a corps, though no reliance could be placed upon his obedience to an order unless it chimed in with his own plans and fancies.[1]

---

1 // This is a frank and accurate assessment of his chief subordinates. Perhaps the greatest irony in the discussion is the value that Smith placed on Richard Taylor as his most capable subordinate. Though Taylor caused Smith a great deal of consternation, as Prushankin points out in his book *A Crisis in Command*, Smith nevertheless recognized the talent Taylor brought to his duties in the Trans-Mississippi.

Smith would obviously have been pleased with the immediate replacement of two of his district commanders, but he also expressed other desires in this letter. He hoped that President Davis would appoint his old friend and medical director, Dr. Sol A. Smith, a brigadier general to replace his chief of staff, General Boggs. If a major general were to be sent to the Trans-Mississippi, an assignment Smith he seemed to anticipate, his preferences were for Patrick R. Cleburne, Simon B. Buckner, or Carter L. Stevenson.[2]

In the next few months, some of the changes that would occur were not all to Smith's liking. Portents of two of these changes arrived a few weeks later in the form of requests from Generals Holmes and Taylor for relief and reassignment. Smith declined to forward Taylor's request on the grounds that he was needed in the department. He returned it to him with assurances that he had repeatedly reported Taylor's outstanding performance to the War Department, and that he hoped soon to see Taylor's promotion to lieutenant general. In a personal note to Taylor at the same time, Smith explained to him that he was indispensable to the Trans-Mississippi and asked him to state frankly "what the matter really is." Taylor could hardly be frank, however, for what troubled him more than promotion was his general dislike of serving under General Smith. As for General Holmes, his request for relief was forwarded with an indorsement asking that one of the three major generals— Cleburne, Buckner, or Stevenson—be sent out to replace him.[3]

Holmes was to display his usual indecision in this last episode of his Trans-Mississippi career. On February 6, 1864, he withdrew his request for relief but renewed it on February 18. Ten days later, in a very bitter letter, Holmes accused General Smith of detaching a brigade from his command for assignment to Indian Territory before adding that he had been subjected to other "indignities." He insisted that he be ordered immediately to the War Department. A little less than a week later Holmes repeated this request, but the next day appeared to have second thoughts and instead apologized to Smith for his angry outburst. Although in this last letter Holmes had again requested relief, he was obviously worried that he would be succeeded by Sterling Price. Probably wisely, Holmes advised that if the enemy threatened Arkansas, General Smith himself should take personal command.[4]

For almost a year, several leading Trans-Mississippians had worked for Holmes's removal, prominent among them Governor Reynolds. With Holmes's latest request for relief Reynolds resumed his campaign for the general's removal. On February 6, the

---

2 Smith to R. W. Johnson, January 15, 1864, *OR* vol. 34, pt. II, 868-869.

3 Taylor to Boggs, February 28, 1864, with endorsement Smith to Taylor, March 4, 1864, Smith to Taylor, March 4, 1864, all in J. L. Brent Collection, Military Archives, Adjutant General's Office Library, Louisiana State Military Department, Jackson Barracks; Taylor to Cooper, February 28, 1864, Holmes to S. S. Anderson, February 1, 1864, with endorsement signed by E. Kirby Smith, March 1, 1864, *OR* vol. 34, pt. II, 935.

4 Holmes to Smith, February 6, 18, March 7, 8, 1864, Holmes to Boggs, February 28, 1864, all in Correspondence of General T. H. Holmes, 1861-1864, Chap. II, Vol. 358, Record Group 109, National Archives.

Simon Bolivar Buckner.

Missouri State Capitol

governor in exile urged a group of medical officers of the District of Arkansas to report Holmes's alleged mental condition to the inspector general on his next district inspection. On February 20, as he had done frequently in the past, Reynolds asked President Davis to remove the enfeebled general. In Shreveport, Reynolds personally urged Smith to accept Holmes's request for relief. By this time it was probable that Smith no longer needed the governor's urging. On March 11, without prior War Department authorization, Smith relieved Holmes of his district command, and on March 16 General Price formally assumed command in Arkansas.[5]

Reynolds remained fearful that Holmes would again change his mind and request reinstatement by the president. His fears were heightened by the rumor that Holmes had been so impressed by the farewell serenades and other departure honors rendered him that he was seriously considering such a step, but this was not to be. On April 18, War Department orders were issued confirming his relief from the Trans-Mississippi Department and reassigning him to command of the reserve forces in North Carolina. Thus the man who had been the Department's first commander quietly disappeared from the Trans Mississippi scene.[6]

After Holmes's relief, Simon Bolivar Buckner, one of the major generals Smith had requested, was posted to the department. Around mid-year, Buckner reached Shreveport and in the absence of Smith on an inspection tour, went on to visit Marshall. There, he seems

5 Reynolds to E. C. Cabell, to Davis, to Shelby, February 6, 20, March 26, 1864, all in Reynolds Papers; Special Orders No. 60, Hdqrs. Trans Miss. Dept., March 11, 1864, Smith to Holmes, March 11, 1864, General Orders Nos. 22 and 23, Hdqrs. District of Arkansas, both March 16, 1864, *OR* vol. 34, pt. II, 1034-1035, 1047.

6 Reynolds to J. P. Benjamin, to Waldo P. Johnson, April 4, 13, 1864, both in Reynolds Papers; Special Orders No. 90, Adj. and Insp. General's Office, Richmond, April 18, 1864, *OR* vol. 34, pt. III, 778.

to have spent considerable time with Governor Reynolds, who hoped Buckner would be made a kind of junior secretary of war, handling the administrative tasks of the department while Smith took the field.[7] Instead, Buckner was assigned on August 4 to the District of West Louisiana, the command by that time vacated by General Taylor because of his increasing antipathy for General Smith.[8]

*   *   *

THE IRRECONCILABLE BITTERNESS between Smith and Taylor, which had resulted in the latter's removal as a district commander, was a byproduct of the combined Red River and Camden campaigns of Union Generals Nathaniel Banks and Frederick Steele in the spring of 1864. These campaigns have been the subjects of much study and it is not my purpose to examine them in detail, but they cannot be totally ignored in any account of the Trans-Mississippi Department.[9]

Nathaniel Banks began his Red River Campaign in March of 1864, marching northward from Berwick Bay toward the Red River. Simultaneously, Rear Admiral David D. Porter's Federal gunboat fleet began ascending the Red River accompanied by transports carrying Brigadier General Andrew J. Smith's Union army corps from Vicksburg. By the last week of March, all the major elements of Banks's invasion force had assembled in the vicinity of Alexandria, Louisiana, and an advance on Shreveport began.

A series of skirmishes ensued between Banks's forces and those of Richard Taylor, culminating in Taylor's major victory at Mansfield on April 8. Banks's advance was not only stopped at Mansfield, but he lost some 2,235 men killed, wounded, and missing, as well as large amounts of materiel. Ironically, April 8 had been declared a fast day for the

---

7   S. Cooper to Buckner, May 2, 1864, ibid., 801; J. G. Walker to Boggs, June 21, 1864, ibid., pt. IV, 688; Reynolds to E. C. Cabell, to L. A. McLean, to W. P. Johnson, to Smith, July 4, 9, 14, 25, 1864, all in Reynolds Papers.

8   General Orders No. 60, Hdqrs. Trans Miss. Dept., August 4, 1864, *OR* vol. 41, pt. II, 1039.

9   // The standard text on the Red River Campaign at the time of Dr. Geise's writing was Ludwell H. Johnson, *Red River Campaign: Politics and Cotton in the Civil War* (Baltimore, MD, 1958). A number of studies have since emerged beginning in the 1990s. These include: William Riley Brooksher, *War Along the Bayous: The Red River Campaign in Louisiana* (Washington, D.C., 1998); Gary D. Joiner, *One Damn Blunder from Beginning to End: The Red River Campaign of 1864* (Wilmington, DE, 2003); Theodore P. Savas, David A. Woodbury, and Gary D. Joiner, eds., *The Red River Campaign: Union and Confederate Leadership and the War in Louisiana* (Shreveport, LA., 1994); and Michael J. Forsyth, *The Red River Campaign of 1864 and the Loss by the Confederacy of the Civil War* (Jefferson, NC, 2001). Each of these studies highlight different aspects of the campaign. For example, Joiner's *One Damn Blunder from Beginning to End* contains a trove of information about the important role of the Federal fleet in the campaign (he is an expert on Civil War inland naval vessels), while the Savas, Woodbury, and Joiner collaboration highlights an eclectic collection of essays on a broad range of subjects.

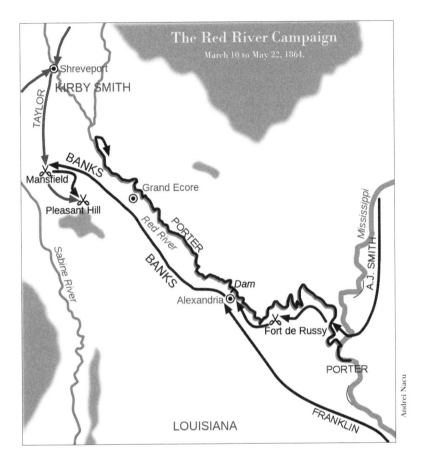

Confederates by President Davis, a day on which "military exercises will be suspended." In the darkness of night immediately following the end of the Mansfield fighting, Banks withdrew his men south to the vicinity of Pleasant Hill, where on April 9 a Confederate attack was driven back with severe loss. Even though he held the field, Banks continued his retreat.[10]

Meanwhile, General Smith had arrived at the scene of action. When he learned that Banks had retreated, Smith ordered most of Taylor's infantry to march north for Shreveport, leaving Taylor only his cavalry and a small infantry division. On April 14, Taylor—still hoping to destroy the retreating Banks—went to Shreveport to plead for the return of his infantry. Smith refused and instead took command himself of Taylor's infantry, which he ordered to march to oppose General Steele in Arkansas. Taylor was left in command at Shreveport. Some days later the thoroughly embittered Taylor returned to

---

10 General Orders No. 8, Hdqrs. Trans-Miss. Dept., March 18, 1864, ibid., vol. 34, pt. II, 1057.

Natchitoches, where he resumed command of his little army. Once again, he took up his pursuit of Banks.[11]

In Arkansas, Steele's advance, which had been intended to coincide with that of Banks in Louisiana, did not get underway until March 23. Throughout the last days of March and the early days of April, Steele moved south occupying Camden, which he hoped to use as a supply base, on April 15. There, he learned of Banks's withdrawal and began to doubt the wisdom of his own farther movement on Shreveport. On April 19, Kirby Smith arrived in the vicinity of Camden with the infantry from Louisiana. Finding that Price had not cut Steele's communications line to the north, Smith ordered James Fagan with a large cavalry command to destroy the Union supply bases on the Arkansas River. He was then to deploy his command astride Steele's communication and supply line to Little Rock. It was obvious that Smith intended no less than the destruction or capture of Steele's entire army.

Unfortunately, Smith's plans were to miscarry badly. Apparently deterred by heavy losses suffered in a desperate but successful action at Marks's Mill on April 25, and unable or unwilling to cross the swollen Sabine River, Fagan did not attack the Union supply bases on the Arkansas River. Alerted to the precariousness of his position at Camden by the Federal defeat at Marks's Mill, Steele began withdrawing northward on April 27. For reasons not entirely clear, perhaps seeking food and forage, Fagan moved too far west to delay Steele's retreat. By the 28th, the Federals had reached Jenkins' Ferry on the Sabine river, which they hastily bridged with pontoons. Before all of Steele's army could cross, however, Kirby Smith's hotly pursuing Confederates appeared on the scene and the bloody battle of Jenkins' Ferry began. Fighting in the flooded river bottom in a nightmare of waist-deep water and mud, hampered by the terrain as well as by questionable tactics, the Confederates were unable to prevent the escape of the Yankees across the river or their destruction of the pontoon bridge. Three days later Steele's men were recuperating in the comparative safety and comfort of Little Rock.[12]

The recriminations called forth by these campaigns would be heard for many months to come. Taylor in particular was so embittered against Smith as to lose all sense of military propriety in his condemnation of his superior for permitting Banks to escape. When Smith could no longer tolerate his subordinate's abuse he relieved him of command and ordered him to Natchitoches to await President Davis's pleasure. Major General John G. Walker became district commander in Louisiana. Smith also forwarded to the President all of

---

11 Discussion of military movements in the Red River Campaign is based primarily on Johnson, *Red River Campaign*, 89-169, 180-183.

12 Discussion of military movements in this campaign is from ibid., 171-180, 184-205. // Two additional studies provide more information on this unknown element of the Red River Campaign: Edwin C. Bearss, *Steele's Retreat from Camden and the Battle of Jenkin's Ferry* (Little Rock, AR, 1961), and Michael J. Forsyth, *The Camden Expedition of 1864 and the Opportunity Lost by the Confederacy to Change the Civil War* (Jefferson, NC, 2003).

Taylor's insubordinate correspondence, along with his own explanations of the recent campaigns.[13]

The feud between Smith and Taylor quickly achieved public notoriety, and both soldiers and civilians began taking sides in the dispute between the two generals. Those supporting Taylor generally limited their argument to the simple charge that Smith let the beaten Banks slip out of Taylor's grasp by weakening his army at the crucial moment. They tended to ignore Banks's impressive numerical superiority over Taylor even in retreat, and the fact that his army had by no means been disorganized by the defeat at Mansfield.[14]

Those who supported Smith tended to agree with a pseudonymous but apparently well-informed letter in the *Richmond Whig*. The writer pointed to Banks's numerical and material strength and to the practical impossibility of Taylor's again defeating Banks were the Federals to entrench, which they did. The writer stressed, moreover, the limited opportunities for the Confederates in Louisiana by pointing out that they could not effectively operate south and east of the Atchafalaya, which was controlled by Federal gunboats. On the other hand, a victory over General Steele's Union army in Arkansas, which was no stronger than the Confederate forces Smith could marshal against him, would open the way to the Arkansas Valley and ultimately to Missouri. The *Whig* correspondent also pointed out, as did other commentators, the probability of a fundamental difference between the perspectives of Smith and Taylor:

> History teaches us that subordinate commanders of armies and districts, with their eyes fixed upon their own localities, and the enemy opposed to them, and with the natural desire of distinction and success, are prone to magnify the importance of their position, and to think that they should be reenforced. But the General commanding a Department, dependent upon itself for its means of defense and offense, must take a survey of the whole field of action, and must decide upon his own responsibility, what is best for the whole cause.[15]

13 Kerby, *Kirby Smith's Confederacy*, 320-321; Winters, *Civil War in Louisiana*, 380; Castel, *Price*, 183-184; Special Orders No. 145, Hdqrs. Trans-Miss. Dept., June 10, 1864, S. S. Anderson to John G. Walker, June 10, 1864, both in *OR* vol. 34, pt. IV, 664.

14 // While it is true that the Union Army enjoyed a large numerical advantage, Taylor recognized a legitimate opportunity to inflict a potentially decisive blow against the Federal forces. General Banks could not abandon the region without losing the entire Federal fleet, which was trapped above the falls at Alexandria due to the low level of the Red River. Thus, with greater forces at hand, as Taylor argued in his memoirs *Destruction and Reconstruction*, he believed he could have trapped both the Union fleet and the army. His failure to convince Smith to provide the available infantry instead of chasing Steele in Arkansas gave Banks and Admiral Porter the breathing space they needed to escape from the Red River Valley and fight another day in other theaters of the war.

15 "Trans-Mississippi" to the editor of the Richmond *Whig*, n.d., quoted in Sarah A. Dorsey, *Recollections of Henry Watkins Allen Brigadier General Confederate States Army Ex-Governor of Louisiana* (New York, NY, 1966), 269-277.

Smith's own correspondence prior to the campaign sustains the view that he had long since settled upon the general plan that he ultimately followed, and that initially at least both Price and Taylor had more or less agreed with him. As early as January 16, Taylor wrote to General Boggs that he expected a Red River invasion in the spring coordinated with an advance by Steele south from Arkansas. Taylor recommended a concentration of forces against one of these columns. "Holding the country in the spring is simply a question of rapid marching. The radii [i.e., roads] from Holmes, Magruder and myself converging to some common center should be put in the best order." A little later, Smith wrote President Davis that he feared a formidable Red River invasion as soon as the river rose. Even before the campaigns began Price was recommending to Smith a concentration against Steele's column because it would be the weaker of the two, and because Steele's destruction would mean the recovery of the Arkansas Valley and the possible opening of the route to Missouri. Smith's reply showed that he agreed with Price's evaluation — "With yourself, General, I feel the importance of this move"—and at the same time revealed Smith's simple basic strategy. The enemy must be permitted to force the defending Confederates in both Louisiana and Arkansas back within close supporting distance of each other, where they could recoil on the Federal thrusts and perhaps effectively concentrate on the weaker force and destroy it.[16]

In the ensuing campaigns Smith never really wavered from his basic design. Steele, commanding the weaker Federal force, was destined to feel the full weight of the Confederate concentration as Price had suggested. Smith's undeviating strategy becomes clearer when one notices that on April 12, after Banks had been turned back by Taylor, Smith's headquarters instructed Price that communication between Banks and Steele must be prevented. "The latter hearing of Banks's defeat might be induced to retreat, whereas it is of paramount importance that he should be drawn into the interior as far as possible."[17] Obviously Smith was no longer really worried about Steele as a threat to Shreveport. He wanted Steele's advance to continue so that he could destroy him.

In view of Smith's consistent strategy, Taylor's attempt on April 13 to persuade Smith that Steele would retreat when he learned of Banks's defeat, and his subsequent criticism that Smith took his infantry from him after it was already known that Steele had stopped his advance on Shreveport, are largely irrelevant. Taylor's infantry did actually begin marching north on the same day, April 14, that Smith learned Steele had stopped his advance and was moving his forces toward Camden. The reason Smith did not then halt Taylor's infantry and

16 Taylor to Boggs, January 16, 1864, Smith to the President, January 20, 1864, Price to Smith, March 8, 1864, Smith to Price, March 16, 1864, *OR* vol. 34, pt. II, 879, 895-896, 1028-1029, 1043-1044. // Price was much more agreeable in his correspondence with Smith, and this may have convinced the department commander to support Price's call for an expedition in Missouri. By contrast, Taylor continued his acerbic diatribe in his discussions with Smith, which pushed the senior commander away from Taylor's point of view.

17 Anderson to Price, April 12, 1864, ibid., pt. III, 761.

send them again against Banks was his belief that the much weaker Steele might still be trapped at Camden. Toward this end, Price was ordered (also on April 14) to throw sufficient cavalry across the Ouachita River to break Steele's lines of supply and communications from Camden northward to the depots in the Arkansas Valley.[18]

Unfortunately, Smith's subordinates in Arkansas could not accomplish the missions he assigned them. The tactical failure of Price to isolate Steele in Camden, as well as the later tactical failure of Fagan to destroy Steele's depots, disrupt his communications, and slow his retreat to the Sabine, do not diminish the soundness of Smith's strategic conception. The tasks assigned were within the Confederates' military capabilities, but circumstances or perhaps a lack of determination, resulted in failure.[19]

In any case, one may continue to believe that the potential advantages of a decisive military victory were greater in Arkansas than in Louisiana. Had Taylor carried the argument, kept his infantry, and miraculously destroyed Banks's army, the way to New Orleans would still have been barred by the Federally controlled the Atchafalaya and Mississippi rivers.[20] On the other hand, had local tactical blunders not caused Smith to fail in Arkansas, the recapture of the Arkansas Valley was almost inevitable, and possession of the Arkansas Valley would have permitted increased pressure on Federal Missouri with all that might mean to the armies east of the river.

After the conclusion of these campaigns, Taylor waited in Natchitoches for some time without a command. On July 18, by direction of President Davis, orders were issued in Richmond for Taylor to cross the river and report by the nearest telegraph to the War Department. He was presumably not to be accompanied by troops. In the meantime, he had recommended a campaign in Missouri and turned down an offer from Smith to command it. In Taylor's words, "Everything [but Camile J. de Polignac's infantry in Louisiana] . . . should be directed to Missouri there can be no doubt but this is the last campaign of the war." The Missouri campaign, however, would have to wait.[21]

On July 9, General Smith had received through Lieutenant General Stephen D. Lee, commanding the Department of Alabama, Mississippi, and East Louisiana, an urgent

---

18 Taylor, *Destruction and Reconstruction*, 217-218; E. Cunningham to Taylor and to Price, April 14, 15, 1864, both in Kirby Smith Papers; Winters, *Civil War in Louisiana*, 361.

19 Castel, *Price*, 177-183; Smith to Jefferson Davis, June 11, 1864, in Kirby Smith Papers.

20 // While it was true that Taylor could not have retaken New Orleans, Banks' forces could not have shifted to other theaters to tip the scales there for the Union. For example, the XIX Corps joined the Army of the Potomac in the Eastern Theater and fought in the Shenandoah Valley in the late summer and fall and, by doing so, helped defeat Jubal Early's Confederate Valley army at Cedar Creek.

21 Taylor to S. S. Anderson, May 14, 1864, in Brent Collection, Louisiana State Military Department; Taylor to Smith, May 24, 1864, in Kirby Smith Papers; Reynolds to T. C. Manning, February 18, 1865, in Reynolds Papers; S. Cooper to E. K. Smith, July 18, 1864, quoted in S. D. Lee to Colonel Gober or Commanding Officer, July 22, 1864, *OR* vol. 41, pt. I, 117.

message from General Braxton Bragg, President Davis's military advisor. According to Bragg, Union Major General Edward R. S. Canby was moving on Mobile with 20,000 men and that Trans-Mississippi troops should be crossed to the east side of the river to create a diversion.[22] There followed a rapid flurry of messages from east of the Mississippi, most of them from Bragg forwarded through Lee to Smith. One such message, on July 22, directed that Taylor not cross the river alone, but that he be accompanied by the infantry of his corps. Smith accordingly ordered Taylor on July 28 to Alexandria to take command of the two infantry divisions there (Polignac's and Walker's) and to move them across the river "with as little delay as possible."[23]

Plans were prepared by the department engineer, Colonel Henry T. Douglas, to lay a pontoon bridge to get Taylor's infantry across the river. Taylor approved Douglas's proposal but Smith did not, thinking the idea highly impractical. The troops should be ferried over at night in pontoon boats, forty-two of which were available. Taylor accepted this idea but recommended a cavalry diversion toward New Orleans to cover the crossing. Smith rejected the diversion on grounds it would require the cavalry to operate in unhealthful country (a somewhat odd objection) and would prevent their best employment, which would be immediate defense of the crossing.

While the generals debated, the troops scheduled for the crossing became increasingly demoralized. Desertion rates soared. Neither Polignac's nor Walker's Texans had ever served east of the Mississippi, and apparently had no desire to do so. In Walker's Division morale was especially low because all three brigades had recently lost their commanders at Jenkins' Ferry—two mortally wounded and one gravely injured. Walker himself, who was popular in the ranks, had left the division to assume command of the District of West Louisiana. His place was taken by Major General John H. Forney, who was unpopular.

Under the circumstances it was highly questionable whether the troops could be persuaded to cross the river in any fashion, and neither Smith nor Taylor seem to have had much hope of success in this undertaking. Besides, as the weeks dragged on it became apparent by the enemy's deployment of his gunboats that he anticipated an attempted crossing. Consequently it must have been a relief for Smith when on August 19 he received a message from Davis stating that the President personally had never directly ordered such a crossing. In spite of its ambiguity the message provided an opportunity to suspend operations and Smith did so. On August 22 orders were issued at Shreveport directing Taylor to proceed across the river without the infantry. Taylor did not receive this message for several days and continued his preparations for a troop crossing until about August 27. A few nights later he quietly slipped across the river accompanied only by personal

22 Kerby, *Kirby Smith's Confederacy*, 324; S. D. Lee to Smith, July 9, 1864, Kirby Smith Papers.

23 S. D. Lee to E. Kirby Smith or Major General Walker, July 16, 1864, to Brigadier General Liddell, July 23, 1864, W, R. Boggs to R. Taylor, July 28, 1864, *OR* vol. 41, pt. I, 89-90.

attendants.[24] Although the troop crossing was not abandoned but only suspended, it was never to take place.[25]

* * *

OUT IN INDIAN Territory, meanwhile, a dispute had arisen over command of that district. Back in December of 1863, General Smith had assigned Samuel B. Maxey to the command in place of General William Steele. Then, in early February 1864, a resident of the Territory brought news from Richmond that the War Department would order Maxey relieved by General Douglas H. Cooper. It was at this point that the controversy began.[26] In a letter to the President, General Cooper claimed that, in making Maxey General Steele's successor, Kirby Smith had ignored him (Cooper) and his War Department assignments as Superintendent of Indian affairs and commander of all Indian troops on the borders of Arkansas.[27]

The War Department attempted to settle the dispute on July 21 by issuing orders making Cooper district commander, but that was not the end of it. Smith initially ignored these orders and Adjutant General Samuel Cooper's "imperative" instructions on the subject, and then tried unsuccessfully to get the orders revoked. Trans-Mississippi Department orders finally designated Douglas Cooper as Superintendent of Indian Affairs in February of 1865. Once that happened the outraged Maxey, who as district commander also superintended Indian affairs, requested relief from command on grounds that intolerable conflict would result if the superintendency were placed in other hands. On February 21, 1865, Maxey was ordered to Texas and Cooper appointed in his stead, thus

24 Kerby, *Kirby Smith's Confederacy*, 329; Winters, *Civil War in Louisiana*, 381-382; Norman Potter Morrow, "Price's Missouri Expedition, 1864," unpublished Master's Thesis, University of Texas, 1949, 12-13; Felix Pierre Poche, *A Louisiana Confederate: Diary of Felix Pierre Poche*, ed. by Edwin C. Bearss, trans. by Eugenie Watson Somdal (Natchitoches, LA, 1972), 159.

25 Discussion of the proposed river crossing is based on *OR* vol. 41, pt. I, 88-124, Kerby, *Kirby Smith's Confederacy*, 324-330; Winters, *Civil War in Louisiana*, 381-382; unsigned memorandum, n.p., n.d., concerning Taylor's river crossing, with unsigned indorsement stating it was written contemporaneously, in Brent Collection, Louisiana State Military Department; "Abstract of Correspondence between Genl's. E. K. Smith, R. Taylor, and B. Bragg," Executive Office, Richmond, July 22, 1864, copy in Jefferson Davis Collection, Louisiana Historical Association Collection.

26 Maxey to S. S. Anderson, February 12, 1864, in Trans Mississippi Department Letters Received 1862-1864, Letters and Telegrams Received and Sent (Incomplete), 1861-1865, Departmental Records, Record Group 109, National Archives.

27 Cooper to Jefferson Davis, February 29, 1864, with two indorsements and three inclosures, *OR* vol. 34, pt. II, 1007-1008.

ending a year of wrangling and Kirby Smith's long and somewhat bizarre defiance of the War Department orders.[28]

The Confederate military posture in Texas improved slightly in 1864. That March, Colonel "Rip" Ford, though an officer in state service, moved out of San Antonio with a mixed Confederate and state command of some 1,500 men bent on retaking the lower Rio Grande Valley. Learning at Ringgold Barracks that the Federals had only a skeleton force at Fort Brown, Ford moved against that place in the last week of July, and after some skirmishing occupied it. The weak Federal force retreated to Brazos Island. This left all the lower Valley in Confederate hands and permitted reopening the convenient Brownsville Matamoras trade. The remainder of 1864 was comparatively quiet in the Valley with only occasional encounters between Ford's Confederates, the Federal troops at Brazos Santiago, and guerrilla bands from Mexico.[29]

*   *   *

ONE CONSEQUENCE OF the comparatively heavy military activity in 1864 was a rash of promotions in the higher ranks. Smith's general orders in April, shortly after the Camden campaign, announced the promotions of six colonels to brigadier general and one brigadier general to major general, and in May the promotions of one colonel and one major to brigadier general, and five brigadier generals to major general. All these promotions were subject to the approval of the President and confirmation by Congress.[30]

Among those pleased at the promotions was Governor Reynolds, who immediately wrote to Senator Waldo P. Johnson (Missouri) in Richmond asking him to try to get the Senate to confirm them as quickly as possible. Others, predictably, were unhappy. Brigadier General McCulloch out in Texas, who appears to have felt himself overlooked, complained of a shortage of Texans on the promotion lists. McCulloch's ire is understandable, for he ranked as brigadier from as long ago as March 4, 1862, making him senior to all those promoted except Samuel Maxey. Under the circumstances, Smith felt constrained to explain to McCulloch that the promotions were based upon the recommendations of commanding officers and "were won by services on the battlefield," and to point out that more than half of

---

28 Special Orders No. 171, Adjt. and Insp. General's Office, Richmond, July 21, 1864, Smith to S. Cooper, October 1, 1864, with indorsement, ibid., vol. 41, pt. II, 1019, pt. III, 971; Maxey to S. S. Anderson, February 11, 1865, in Trans-Mississippi Department, Letters Received 1862-1864, Letters and Telegrams Received and Sent (Incomplete), 1861-1865, Departmental Records, Record Group 109, National Archives; George H. Shirk, "Indian Territory Command in the Civil War," *Chronicles of Oklahoma*, XLV (Winter, 1967-1968), 471.

29 Oates, *Rip Ford's Texas*, 352-387.

30 General Orders No. 13, 15, 21, 24, Hdqrs. Trans-Miss. Dept., April 13, 15, May 13, 19, 1864, *OR* vol. 34, pt. III, 764, 768, pt. II, 823, pt. III, 828.

the new appointees were in fact Texans. Smith closed tactfully by expressing sympathy with McCulloch's internal difficulties in his district and confidence that he would "triumph."[31]

In Richmond, meanwhile, Smith's promotions appear to have been received with more neglect than enthusiasm. On October 28, Smith wrote Adjutant General Cooper seeking to have the president act upon them. The officers in question had, he pointed out, been serving in their new capacities for some months. At the same time Smith recommended the promotion of four colonels he had not yet ventured to announce in department orders. On December 23, General Cooper conveyed Richmond's rebuke to Smith: "The President instructs me to say that it is improper for you to announce the promotion of general officers and assign them to duty before they are appointed by him." Only three of those Smith had appointed to brigadier general would be nominated by the president to the Senate. Subsequently, however, others were nominated and confirmed; even those who were not acted upon in Richmond continued to enjoy the titles and privileges of their new ranks, at least within the Trans-Mississippi Department.[32]

One promotion, this one made in Richmond, mightily rankled General Magruder: the elevation on October 11, 1864, of General Buckner to lieutenant general. The promotion made him senior to Magruder and junior only to the department commander. A few weeks later Magruder wrote directly to the president concerning the "herculean task" he had accomplished in Texas and reminding Davis that he had always supported the administration "undeviatingly and most faithfully." Magruder's concluding herculean sentence relative to Buckner's promotion said it all:

> Whilst claiming to be as little selfish as any officer can be, I cannot feel otherwise than humiliated that this officer much my junior in rank, Commanding like myself a District of the Trans Mississippi Department, whose advent is comparatively recent, and whose name has not been that I am aware of, connected with any successful service to the Republic, should be placed over me in the presence of the Army which I command and of the troops and people of Texas, whose confidence during a period I have enjoyed, in a high degree, of which have received the most gratifying and unequivocal evidence.[33]

31 Reynolds to Waldo P. Johnson, May 24, 1864, in Reynolds Papers; Smith to McCulloch, June 7, 1864, photostat in McCulloch Papers; "List Brigadier Generals in Trans-Miss. Dept., and their respective ranks," A. & IGO, December 2, 1863, signed by Ed. A. Palfrey, in Trans-Mississippi Department, Letters Received, 1862-1864, Letters and Telegrams Received and Sent (Incomplete), 1861-1865, Departmental Records, Record Group 109, National Archives.

32 Smith to Cooper, Cooper to Smith, October 28, December 23, 1864, *OR* vol. 41, pt. IV, 1016-1017, 1121-1122.

33 General Orders No. 80, Hdqrs. Trans-Miss. Dept., October 11, 1864, ibid., pt. III, 1001; Magruder to Davis, November 5, 1864, in Jefferson Davis Collection, Louisiana Historical Association Collection.

Magruder was by this time no longer commanding in Texas, a state with which he felt a special identity. On August 4, 1864, he had been shifted to the District of Arkansas and his place in Texas taken by John G. Walker. Sterling Price, who was scheduled to lead an impending invasion of Missouri, moved from command of the district to command of the cavalry in Arkansas. At the same time, Simon Buckner was assigned to the District of West Louisiana to replace Walker.[34]

*   *   *

THE IDEA OF the 1864 campaign into Missouri had had a long period of germination in the minds of various Trans-Mississippi leaders. General Smith no doubt was influenced by the idea when he determined to concentrate against Frederick Steele's Union column, and, even though real victory eluded him at the Battle of Jenkins' Ferry, he put the invasion wheels in motion some two weeks after that battle. On May 16, both Major Generals Thomas J. Churchill and Mosby M. Parsons were ordered to march their infantry divisions to Camden, "preparatory to a movement in the direction of Missouri." Three days later Price was notified by Department Headquarters that General Smith proposed "to make the Arkansas Valley and Missouri the theatre of operations." Price, therefore, was to employ his staff in establishing depots and supply trains and to prepare to receive "the bulk of the forces in Louisiana." The invasion of Missouri was to be made with the concentrated resources of the Department.[35]

Smith's timetable and plans were drastically altered between May 16 and late August of 1864, when the campaign actually started, chiefly, as he later explained, because of the orders from General Braxton Bragg to send the infantry east of the Mississippi River. Instead of a comparatively slow advance north utilizing infantry, cavalry, and artillery and based on the Arkansas Valley, there would now be a massive cavalry diversion aimed at Missouri. As a result, the final orders to Sterling Price to command head the expedition put him in

34 General Orders No. 60, Hdqrs. Trans-Miss. Dept., August 4, 1864, *OR* vol. 34, pt. II, 1039; General Orders No. 1, Headquarters Army in the Field, August 29, 1864, ibid., vol. 41, pt. II, 1090.

35 C. S. West to T. J. Churchill and to M. M. Parsons, both May 16, 1864, Boggs to Price, S, S. Anderson to Price, both May 19, 1864, all ibid., vol. 34, pt. III, 820-821, 828-829. / / Since the time of Dr. Geise's writing, several studies have appeared about Sterling Price's invasion of Missouri in 1864. These include Mark A. Lause, *Price's Lost Campaign: The 1864 Invasion of Missouri* (Columbia, MO, 2011); Kyle S. Sinisi, *The Last Hurrah: Sterling Price's Missouri Expedition of 1864* (New York, NY, 2015), and Michael J. Forsyth, *The Great Missouri Raid: The Last Confederate Invasion of the North* (Jefferson, NC, 2015). Each of these studies focus on various aspects of the expedition, such as its impact on the United States elections in 1864, or the privations suffered by the soldiers of both sides during the course of the grueling campaign.

command only of "the cavalry of the District of Arkansas." In other words, "the bulk of the forces in Louisiana" would not be joining him.[36]

The story of Price's invasion of Missouri is almost told by the various official designations of his army during that fall and winter. On August 29, the first general order issued in his new command was headed "Army in the Field." Two days later Price's command began marching northward from Princeton, Arkansas, with the city of St. Louis the first major objective. On September 18, the day before this force crossed the Missouri border, Price redesignated his command the "Army of Missouri."[37]

The grandly named "Army of Missouri" would not remain long in that state. After what can only be described as sluggish movement, Price suffered a bloody repulse at Pilot Knob in the southeastern part of the state and was forced to abandon St. Louis as an objective. Turning northwest toward Jefferson City he bypassed that place after finding it too well fortified and continued his march in the direction of the Kansas border, fighting several successful skirmishes along the way. As his army approached Kansas City, however, Federal resistance began stiffening. By October 22, he had given up all thought of capturing Kansas City or Leavenworth and decided to retreat southward. The following day, just south of Kansas City, he fought the critical battle of Westport. The engagement was a Confederate disaster that cost his army perhaps as many as 1,500 casualties, though Price did succeed in extricating the main body of his command, as well as his supply train.[38]

---

36 Castel, *Price*, 196-201; Reynolds to Price, and to George G. Vest, July 18, August 6, 1864, both in Reynolds Papers; General Orders No. 1, Headquarters Army in the Field, August 29, 1864, *OR* vol. 41, pt. II, 1090. General Smith's explanations of his change of plans for the Missouri invasion leave much unanswered. In at least two letters in 1865, he stated that at the end of the spring 1864 campaigns, he intended to use all his "available" or "disposable" forces for a campaign in Missouri, but that receipt of General Bragg's order for a river crossing of the infantry in mid-July convinced him to decide on a cavalry raid only. See Smith to Jefferson Davis, and Smith to Samuel Cooper, March 11, 16, 1865, ibid., vol. 48, pt. I, 1418-1419, lt.27-1428. In an earlier letter, however, Smith explained that by the time he received Bragg's order regarding the crossing, he had already determined on a cavalry invasion of Missouri augmented by infantry operations against Steele in the Arkansas Valley. See Smith to the President, August 21, 1864, ibid., vol. 41, pt. I, 113-117. Perhaps as Morrow suggests in "Price's Missouri Expedition," 29, Smith's plans for the invasion had never fully matured. // Dr. Geise illustrates one of the major problems with the execution of Price's raid into Missouri, i.e., the lack of understanding of what expedition's real objective. Further, the objective seemed to shift with every Rebel setback. The lack of a clearly defined objective ensured that Price's raid would amount to little more than a waste of resources that the Confederate Trans-Mississippi Department could not afford.

37 General Orders No. 1, Headquarters Army in the Field, August 29, 1864, *OR* vol. 41, pt. II, 1090; Castel, *Price*, 201-207; General Orders No. 8, Hdqrs. Army of Missouri, September 18, 1864, *OR* vol. 41, pt. III, 943.

38 Discussion of military movements in the 1864 Missouri campaign is based on Castel, *Price*, 200-250; General Orders No. 23, Hdqrs. Price's Army, December 3, 1864, in Maj. Gen. Sterling Price, General Orders, Circulars, 1863-1864, Army in the Field, District of Arkansas, Trans-

As Price retreated southwesterly his troops were to have their last fight of the campaign at Mine Creek, Kansas. In addition to the 300 Confederates killed and wounded there, some 900 more were taken prisoner, including two general officers. On December 2, the starving and weary remnants of Price's invasion army finally came to rest at Laynesport, Arkansas. The following day's general order bore the unpretentious heading, "Hd. Qrs. Price's Army." The so-called Army of Missouri had ceased to exist. Ironically, only the day before at Montgomery, Alabama, General Pierre G. T. Beauregard had dispatched a message asking Smith to aid General John Bell Hood in Tennessee by launching a powerful diversion in Missouri. Beauregard was apparently unaware the effort had already been made and had already failed miserably.[39]

Both Sterling Price and Kirby Smith immediately proclaimed Price's meandering operations a great success. Their reports stressed the numbers of Missourians recruited, prisoners taken, and large amount of Federal property destroyed. Smith claimed also that Price had prevented a Federal campaign from New Orleans to capture Mobile and hampered Union operations in Tennessee and Georgia by occupying the attention of Union troops who would otherwise have been available for duty east of the Mississippi.[40] Other assessments, including some issued soon after the end of the campaign, described it as a dismal failure.[41]

As was to be expected, perhaps, Governor Reynolds was embittered by what he considered to be Price's great failings. Calling the expedition "a weak and disgraceful plundering raid," he determined to drive Price from command and indeed from the army itself. Because of Reynold's public attacks on him, Price on January 6 requested that Smith try him by court martial, hoping in that way to clear his name. Since Price's principal accuser was not in the army and could not prefer court martial charges, Smith instead appointed a court of inquiry to examine Reynolds's accusations. The court finally convened on April 21, 1865, at Shreveport. On May 3, the court, not yet having heard all the witnesses, was

---

Mississippi Department, Departmental Records, Record Group 109, National Archives. // Although dated, the best study about the battle of Westport may well be Howard N. Monnett, *Action Before Westport, 1864* (Boulder, Colorado, 1964). The author was a local expert on the battle who lived in Kansas City. Westport was the largest battle fought west of the Mississippi River during the war, and it was an unmitigated disaster for Price's army.

39 Beauregard to Smith, December 2, 1864, *OR* vol. 41, pt. IV, 1092. // The two captured officers were Major General John S. Marmaduke and. Brigadier General William L. Cabell. See *OR* vol. 41, Pt. 1, 332, 335, 337-338, 352.

40 Castel, *Price*, 250-251.

41 Oldham, "Memoirs," 392-394; John N. Edwards, *Shelby and His Men*, 465, 482-484. // Contemporary scholars agree with Dr. Geise's assessment that Price's Missouri expedition was a failure.

adjourned to Washington, Arkansas, but because of the collapse of the Confederacy it did not meet again.[42]

Although Reynolds's attack on Price, even today, comes across as unnecessarily bitter and in some respects unfair, recent writers on the 1864 Missouri Campaign seem to agree on Price's failure. Albert Castel, whose study of Price in the Civil War is generally sympathetic, sums up the failings of Price's campaign thusly:

> Neither Kirby Smith nor Price mentioned that this expedition failed to seize St. Louis or occupy Jefferson City and install a Confederate government, failed to bring about a mass uprising of Southern sympathizers, failed to influence the state elections except probably to increase the Republican vote, and failed to do any damage to the Union military installations in Kansas.[43]

One thing Price did achieve, however, was the destruction of any combat effectiveness his army had originally possessed. The rest of 1864 and a good part of early 1865 were spent reorganizing, rearming, remounting, and in some cases dismounting, the cavalry stationed in Arkansas. During this lengthy process the men and units successful in bringing their horses out of Missouri received first priority to continue as cavalry. Some units that had resorted to horse stealing to retain their status as cavalry were dismounted. In the end, only the brigades of Jo Shelby and John B. Clark, Jr, were retained as cavalry. Missouri was now safe from further mounted invasion.[44]

Price's campaign would be the last initiated anywhere by the Confederates of the Trans-Mississippi Theater.

---

42 Reynolds to Waldo P. Johnson, March 2, 1665, in Reynolds Papers; Castel, *Price*, 256-262, 264. // See Governor Reynolds' biography *Sterling Price and the Confederacy*, for additional primary source information on the failures of Price's expedition, including Reynolds' effort to remove Price from command.

43 Castel does acknowledge, however (*Price*, 252), as do both Morrow ("Price's Missouri Expedition," 170), and Robert E. Shalhope, in *Sterling Price, Portrait of a Southerner* (Columbia, Mo., 1971), 275, that Price's raid delayed Federal capture of Mobile. See also Kerby, *Kirby Smith's Confederacy*, 358-360. // Contemporary scholars, including this editor, are less convinced of Shalhope's claim, but most would agree with Castel's assessment above.

44 Reynolds to Smith, December 16, 1864, to Magruder, December 28, 1864, January 5, 1865, to S. D. Jackman, January 5, 1865, all in Reynolds Papers; Magruder to Boggs, November 16, 26, December 4, 1864, Price to W. A. Alston, December 10, 1864, *OR* vol. 41, pt. IV, 1053, 1077-1079, 1096-1098, 1105-1106.

Chapter 14

Decline and Collapse
December 1864 – June 1865

By THE END of 1864, signs of decay were evident almost everywhere in the Trans-Mississippi Department.

The department's inspector general reported in December that the cavalry regiments in Louisiana were, with only two exceptions, totally deficient in "drill, discipline, order, appearance, police of camps, care of animals, and public property." The infantry in that state was "under generally a poor state of discipline." In Texas, an observer newly arrived from east of the Mississippi reported back to Richmond, "This side of the Mississippi River is badly whipped."[1]

In Arkansas, court martial rates appear to have increased steadily from October 1864 through February 1865, and one of the first general orders of the new year dealt with the "repeated . . . outrages committed upon the property of citizens by the Cavalry of this District."[2] Perhaps it was only another sign of the times there when on Christmas Day of 1864, James S. Rains, one of Reynolds's favorite generals in the Missouri State Guard, borrowed an ambulance Kirby Smith had previously lent to the exiled governor and wrecked the vehicle in an episode of drunken driving that reads as if it is a century ahead of its time.[3]

The pace of at least one salutary reform was accelerated in January of 1865: the wholesale dismounting of cavalry regiments. On January 30, Major General John A.

---

1 W. C. Schaumburg to E. K. Smith, November 21, 1864, J. P. Jones to "(Generals. Cooper . . .)," November 21, December 27, 1864, *OR* vol. 41, pt. IV, 1070-1072, 1124-1125.

2 General Orders No. 3, Headquarters, Dist. of Ark., January 6, 1865, in Maj. Gen. J. B. Magruder, General Orders 1864-1865, Dist. of Ark., Departmental Records, Trans-Miss. Dept., Record Group 109, National Archives. Monthly court martial frequency in Arkansas was determined by examining orders pertaining to courts martial in the file cited above.

3 Reynolds to Boggs, January 10, 1865, in Reynolds Papers.

Wharton was directed to unhorse nine Texas regiments, and Major General John G. Walker three regiments, to form an infantry division and an infantry brigade to be used at Galveston. A week later Smith strongly recommended that General Simon Buckner dismount four Louisiana cavalry regiments.[4] Apparently the horses relinquished by these regiments were bought by the government for use in artillery and other transportation. To one observer, at least some of the former cavalrymen seemed satisfied in "Infantry harness."[5] Smith's reason for the conversion, as stated to General Wharton, was that the cavalry "numbers more than half of the whole army in the department and its further maintenance has become an impossibility." He did not, however, touch the cavalry in Arkansas, most of which had been unintentionally dismounted by Price's disastrous Missouri raid.[6]

*   *   *

THE NEW YEAR brought constant pressure on Kirby Smith from Richmond to do something to aid the Confederates east of the river. A previous letter from the secretary of war had urged a Mississippi River crossing or a diversion into Missouri, to which Smith responded on January 6, 1865, that an exhausted countryside, heavy rains, and limited transportation prevented either movement before summer.[7]

Nevertheless, Jefferson Davis renewed the pressure on January 31, telegraphing Smith that it was "advisable" that he be charged with "military operations" on both banks of the Mississippi and instructing him to cross as many men as possible as soon as possible. Though Davis wanted an immediate answer, Smith did not receive the message until February 23. Five days later he replied to Davis that it was "physically impossible to cross troops over the Mississippi" until June brought low water. For him to assume command of both banks of the river was equally impossible during winter, he added, and would be practicable only "to a certain extent" in the summer.[8]

That same day, Smith sent a second dispatch reassuring the president of his intense desire to cooperate with the armies east of the river. He also pointed out what was rather obvious: there were the only two ways he could aid the states east of the Mississippi—by a river crossing in force or by an invasion of Missouri. He repeated his doubts about both those

4 Smith to Walker and to Wharton, January 30, February 22, 1865, J. F. Belton to Buckner, February 7, 1865, *OR* vol. 48, pt. I, 1353, 1396-1397, 1371.

5 R. L. Upshaw to Guy M. Bryan, April 9, 1865, in Bryan Papers.

6 Smith to Wharton, January 30, 1865, *OR* vol. 48, pt. I, 1351-1352.

7 Smith to S. Cooper, January 6, 1865, in Confidential Letters and Telegrams Sent, Department of the Trans-Mississippi, 1865, Chap. II, vol. 71 1/2, Military Departments, Record Group 109, National Archives.

8 Davis to Smith, January 31, 1865, *OR* vol. 41, pt. I, 124; Smith to Davis, February 28, 1865, ibid., vol. 48, pt. I, 1406.

operations. The president directed that this letter, along with other dispatches of General Smith's, be forwarded to General Robert E. Lee for comment.[9]

On the basis of Davis's original suggestion to Smith that he assume command of both banks of the Mississippi, Lee issued an order to Smith to that effect on March 28, but promptly diluted it by requesting Smith's views of the "practicability" of this assignment. Lee was not then aware of Smith's objections because Smith's correspondence on the subject was not forwarded to him until that same date, apparently after he had already issued the order.[10] The next day, Lee commented to the president that Smith was probably right about the physical impossibility of crossing troops before the spring, but he saw no reason why Smith could not command on both banks if the enterprise were attempted later. An invasion of Missouri would be as effective as a river crossing, but only if the Confederates could remain there. "A mere expedition into Missouri, similar to those previously undertaken," explained the beleaguered Virginia commander, "will give no material benefit."[11]

Though Richmond did not directly order Smith to carry out either a Missouri invasion or a river crossing, the possibility of a crossing had aroused anew the apprehensions of Trans-Mississippi state officials that their states would be denuded of troops in an attempt to save the faltering East. According to Guy M. Bryan, Governor Allen of Louisiana wrote the president taking the "high ground" against a river crossing. Bryan, a Confederate colonel and acting agent of the state of Texas at department headquarters, informed Governor Pendleton Murrah of Allen's eagerness for a governors' conference on the subject. He also warned the Texas delegation in the Confederate Congress that removing the troops would mean the surrender of the Trans-Mississippi states. He may even have intended a dark hint of "reconstruction" or secession when he remarked that "self preservation is the first law of nations."[12]

In the face of vigorous state opposition and his own pessimistic evaluation of the chances of a winter river crossing, Smith on February 24 had his adjutant general dispatch a curiously ambiguous message to General Magruder in Arkansas. In it, Smith suggested that it might be possible to cross the troops of the northern subdistrict of Arkansas to the east of the Mississippi, and he requested that if Magruder considered the movement feasible, he

---

9   Smith to Davis, February 28, 1865, with indorsement, n.d., "B. N. H. [i.e., Burton N. Harrison], send copies to Genl. R. E. Lee, J. D.," and memorandum, n.d., "Copy forwarded to Genl. R. E. Lee, March 28, 1865, B. N. H.," in Jefferson Davis Collection, Louisiana Historical Association Collection.

10   Lee to Smith, March 28, 1865, copy in Brent Collection, Louisiana State Military Department.

11   Lee to Mr. President, March 29, 1865, Douglas S. Freeman, ed., *Lee's Dispatches: Unpublished Letters of General Robert E. Lee, C.S.A. to Jefferson Davis and the War Department of the Confederate States of America from the Private Collection of Wymberley Jones de Renne of Wormsloe, Georgia* (New York, NY, 1957), 347-348.

12   Bryan to Governor and to Texas Delegation, both February 8, 1865, in Bryan Papers.

should issue the necessary orders immediately. Later in the same message Magruder was directed to move all troops of the northern subdistrict to the south of the Arkansas River as soon as the weather permitted, an amendment that surely indicated both Smith's irresolution and his pessimism about a crossing of the Mississippi.[13]

Indeed, pessimism and even a note of despair are sometimes apparent in Smith's correspondence in early 1865. By then, he had determined to abandon Galveston in the event of a Yankee attack in force on the city because "of the impossibility of contending against the heavy armaments the enemy can concentrate for the attack of a position."[14] Earlier in January, his comments bordered on desperation in a letter to John Slidell, the Confederate representative in Paris, France, urging Slidell to remind the Emperor that the French empire in Mexico was dependent upon Confederate independence. Perhaps clutching at the straw of French support of a separate Trans-Mississippi, Smith offered his opinion that "nineteen-twentieths of the planters" of the slave areas of the Trans-Mississippi would accept gradual emancipation as the price of independence.[15] On the other hand, Smith may have already heard and half-believed a rumor, certainly current west of the river by the following month, that Confederate independence would soon be recognized by Britain, France, and Mexico on the condition of gradual emancipation.[16]

No doubt Smith's confidence had been injured in part by widespread public criticism of his administration of the department, criticism which had in some quarters reached the proportions of an organized campaign against his retaining the command. The *Whig* led the attack in Richmond, and the *Whig's* editorials were echoed elsewhere.[17] Some members of the Trans-Mississippi Congressional delegations were also critical of Smith's performance. A number of the Louisiana delegates wanted General Braxton Bragg, whose home was in Louisiana, to supersede Smith. Other delegations supported General Joseph E. Johnston for the position. Several felt that Smith, as both a military commander and a civil administrator, was overburdened with responsibilities; others simply considered him incompetent.[18]

In every case of severe criticism the complaints arose in three general areas: Smith's alleged thwarting of Richard Taylor during the Red River Campaign, his inactivity as a field

---

13 J. F. Belton to Magruder, February 24, 1865, *OR* vol. 48, pt. I, 1402.

14 Smith to J. G. Walker, January 30, 1865, ibid., 1353.

15 Smith to Slidell, January 9, 1865, ibid., 1319-1320.

16 For this rumor see Cattie to Husband, February 11, 1865, in Coit Family Papers, Dallas Historical Society.

17 John H. Reagan to Guy M. Bryan, January 18, 1865, in Bryan Papers; Thos. C. Manning to Thos, C. Moore, March 30, 1865, in Thomas O. Moore Papers, Department of Archives and Manuscripts, Louisiana State University Library; Thomas C. Reynolds to Smith, March 11, 1865, in Reynolds Papers.

18 Thomas L. Snead to Sterling Price, January 10, 1865, *OR* vol. 48, pt. I, 1320-1322.

general,[19] and most often heard, his failure to control cotton transactions in the Trans-Mississippi Department. Indeed, so frequent was this last complaint that one friend of Smith's at Richmond advised Colonel Guy Bryan to tell Smith, "if he can find anybody who has been acting the rascal about cotton—to have him shot. The Cotton Bureau is made the excuse for abusing everybody in the T.M.D."[20]

Complaints about cotton transactions did not always come from Richmond. On January 5, 1865, Robert W. McHenry, a citizen of Union County, Arkansas, wrote President Davis that the cotton trade with the enemy along the Mississippi River under the pretense of obtaining needed military supplies had reached such proportions as to demoralize the army.[21] Smith was, of course, aware of the problem and had already taken steps to appoint General Buckner to control the illicit (but apparently useful) trade and to prevent flagrant abuses in the name of military necessity. Assisting Buckner would be Major John A. Buckner in Louisiana and Captain John W. Polk in Arkansas.[22]

By February 4, 1865, General Buckner had submitted to department headquarters a plan for controlling the cotton trade. Buckner's proposed regulations did not, apparently, include sufficiently strong justification for officially violating Confederate law by trading with the enemy. He was therefore required to incorporate in them the rather delicate remark, "the pressing wants of the army create a military necessity for rendering available for supplies the cotton near the enemy lines."[23]

Shortly thereafter, Smith authorized Buckner to make an agreement with Governor Allen permitting Louisiana to export cotton to the enemy for state needs. He warned Buckner that Judge Gray, the Treasury agent, would probably disapprove all trading of cotton with the enemy, and if he did so, Smith would close the lines.[24] Meanwhile, some small contracts already made by Louisiana state officials and by Major S. K. Hays, chief quartermaster of the District of West Louisiana, would be honored, the cotton involved being slightly in excess of 400 bales.

19 T. Douglas to D. F. Boyd March 31, 1865, in David F. Boyd Civil War Papers, Department of Archives and Manuscripts, Louisiana State University Library. // Prushankin discusses these oft-heard complaints in his book *Crisis in Command* and in essays he wrote profiling General Smith in the series of *Confederate Generals of the Trans-Mississippi* volumes. The first essay, found in volume one, reviews events in 1864 titled "To Carry Off Glory: Edmund Kirby Smith in 1864," while the second essay in volume three steps back to events of the previous year with the title, "'I Feed my Responsibilities are Great': Edmund Kirby Smith in 1863."

20 J. B. Sexton to Bryan, January 30, 1865, in Bryan Papers.

21 McHenry to Davis, January 5, 1865, *OR* vol. 48, pt. I, 1316.

22 J. F. Belton to Buckner, January 6, 1865, ibid., 1318.

23 J. F. Belton to Buckner, February 4, 1865, ibid., 1364-1365.

24 Smith to Buckner, February 15, 1865, ibid., 1389.

As Smith had anticipated, Gray would not approve this illicit traffic in cotton. On March 2, General Buckner was instructed to issue a general order suppressing it.[25] Smith, however, had no faith in Gray's ability to supply the army through regular channels. A week after the instructions to Buckner, Smith confided to Senator Robert W. Johnson that Gray "has tendered his resignation, is overwhelmed by the responsibilities thrown upon him, and has not the business capacity for conducting the purchasing bureau upon a scale commensurate with our wants."[26] The lines would not remain closed for long.

In spite of the ambiguity of the official attitude toward the cotton trade, some front-line officers made vigorous attempts to suppress it in the weeks after March 2. Among them was Joseph L. Brent, erstwhile chief of ordnance in Louisiana and now a brigadier general commanding a Louisiana cavalry brigade. "You will investigate every attempt, whether successful or not, to pass cotton; and it is strange to me that you cannot break it up," Brent admonished one of his outpost commanders on March 13. "If cotton passes over illegally at Pointe Coupee, pursue and burn it, impressing the teams and arresting every one concerned in it. If you do not break up this cotton trade with the means at your command," he added, "I will regretfully be forced to the conclusion that you are not vigilant and energetic."[27]

In spite of the zeal demonstrated by officers like Brent, cotton continued to pass through the lines with and without military permits. By the last week of March, Brent had become cynical about the determination of his superiors to halt the traffic. On March 24, he observed four Federal steamers lying in the Ouachita River under control of Major Buckner, and no one could board them without permission from the major. Consequently, said Brent, he would no longer issue orders enforcing the cotton ban since Major Buckner seemed to have special instructions on that point.[28]

As late as May 7, 1865, Brent was still complaining that blank cotton export permits signed by Major Hays, district quartermaster, were circulating freely in his area and might be used by Yankee spies to break his security. Brigadier General Harry T. Hays, who had led a brigade in Lee's Virginia army before being severely wounded in May of 1864, was at that time commanding the subdistrict. Hays replied sympathetically the next day that until he could get a firm decision from General Buckner or General Smith, he would suspend the trade on his own initiative. He patiently explained to Brent that the necessities of the

25 Smith to Gray, March 8, 1865, ibid., 1414-1415.

26 Smith to Johnson, March 16, 1865, ibid., 1428-1429.

27 Brent to A. O. P. Pickens, March 13, 1865, ibid., 1423. Brent's zeal had long since become legendary in the ordnance department in Louisiana. As Brent's cavalry brigade was stationed in alligator country, a standing joke among ordnance men was that he probably had alligator hunting details out to provide alligator oil for the brigade ordnance. Powhatan Clarke to David F, Boyd, February 17, 1865, in Boyd Civil War Papers.

28 Brent to J. G. Clarke, March 23, 1865, *OR* vol. 48, pt, I, 1443.

department had forced the continuance of the illegal practice, and that only recently 15,000 barrels of much-needed flour had been contracted for in this way.[29]

Under these circumstances it is small wonder that the senior military commanders continued to equivocate and to evade Judge Gray's disapproval of the trade through the lines until the very last days of the war. Perhaps the last project to run cotton through the lines was considered on May 12, by which time surrender negotiations for the department had already begun. On that day Major Buckner consulted with General Brent about passing 10,000 bales of government cotton through the lines by steamboat and exchanging it for gold. Brent explained that his troops, already demoralized and out of hand, were so bitter about the cotton trade with the enemy that they would probably destroy both steamers and cargoes.[30]

While Brent had been admonishing his junior officers to track down cotton traffickers, one of his subordinates, a captain commanding the troops east of the Atchafalaya and south of Morganza, had succeeded in negotiating a curious truce with the Union officer commanding at Morganza. On March 27, the Confederate captain had agreed that the troops under his command would not fire on Federal transports navigating the Mississippi, nor would they attempt to capture the pickets at Morganza or interfere with persons working on the Mississippi levees. The Federal officer, in turn, agreed he would not send out raiding parties and would keep his men "confined within the limits necessary for their comfort." Neither side would interfere with unarmed officers and men passing up and down the river. This remarkable arrangement was to be permanent unless rescinded by superior authority, in which case due notice would be given. Meanwhile, both officers were to attempt to persuade their seniors of its merits, and indeed this truce seems to have prevailed until the war's end.[31]

Over in Texas, meanwhile, a more ambitious truce was attempted that same March by Union Major General Lew Wallace. The general was convinced that West Texas could be detached from the Confederacy and obtained permission to visit the Texas coast under a flag of truce. In an interview at Port Isabel on March 11, Brigadier General James E. Slaughter, commanding the "Western Sub-District of Texas," and Colonel John "Rip" Ford, commanding at Brownsville, agreed to forward Wallace's "propositions" to General Smith through General Walker. Wallace arrived off Galveston on March 27 and apparently expected to be as cordially received by Walker as he had been by Slaughter and Ford.

29 Brent to H. T. Hays, Hays to Brent, May 7, 8, 1865, both in Boyd Civil War Papers.

30 Brent to S. B. Buckner, May 13, 1865, in J. L. Brent Papers, Louisiana Historical Association Collection.

31 Agreement between Captain Bailie, U.S.A. and W. B. Ratliff, C.S.A., March 27, 1865, J. A. Collins to A. O. P. Pickens and to J. L. Brent, both March 29, 1865, all in Brent Collection, Louisiana State Military Department.

Instead, General Walker rebuffed him coldly.[32] In a letter to Slaughter, Walker explained that he well understood the delicate circumstances under which the discussions with Wallace took place,

> Yet I regret you should have consented to entertain, or rather receive, the proposals actually made, since to have acceded to them would be the blackest treason to the Confederacy. No one is more desirous of terminating this war honorably than myself, but I beg that in future you will exercise the greatest caution and that you will not permit yourself to be drawn into such discussions as took place in your interviews with Major-General Wallace.[33]

* * *

SHORTLY AFTER THIS episode, but quite unconnected with it, came the last series of major command changes to take place in the Trans-Mississippi Department. General Walker was relieved of command of the District of Texas and reassigned to the command of his old division. In his place, General Magruder was returned to Texas, leaving Major General James F. Fagan in command in Arkansas.[34] On April 19, the Districts of Arkansas and West Louisiana were reduced to the status of subdistricts and merged under General Buckner as the "District of Arkansas and West Louisiana."[35] On May 9—one month after General Lee's surrender at Appomattox Court House in Virginia—Buckner was given additional duty as chief of staff to General Smith, William Boggs having been reassigned to the command of the Louisiana subdistrict on April 24. Subsequently, Boggs would be relieved of his command by General Harry Hays.[36]

Early in that last April of the war, Smith—not knowing that the march of events east of the river was making actions in the Trans-Mississippi more futile with each passing day—authorized Fagan to attack Little Rock, Arkansas. General Joseph "Jo" Shelby's cavalry was placed at Fagan's disposal, and on April 11 an additional infantry division was offered to him

---

32 Wallace to Grant, April 18, May 16, 1865, Wallace to Slaughter, March 17, 1865, Ford to Wallace, March 19, 26, 1865, Wallace to Ford and to J. M. Hawes, March 24, 30, 1865, Walker to Wallace, March 25, 1865, Wallace to Walker, March 30, April 2, 1865, Wallace to Slaughter and to Ford, both April 6, 1865, *OR* vol. 48, pt. II, 457-463.

33 Walker to Slaughter, March 27, 1865, ibid., pt. I, 1448.

34 General Orders No. 30, Hdqrs. Trans-Miss. Dept., March 31, 1865, Special Orders No. —, Hdqrs. Trans-Miss. Dept., May 12, 1865, ibid., 1455, pt. II, 1300; Reynolds to James F. Fagan, March 24, 1865, in Reynolds Papers.

35 General Orders No. 39, Hdqrs. Trans-Miss. Dept., April 19, 1865, *OR* vol. 48, pt. II, 1283.

36 General Orders No. 43, Hdqrs. Trans-Miss. Dept., May 9, 1865, ibid., 1295-1296; General Orders No. 3, Hdqrs. Dist. of Ark. And West La., April 24, 1865, in J. L. Brent Papers, Louisiana Historical Association Collection.

with the explanation on April 15 that it was to be used solely for support after the cavalry had taken the city.[37]

On the previous day (April 15), Union Major General Joseph J. Reynolds at Little Rock had addressed a letter to Fagan advising him of General Lee's surrender and offering the same terms to him that General Grant had given Lee. A few days later Governor Reynolds dispatched a similar letter to M. Jeff Thompson, then commanding north of the Arkansas River. When Union couriers under flag of truce found Fagan on April 24 and handed him the governor's letter, the general scornfully turned it down. On April 30, Reynolds's message was delivered to Thompson at Harrisburg, Arkansas, again under a flag of truce. Thompson also refused the terms, but he was less curt about it than Fagan and took time to express to Reynolds his "sincere regret and horror at the manner in which President Lincoln came to his death."[38]

Down in Louisiana, meanwhile, the news of Lee's surrender reached General Brent from the Union forces at Morganza on April 17. Brent decided immediately not to give it any publicity, but such momentous news could not be long suppressed. The information must have reached department headquarters within the next three days, for on April 21 General Smith announced the surrender of the Army of Northern Virginia and called on his soldiers to continue "to sustain the holy cause." Smith held out to his men the possibility of foreign intervention, but revealed his real hope when he remarked that further resistance would "secure to our country terms that a proud people can with honor accept.[39]

Many soldiers ignored Smith's orders to "stand by your colors—maintain your discipline." Desertion rates, already high, soared. At Warrensburg, Missouri, the Federal commander reported on April 24 that large bands of men were returning from the Rebel army, several parties of forty or fifty having been seen moving northward through the southeastern part of the state.[40] Two days later Federal Brigadier General Powell Clayton

---

37 P. H. Thompson to Fagan, April 4, 1865, John G. Meem, Jr., to Fagan, April 11, 1865, Smith to Fagan, April 15, 1865, OR vol. 48, pt. II, 1262-1263, 1276, 1281. Several weeks later a Union spy accurately described these preparations. He reported that 10,000 infantry, 5,500 cavalry, plus nineteen pieces of artillery, were destined for an assault on either Little Rock or Pine Bluff, that one infantry division had marched northward from Shreveport on April 18, and that another at Marshall had been alerted to move north. In addition, Shelby's and other cavalry commands were riding northward, and large amounts of ammunition had been issued to all these units. The spy sensibly predicted that news of General Lee's surrender would stop this operation. F. J. Herron to J. J. Reynolds, May 11, 1865, with enclosure, Report of C. S, Bell, scout, ibid., 397-403.

38 Reynolds to Fagan, April 14, 1865, ibid., 98; Reynolds to Thompson, April 18, 1865, ibid., 117; Fagan to Reynolds, April 25, 1865, ibid., 190; Thompson to Reynolds, April 30, 1865, ibid., 249.

39 Brent to General [illegible] April 17, 1865, in J. L. Brent Papers, Louisiana Historical Association Collection; Smith to Soldiers of the Trans-Mississippi Army, April 21, 1865, OR, vol. 48, pt. II, 1284.

40 C. G. Laurant to Commanding Officer First Subdistrict and to C. E. Spedden, both April 24, 1865, ibid., 183-184.

reported that about five rebel deserters a day were surrendering at Pine Bluff, Arkansas. By April 29, Magruder was reporting from Texas that the "men are deserting by tens and twenties at night." In Louisiana General Brent had almost lost control of his front-line troops. He reported on May 4 that twenty men had deserted from his infantry and thirty-six from the 7th Louisiana cavalry in the previous three or four days, and that very morning he had arrested an entire Texas artillery company that had started for home. The next day Brent concluded that the morale of the troops manning the Red River forts near Alexandria was so low "as to forbid the belief that they can be relied on." He recommended mixing troops from different states and asked, because of their steady and loyal reputation, for 250 Missouri troops to relieve a like number of the existing garrisons.[41]

It would seem that only in the Indian Territory, where the news from the East had not fully penetrated, was there any semblance of normality. A meeting was being arranged there at Council Grove between Confederate commissioners General James W. Throckmorton and Colonel William D. Reagan, several representatives of the Confederate tribes, and certain chiefs of the so-called wild tribes of the prairies. A military alliance against the Yankees was to be discussed. Upon learning that the Plains Indians were "thirsting for revenge on the frontier of Kansas," Cooper began to have second thoughts about loosing Comanche, Kiowa, and Arapahoe war parties on the Federal settlements.[42] Only vaguely aware of the rapid developments east of the Mississippi, Cooper on May 10 sounded almost complacent and even naive. "What does all this Federal news about Sherman and Johnston mean?" Cooper continued:

> A friend writes me that up to 1st of May no official or even Southern accounts of Lee's surrender had reached Shreveport. It is very strange the country should be flooded with alarming reports relative to our army east. I shall advise all commissioners and delegates to Council Grove and the people generally to go ahead just the same as if no bad news had reached us. Please keep everything rocking along just as usual, especially in the quartermaster and commissary departments. The people and soldiers must be fed, come what may. The Indians are not scared yet.[43]

In spite of Cooper's desire to keep things "rocking along just as usual," the end of the war had by then approached much closer to him than Johnston's surrender to Sherman in distant North Carolina. That very day in neighboring Arkansas, M. Jeff Thompson was preparing to surrender the northern subdistrict to representatives of Major General

41 Powell Clayton to John Levering, April 26, 1865, ibid., 207; Magruder to Boggs, April 29, 1865, ibid., 1291; J. L. Brent to A. P. Bagby, May 4, 5, 1865, both in J. L. Brent Papers, Louisiana Historical Association Collection.

42 E. Kirby Smith to Albert Pike, C. S. West to W. D. Reagan, D. H. Cooper to S. S. Anderson, April 8, 15, May 15, 1865, *OR* vol. 48, pt. II, 1266-1269, 1279-1280.

43 D. H. Cooper to T. M. Scott, May 10, 1865, ibid., 1297.

Grenville M. Dodge, the commander of the Union Department of the Missouri. The formal surrender, signed on May 11 at Chalk Bluff, Missouri, gave Thompson the same generous terms Grant had given Lee.[44]

Because most of Thompson's troops were hiding out in the thickets and swamps, the Federals were inclined to disbelieve his estimate that they numbered upwards of 5,000. By June 30, however, paroles had been issued to 7,454 officers and men ostensibly belonging to him.[45] Thompson reacted with bitter irony when news of his negotiations prompted Confederate soldiers to begin appearing out of the swamps in boats and canoes to accept Federal paroles and Federal rations. According to Thompson's own account, he gave some of these men a farewell speech expressing the hope the Yankees would provide them the hanging they deserved. He reminded the Missourians among them that during Price's raid they had boasted of hanging Unionists, and wondered aloud how they would now fare amidst their victims' compatriots.[46]

Thompson's surrender did not mean that every Confederate north of the Arkansas River ceased hostilities on May 11, 1865, but General Powell Clayton could report in less than a week that organized Rebel resistance no longer existed there. South of the river, however, where General Fagan was still in command, Thompson's surrender had no effect. When Simon Buckner, as Smith's chief of staff, left Shreveport on May 20 to negotiate with the Federals at the mouth of the Red River, Fagan assumed temporary command of the District of Arkansas and West Louisiana. During Fagan's absence at Shreveport, Brigadier General Thomas P. Dockery, commander of the Reserve Forces of Arkansas and the senior Confederate officer remaining in the state, assumed command. On May 29, Dockery arrived

44 Report of Maj. Gen. Grenville M. Dodge, U.S. Army, Commanding Department of the Missouri with Inclosures A and B and Report of Lieut. Col. Charles W. Davis, Fifty-first Illinois Infantry, Assistant Provost-Marshal-General with Inclosures A through P and Subinclosures Nos. 1 and 2, June 24, May 15, 1865, ibid., pt. I, 227-237.

45 C. W. Davis to G. M. Dodge, June 20, 1865, ibid., 237.

46 Thompson's War Account, 1861-1865, in M. Jeff Thompson Collection, Tulane University Library. Although there was more bitterness than humor in Thompson's comments on his invisible command, he was known as a "witty fellow" even among his enemies. C. W. Davis to G. M. Dodge, May 10, 1865, *OR* vol. 48, pt. II, 386. During Price's 1864 raid into Missouri, Thompson "liberated" at Sedalia, Missouri, a saber and a pair of Colt navy revolvers belonging to a federal colonel. Shortly after the surrender negotiations began, Thompson received a peremptory, even insulting, letter addressed to him as "Late Brig. Genl. C.S.A," demanding return of these weapons. In this letter, the aggrieved Yankee colonel referred to his sidearms as "sacred to me as my honor." Although it would be difficult to prove whether or not he actually sent it, Thompson penned a reply worthy of his reputation: "Should you ever have another Sabre and Pistols that are as 'Sacred to you as your honor'—defend them better than you did these at Sedalia or save them as you did your body on that occasion." He signed himself "M. Jeff Thompson, Still Brig. Genl. M. S. G., Comdg., Nor. Sub. Dist. of Ark." John F. Phillip Thompson, Thompson to John F. Phillips, May 16, 26, 1865, copies of both in Thompson Collection, Tulane University Library.

at Pine Bluff fully prepared to discuss surrender terms, and on June 2, near Little Rock, Dockery and Union General Reynolds agreed on terms similar to those given General Lee. By that time the terms upon which the department had been surrendered were known to Dockery.[47]

The negotiations for the surrender of the entire department were more complex and lasted about a month. As early as April 19, Major General John Pope, commanding the Military Division of the Missouri at St. Louis, had dispatched his chief of staff, Lieutenant Colonel John T. Sprague, down the Mississippi to the mouth of the Red River to attempt to open negotiations with General Smith.[48] Sprague arrived there on April 23, and six days later Brent was ordered to dispatch a steamer to the river mouth to pick him up and bring him to Alexandria where Smith would meet him.[49] On May 5, Brent reported that his flag of truce officers had returned from the mouth of the Red with the news that Colonel Benjamin Allston of Smith's staff was at the river mouth and would conduct Sprague to Shreveport.[50] That same day, Sprague reported to Pope that Colonels Allston and George Flournoy would accompany him to Shreveport.[51]

General Pope, meanwhile, was becoming impatient. Without any definite news from Sprague by May 10, he ordered Sprague to return to St. Louis as soon as he had heard from Smith—even if the Confederate reply was negative. Pope commented sourly that Joseph E. Johnston and Richard Taylor had already surrendered, and implied that Smith's surrender was simply a matter of time given the demoralization of the Confederate Trans-Mississippi troops. A week later Pope informed General Grant that a campaign in Texas would probably not be necessary.[52]

Accurate Yankee assessments of the general Confederate breakdown, such as Pope's, were based not only on the reports of Union agents but on information supplied by military deserters, parolees, and civilian defectors pouring into the Union lines. One was a "Major" McKee who had escaped from the Shreveport jail on May 10 to report the Confederates "very much disaffected." McKee also supplied information on troop strengths in Louisiana and the placement of torpedoes (floating mines) in the Red River. He also disclosed that a

---

47 J. J. Reynolds to Grant, May 29, 1865, Thomas P. Dockery to Officers and Soldiers of Reserve Forces of the State of Arkansas, June 2, 1865, *OR* vol. 48, pt. II, 658, 894.

48 John T. Sprague to S. P. Lee, April 18, 19, 1865, John Pope to J. J. Reynolds, April 20, 1865, 117, 133, 138-140.

49 Sprague to Pope, April 24, May 2, 1865, ibid., 177, 292; S. B. Buckner to William R. Boggs, April 29, 1865, in Boyd Civil War Papers.

50 Brent to William R. Boggs, May 5, 1865, in J. L. Brent Papers, Louisiana Historical Association Collection.

51 Sprague to Pope, May 5, 1865, *OR* vol. 48, pt. II, 322.

52 Pope to Sprague and to Grant, May 10, 17, 1865, ibid., 384, 481-482.

conference of Trans-Mississippi generals and governors was scheduled to be held at Marshall, Texas, about May 19.[53]

The Marshall conference reported by McKee began on May 10 and lasted for three days. Although the proceedings were secret, the meeting was not, for Colonel Sprague was invited to await the results of this conference in Shreveport. In addition to Smith, the principals attending were Governors Flanagin, Allen, and Reynolds, and Colonel Bryan representing Murrah of Texas, who was too ill to attend in person. The governors recommended to Smith that he surrender the entire department immediately, but not on the terms presented by Sprague, which were similar to those granted to Lee. Instead, they proposed the following:

— that no ex-Confederate, civilian or military, be prosecuted for offenses against the United States committed during the war;

— that anyone, civilian or military, desiring to leave the Department be permitted to depart for any place outside the United States he wished, with all his possessions, including arms;

— that the existing state governments be recognized by the Federals until state conventions could be called, and that each state be permitted to retain a small military guard to preserve law and order.

The governors also suggested that Governor Allen accompany Sprague on his return trip to St. Louis in order to explain their views in person. Following the conference Smith, acting on the governors' recommendations, prepared a memorandum for Sprague offering surrender not on Pope's terms but on the lines proposed by the governors. Upon receipt of Smith's memorandum Sprague, having declined Allen's request to accompany him, set out for St. Louis, which city he reached about May 27.[54]

Meanwhile, under Buckner's direction, preparations were underway in Louisiana to offer a show of resistance until the last possible moment and then to withdraw in the

---

53 P. J. Osterhaus to E. R. S. Canby, May 19, 1865, ibid., 502. Although identified in the index of *OR* vol. 48, pt. II, 1416, as E. W. McKee, this "Major McKee" was more likely "A. W. McKee," who was once chief purchasing agent for the Cotton Bureau at Shreveport. McKee had been convicted of corresponding with the enemy, among other things, in 1864. Because he had never been formally commissioned in the Confederate Army, he was released by the military to the custody of Judge Warren F. Moise, who discharged him upon bail, whereupon McKee jumped his bail. See William M. Robinson, Jr., *Justice in Grey, A History of the Judicial System of the Confederate States of America* (Cambridge, MA, 1941), 199-201. According to Kerby, *Kirby Smith's Confederacy*, 274-275, after jumping bail, McKee disappeared forever, but it seems quite likely that he was recaptured and housed in the Shreveport jail until he made his second escape on May 10, 1865.

54 Report of Lieut. Colonel John T. Sprague, Eleventh U.S. Infantry, Chief of Staff, St. Louis, Mo., May 27, 1865, with enclosures Nos. 1 through 7, *OR* vol. 48, pt. I, 188-193. // Pendleton Murrah had suffered for years from tuberculosis and would die on August 4, 1865.

direction of Texas. General Brent, in command of the "Front Line Forces" in Louisiana, before evacuating the Red River forts below Alexandria, was to have the fortifications and guns destroyed and only then withdraw all of his troops to the vicinity of Natchitoches. The pontoon bridge train then being used to bridge the Cane River was also ordered to be withdrawn to Natchitoches and held in readiness to bridge the Sabine. Wood was to be stockpiled along the Red River between Alexandria and Shreveport to fuel steamers used in the evacuation.[55]

These preparations, mostly ordered by General Buckner, reflected agreements to fight on, even if General Smith surrendered. Buckner was to lead this movement, but it is difficult to assess what he and the others intended. In any case, Smith's refusal of immediate surrender on Pope's terms meant continued preparations for resistance.[56] The staff officers at Shreveport were far from one mind in the rapidly deteriorating situation. "The policy of Genl. Smith has been determined, we are to fight thank God even if it be with but a hand full [sic] of men," penned Colonel Henry T. Douglas, the chief engineer, to Brent on May 11. "Of course this must be in Texas-La. and Arks will be abandoned & with the few troops that remain true to us we will fight to the Rio Grande . . . I feel more cheerful now. We shall be able to die like men," concluded Douglas, "or depart in honorable exile, either better far than Yankee domination."[57]

In far different vein eight days later, Major William H. Thomas, the Trans-Mississippi's chief commissary of subsistence, confided to his friend, Major John Reid, that he considered the Texas movement a "farce," but that he had to obey orders. His reasoning at the time would come close to the later truth:

> I consider the army all over the dept. as completely demoralized and do not believe General Buckner can move outside of the Mo. troops 200 men to Texas. I think this is a good deal of Gas with the Mo. troops and when the time comes for them to move which is next Sunday I believe one half of them will quit. I see no chance but to send word to the Yankees that this fight is over.[58]

Whatever exciting talk there had been at Marshall and Shreveport about do-or-die stands, it would seem that Buckner's main objective was to continue to resist in order to secure better peace terms. He was particularly interested in the agreement that would

---

55 S. B. Buckner to Harry T. Hays, H. T. Douglas to C. M. Randolph, both May 10, 1865, Special Orders No. 21, Hdqrs. Subdist, West La., May 16, 1865, all in Boyd Civil War Papers.

56 Castel, *Price*, 270.

57 H. T. Douglas to Brent, May 11, 1865, in J. L. Brent Papers, Louisiana Historical Association Collection.

58 William H. Thomas to John Reid, May 19, 1865, in Confederate States Army Papers (B), May 30, 1861-July 26, 1867, Department of Archives and Manuscripts, Louisiana State University Library.

permit officers and men to leave the country with their arms. This is clearly implied in a letter he wrote General Harry Hays on May 15 authorizing Hays to tell his men that plans were underway for an expedition to Mexico, that they might retain their organizations, and that he (Buckner) had been chosen as the tentative leader. In closing, however, he admitted that the army might "melt" and spoil the scheme.[59]

The melting Buckner feared came faster than he probably expected. On May 18 General Smith departed for Houston, where he intended to establish a new headquarters. He left Buckner in temporary command at Shreveport. That same day Buckner, recognizing the hopelessness of the situation, authorized his immediate junior, Harry Hays, not only to make a truce for the subdistrict of West Louisiana along the lines proposed at Marshall, but to also "make propositions on the Same basis, for the entire Trans-Mississippi Department; with an assurance, that if accorded, the entire Department will be at once pacified, and resistance to the U.S. Government shall cease." Hays was allowed some latitude. If the Federals refused terms for civilians, Hays might accept for the military only; if they insisted upon the surrender of the heavy artillery, gunboats, and the arms of the men who were to remain in the United States, he might yield those points also. Furthermore, if the Federals refused these modified terms for the entire department, Hays might surrender his subdistrict at his own discretion.[60]

Buckner's subordinate had anticipated him by at least one day. On May 16, Hays and Brent had conferred at Natchitoches on their hopeless situation, and the following day Hays had given Brent a written order that if the enemy advanced Brent was to ask for surrender terms.[61] That same day, Brent received word that the United States 16th Army Corps at New Orleans was under orders to move on the Red River, and that a Union advance party had captured the pickets and public property at Harrisonburg. The officer reporting this information added that the morale of the remaining forward pickets was so low and the communication with them so bad that they could not be relied on for future warnings "until the enemy is in the immediate vicinity of Alexandria."

This news was enough for General Brent. The following day he informed Hays that "the contingency contemplated in your written instructions to me and in date of the 17th has occurred, and I shall according to your orders proceed this evening to the mouth of Red River & send in your name to the Com. officer of the U.S. Forces threatening your District & enter into negotiations for the surrender of its troops, public property etc." In further justification of this action, Brent forwarded a letter signed by his two senior subordinates, as well as twenty-one other unit commanders and members of his immediate staff, and another

---

59 Buckner to Hays, May 15, 1865, in Boyd Civil War Papers.

60 Buckner to Hays, May 18, 1865, ibid.

61 Hays to Brent, May 16, 17, 1865, both ibid.

letter signed by some twenty-four leading citizens in his area; both letters called upon him to surrender.[62]

Hays responded the same day with an authorization for Brent to surrender. He had not heard from Buckner and, consequently, "It is no use, I think of delaying longer and you may as well open negocations [sic] at once. In five days we will have no army or anything to surrender."[63] Hays, not yet informed of Buckner's authorization for him to surrender, had acted on his own, but on that same day Buckner reiterated his previous authorization and asked Hays to remind the Federal commander that acceptance of Buckner's terms for the entire Department would pacify the whole country immediately without the difficulties of a campaign and "avoid all risk of foreign complications."[64]

Brent presented his proposals on May 19 to the Union naval officer commanding at the mouth of the Red River to be forwarded to General Canby at New Orleans. Brent also proposed a truce to the Union authorities while negotiations were underway.[65] Hays, meanwhile, appointed two other officers, Colonels Alcibiade De Blanc and John E. Burke, to assist Brent. On May 23, this trio proceeded to Baton Rouge en route to New Orleans to confer with Union General Edward Canby. As Buckner's instructions had by then been received, they claimed authority to negotiate for surrender of the department as well as for Louisiana, but insisted that Kirby Smith would have to approve any negotiations for the department. They could guarantee only the surrender of the subdistrict.[66]

Before they could leave Baton Rouge, however, Buckner himself, accompanied by Sterling Price, arrived in the city. On May 24, Buckner and Price, accompanied by Brent, proceeded on to New Orleans.[67] There, late on the afternoon of May 26, the Confederate delegation met a group of Union officers at the library of a mansion at the corner of St. Charles Avenue and St. Joseph Street, which General Canby used as his quarters. At four o'clock a military convention, signed by Major General Peter J. Osterhaus for Canby and by Buckner for Smith, surrendered the Trans-Mississippi Department. The terms were those tendered to Lee, Johnston, and Taylor, not those that Smith and the governors had wanted; consequently, there was no mention of civilians or of permitting military veterans to reside

62 W. G. Vincent to Sam Flower, May 17, 1865, Brent to Hays, W. G. Vincent and others to Brent, E. R. Biossat and others to Brent, all May 18, 1865, all in J. L. Brent Papers, Louisiana Historical Association Collection; William R. Purvis to D. F. Boyd, May 17, 1865, in Boyd Civil War Papers.

63 Hays to Brent, May 18, 1865, copy in J. L. Brent Papers, Louisiana Historical Association Collection and in Boyd Civil War Papers.

64 Buckner to Hays, May 18, 1865, ibid., and in J. L. Brent Papers, Louisiana Historical Association Collection.

65 Brent to Hays, May 19, 1865, ibid.; Brent to E. R. S. Canby, May 19, 1865, James P. Foster to E. R. S. Canby, May 20, 1865, *OR* vol. 48, pt. II, 503-504, 516.

66 Brent to Hays, May 24, 1865, in Boyd Civil War Papers.

67 W. G. Fuller to Thomas T. Eckert, May 24, 1865, *OR* vol. 48, pt. II, 581.

in or out of the United States. In brief, officers and men would be paroled to their homes. All Confederate property would be surrendered, but officers would be permitted to retain their sidearms and both officers and men their horses. Although effective immediately, these terms still required General Smith's final ratification.[68]

While these events were taking place in Louisiana, military discipline and organization in Texas were crumbling rapidly. On May 16, Magruder reported to Smith that an attempted mutiny had occurred in Galveston two days earlier and that both Generals Maxey and Walker had reported their divisions unreliable. Magruder's conclusion about his district was stark: "Nothing more can be done except to satisfy the soldiers, to induce them to preserve their organization, and to send them in regiments, etc., to their homes, with as little damage to the community as possible. For God's sake act," he begged Smith, "or let me act."[69]

Less than a week later Magruder, after consultation with an ill Governor Murrah, acted on his own. On May 22, Colonel Ashbel Smith, commanding the defenses at Galveston, notified Captain Benjamin F. Sands, commanding the blockading squadron off the city, that Magruder wanted to open negotiations with General Canby. He requested that a steamer be readied to take a Confederate delegation to New Orleans as soon as possible. The same day Captain Sands confirmed a steamer would be available immediately.[70]

On May 25, Colonel Smith, representing Magruder, and William Pitt Ballinger, representing Governor Murrah, were carried out to Captain Sands's flagship and after consultation with Sands transferred to the fast steamer *Antona* for the trip to New Orleans. Their instructions were to attempt to get special terms for Texas and to try to prevent military government and Federal occupation of the state. They arrived at New Orleans early in the morning of May 29. When they learned that Buckner was already there on behalf of General Smith, they decided to proceed independently on the grounds that "the troops of Texas again become Texas troops." Nevertheless, they immediately conferred with Buckner at the St. Charles Hotel and later with the well-known Texas Unionist, Judge John Hancock. Hancock advised them that a military occupation of Texas was both inevitable and necessary, and he accurately explained to them that by the Reconstruction policy then in effect, the Rebel states were still in the Union, but individual Rebels would undergo "some healing process." Hancock promised to try to get Canby to keep the former slaves on the plantations at fair wages until their status was settled.

68 Terms of a military convention, May 26, 1865, with first and second indorsements, both June 2, 1865, ibid., 600.601; Shreveport, *South-Western*, June 7, 1865.

69 Magruder to Smith, May 16, 1865, *OR* vol. 48, pt. II, 1308.

70 Ashbel Smith to B. F. Sands, May 22, 1865, in Ashbel Smith Papers, Archives Collection, University of Texas Library; H. K. Thatcher to E. R. S, Canby, May 26, 1865, *OR* vol. 48, pt. II, 603; B. F. Sands to Ashbel Smith, May 22, 1865, Galveston *News*, May 26, 1865, as quoted in Shreveport *South-Western*, June 7, 1865.

That same evening at 8:00 p.m., Hancock accompanied Colonel Smith and Ballinger to General Canby's quarters for a conference. Shortly after their arrival General Buckner appeared and the meeting began. Canby was friendly, but noncommittal. He informed the gathering that General Philip Sheridan would command in Texas rather than himself, and he thought they should wait to talk to him. He did assure them there would be no serious difficulties about public property and no need to worry over the fact that most Confederate soldiers had gone home, taking their weapons with them. He implied that the blacks would be kept on the plantations, and he expressed his personal preference for a total stranger rather than a Texas Unionist as military governor of Texas. When pressed by Smith and Ballinger for further advice, he suggested they travel on to Washington, D.C.

About the first or second of June, after General Sheridan's arrival in New Orleans, Smith and Ballinger attended a second meeting with Canby, with Sheridan present. They decided that Ballinger should indeed travel on to Washington, and that Smith should return to Texas to influence the army and the people. Smith left soon thereafter while Ballinger remained at New Orleans awaiting accreditation by Canby to the Federal authorities at Washington. After a week of no communications of substance from Canby's headquarters except excuses, Ballinger went to see Canby personally on June 9. The general informed him that further consideration of Federal policy toward the Confederate states and their civil officials had convinced him that a journey by Ballinger to Washington would be futile. Thus ended the hope of separate negotiations for Texas.[71]

While Smith and Ballinger were on their mission to New Orleans, General Kirby Smith arrived at Houston. He had hoped to establish a new headquarters, there but found the District of Texas in the last stages of deterioration. He contented himself by composing three messages on May 30. The first was to Governor Murrah requesting that state troops protect public property since the Confederate troops had disbanded. The second message was to his "Soldiers." "I am left a Commander without an army—a General without troops," explained Smith. "You have made the choice. It was unwise and unpatriotic. But it is final. I pray you may not live to regret it." The third message, couched in much the same self-pitying vein and dispatched to Colonel Sprague, belatedly conceded, "The department is now open to occupation by your Government."[72]

Kirby Smith's last role in the sprawling surrender drama was played off Galveston aboard the Federal vessel *Fort Jackson*. There, on June 2, he endorsed the surrender document signed previously by Buckner and forwarded to him by Canby. In approving it, he

---

71 This account of the Smith-Ballinger mission to New Orleans is based entirely upon Ballinger, Diary, May 17-June 11, 1865. Parks, *Kirby Smith*, 478 n, appears to assume erroneously that Ballinger and Smith did not confer with Canby in New Orleans. Kerby, *Kirby Smith's Confederacy*, 424, seems to make a similar assumption.

72 Smith to Murrah and to Soldiers, both May 30, 1865, both in Kirby Smith Papers; Smith to Sprague, May 30, 1865, *OR* vol. 48, pt. I, 193-194.

added the remark that it was his understanding that paroled officers would be permitted to reside in or out of the United States. Canby endorsed this document by writing that he had made no such stipulation and had no authority to do so.[73]

The Trans-Mississippi Department was thus officially dead as of June 2, but a number of last acts still remained to be played out by its survivors. Commissioners had to be appointed to supervise both the paroling of Confederate troops and the turnover of whatever government property had not been stolen by the departed. These were difficult tasks in difficult times. When Senator Williamson Oldham of Texas, on his way home from Richmond, passed through Shreveport on or about June 5, he found hundreds of disbanded soldiers camped around the town awaiting parole.[74] General Boggs, commenting later on those days, remarked that the soldiers around Shreveport behaved surprisingly well under the circumstances, but it was still necessary for the headquarters clerks to sit up each night with loaded weapons to protect against marauders.[75]

Farther west in Texas, General Magruder abandoned his chaotic district on June 9 for voluntary exile in Mexico. On the following day General Smith, to help wind up affairs there, asked General Hebert to assume district command. The wheel had turned full circle for Texas, with its first "district commander" about to become, after three long years, its final "caretaker."[76]

*   *   *

MEANWHILE, A MORE exciting role was being played by those officers and men who preferred a life of exile in Mexico to Yankee domination at home.

The Mexican enterprise, as originally conceived at Marshall with Simon Buckner as its prospective leader, had caused some concern among senior Federal officers, but the rapid collapse of the department had no doubt greatly reduced its scope.[77] In the end, only remnants of Jo Shelby's Missouri cavalry brigade, perhaps no more than 300 men, together with a scattering of soldiers from other units, formed the expedition. Accompanying them were a number of distinguished citizens including Governors Allen, Murrah, Moore, and Reynolds, and Generals Magruder, Price, and Kirby Smith himself, who had decided to head

73 Terms of a military convention with two indorsements, May 26, 1865, ibid., pt. II, 600-601.

74 Oldham, "Memoirs," 331.

75 Boggs, *Reminiscences*, 83.

76 Oldham, "Memoirs," 340; H. T. Douglas to J. B. Harrison and to P. O. Hebert, both June 10, 1865, both in Kirby Smith Papers.

77 Kirby Smith to Robert Rose, May 2, 1865, F. L. Claiborne to H. N. Frisbee, May 22, 1865, with first endorsement, May 26, 1865, and second indorsement, Hay 27, 1865, P. H. Sheridan to U. S. Grant, May 27, 1865, *OR* vol. 48, pt. II, 1292-1293, 538-539, 625-626.

for Mexico on June 14 to avoid possible arrest. Late in the month the forlorn members of this party crossed the Rio Grande at Eagle Pass to begin their self-imposed exile.[78]

Smith would perform his last duty as a Confederate general while in Mexico. At Monterrey on July 4, he directed "Major Ducayet, Qr. Mr. C.S. Army," to distribute some $100,000 in specie as back pay to Confederate officers west of the Rio Grande "upon proper vouchers." The money was not to be distributed, however, if at the time of surrender it was in the Trans-Mississippi Department and had thus become Federal property. Smith signed himself simply, "Genl."[79]

*   *   *

IN THE FLURRY of surrender negotiations that May, one part of the department had been almost entirely forgotten, namely, the District of Indian Territory.

It was not until June 6 that notice of the convention between Smith and Canby was sent there to General Douglas Cooper, although by that time department headquarters had designated paroling stations for the Territory. Even this message would not be received for weeks. On June 16, Cooper authorized one of his aides to return home saying, "I have recently learned unofficially, through the newspapers, that the C. S. forces in the Trans-Mississippi Department have been surrendered on the same terms as were accepted by Generals Lee, Johnston, and Taylor, east of the Mississippi River"—an astonishing revelation of official ignorance. Cooper sent word to the district adjutant general on June 28 that he had finally read the full terms of the surrender in the *Houston Telegraph*, but "had received no official information or instructions' from Department headquarters." He forwarded the terms, however, so that preparations could be made to comply with them.[80]

Cooper finally received the official notice to surrender on the same day he read the capitulation terms in the *Telegraph*. By then he no longer had a command. As he immediately explained in a letter to Simon Buckner, the only organized military unit remaining in the district as late as June 2 was Brigadier General Stand Watie's Indian division, and this division had been surrendered by its commander on June 23. The Indian leaders, as the representatives of independent nations, had by now begun signing temporary treaties with

---

78 Parks, *Kirby Smith*, 481-482; Kerby, *Kirby Smith's Confederacy*, 428; Castel, *Price*, 273. The idea that General Smith decided to head for Mexico on June 14 is supported by Parks, *Kirby Smith*, 481, and Oldham, "Memoirs," 340, though an alleged eyewitness account of his having met with General Gordon Granger aboard the U.S.S. *San Jacinto* on June 18 off Galveston is contained in "Reminiscences of the Last Vestiges of a Lost Cause, Recollection's, 1865" (typescript), in H. A. Wallace Papers, Archives Collection, University of Texas Library.

79 Smith to F. Ducayet, July 4, 1865, in Kirby Smith Papers.

80 Special Orders No. -, Hdqrs. Trans. Miss. Dept., June 2, 1865, ibid.; Douglas H. Cooper to George Weissinger and to T. M. Scott both June 16, 1865, both in *OR* vol. 48, pt. II, 1323-1324.

Federal commissioners appointed for that purpose, and consequently Cooper's effective authority had already completely disappeared. All he asked was that convenient paroling stations be designated for the scattered white men of his vanished command.[81]

Thus finally came to an end the military district that had been the first one organized on the Confederacy's northwest frontier. And with it went the last vestiges of Confederate military organization west of the Mississippi River.

81 James C. Veatch to J. Schuyler Crosby with Inclosures Nos. 1 through 11 and subinclosure titled "Treaty stipulations made and entered into this 23d day of June, A.D. 1865, near Doaksville, Chocktaw Nation . . ." ibid., 1095-1107.

Postscript

It is perhaps futile either to ask why the comparatively untouched Trans-Mississippi Department did not continue to resist in 1865 or to count its still considerable military potential at that time.

Rapid and total collapse of the department within two months of General Lee's surrender seems ample proof that it was indeed a mere satellite of the Eastern Theater. Despite a very considerable amount of independence after Vicksburg, the department remained both morally and physically part of the Confederacy, and when the main body died, the Western arm quickly atrophied and died as well. Except among a handful of diehards, no real spirit of resistance was left anywhere in the southwest by May 1865. Only those few who feared harsh punishment—generals, governors, judges, and those less distinguished Confederates, principally Missourians who were afraid to go home— accepted Mexican exile rather than a return, however protracted, to full United States citizenship.

It is probably more useful to inquire briefly into the influences which the Trans-Mississippi Department did exert on the course and outcome of the war. As was frequently asserted during the Civil War, and has been reasserted many times since, the Trans Mississippi was a peripheral area. After 1863, Confederate successes or failures there did not have the impact of similar events east of the river. This is not to say that the influence of the department on the war after 1863 was of no effect or insignificant, even though it defies specific proof.

In the sphere of military operations, specific proof is not required to support the idea that the presence of 50,000 or 60,000 reasonably well-armed Confederate troops west of the Mississippi, organized under a single commander-in-chief, constituted a sufficient threat to occupy the full attentions of even more thousands of Federal soldiers who might have been used east of the river to shorten the war. Neither does specific proof seem required that continued occupation by the department's troops of the Texas Gulf Coast, and especially of the busy port of Galveston, as well as access to the Mexican coast through the border towns, kept numerous men and ships of the United States Navy on duty in the western Gulf until the war's end. The consequent prolongation of the war and the enhanced chances for survival of the eastern Confederacy can scarcely be calculated.[1]

In this respect it should also be recalled that during the course of the war, the Trans-Mississippi was never a drain on eastern Confederate military resources. Rather, in almost every way, it bolstered eastern resources. Whenever it was possible for men, lead, grain, cattle, horses, clothing, and imported goods to flow, they almost always flowed east across the Mississippi. Seldom was the direction reversed except in the case of arms or when a comfortable berth was needed for a high-ranking failures from east of the river like Holmes, Huger, or Magruder.

Overall Confederate ability to sustain the burdens of war did not, of course, rest upon military foundations alone. Beyond the military sphere, the Trans-Mississippi also contributed substantially to the Southern war effort. The department provided a viable Confederate presence west of the river around which the individual Trans-Mississippi states could rally in times of crisis. More specifically, in all matters of interstate interest, such as the original creation of the department, the loss of Vicksburg, and the surrender negotiations, the governors and their assistants and representatives assembled both to advise the department commander and to be guided by him. Certain civil duties of the central government were either directly or indirectly controlled by the commanding general over long periods of time, especially treasury and post office functions, the regulation of the cotton trade and of international trade in general. Kirby Smith even attempted some very rudimentary diplomacy, particularly in regard to neighboring Mexico. Furthermore, while the Trans-Mississippi maintained a sturdy Confederate military presence along the Texas-Mexico border, the possibilities of foreign aid and recognition for the entire Confederacy were kept alive and even enhanced. This was particularly true for France, whose puppet government in Mexico was shielded from the hostile Yankees by Kirby Smith's soldiers to the north.

Finally, the Trans-Mississippi Department unquestionably provided the Confederate cement necessary to hold the crumbling blocks of the southwestern states both to each other

---

1   // This assessment squares with the opinions of recent scholarship. See, for example, Prushankin, *Crisis in Command*, 232-233; Joiner, *One Damn Blunder From Beginning to End*, 174-175; Brooksher, *War Along the Bayous*, 226-237; Forsyth, "The Forgotten Trans-Mississippi Theater and Confederate Strategy," in *Southern Strategies*, 250-253; and Sinisi, *The Last Hurrah*, 360-362. Each publication notes that the presence of Confederate forces in the Trans-Mississippi forced the Union to deal with them, which tended to drain resources better utilized east of the river. It was not until General Ulysses S. Grant became the Union General-in-Chief that resources in the West shifted to higher priorities in the Eastern theaters of the war. Nevertheless, as Price's Raid into Missouri demonstrates, even then the Federal high command had to pay attention to events west of the river lest they derail progress toward winning the war in Virginia, Tennessee, and Georgia.

and to the Confederate states as a whole. Without its vital presence after July 1863, it seems likely that the Confederate Trans-Mississippi would have sunk quickly into the anarchy of separate state action and very possibly into the horrors of widespread guerrilla warfare, and that long before May 1865, the fragmented states of that region would have drifted back, one by one, into the orbit of the Federal Union.[2]

2 // See Anne J. Bailey, "The Abandoned Western Theater: Confederate National Policy Toward the Trans-Mississippi Region" *Journal of Confederate History*, V (1990), 35-54, and Michael J. Forsyth, "The Forgotten Trans-Mississippi Theater and Confederate Strategy," in *Southern Strategies*, 217-253. The Trans-Mississippi Department was a region of vast resources and potential as part of the Confederacy. However, lack of strategic vision by the Confederate national authorities condemned the region as a backwater early in the war. Federal leaders, on the other hand, recognized early the criticality of controlling the region and implemented a policy to gain control of the Mississippi Valley quickly, which paid significant dividends to the Union war effort.

Bibliography

Manuscripts

Arkansas, District of, Trans-Mississippi Department, Departmental Records. Record Group 109, National Archives.

Ballinger, William Pitt Papers, 1816-1899. Archives Collection, University of Texas Library. This large and valuable collection contains correspondence to and from a number of figures important to the Trans Mississippi South, among them Jefferson Davis, Guy M. Bryan, John Hancock, P. O. Hebert, Albert Sidney Johnston, John B. Magruder, and Pendleton Murrah. Ballinger's diary is particularly informative on the Texas surrender negotiations.

Barry, James Buckner Papers, 1847-1947. Archives Collection, University of Texas Library. The Civil War materials among these papers relate principally to operations on the northwest Texas Indian frontier.

Baylor, John R. Transcripts. Archives Collection, University of Texas Library. Three volumes of typescripts and photocopies of personal letters comprise this collection. Some information on Baylor's Civil War activities in far west Texas is contained in them.

Bourland, James A. Papers, 1837-1876. Manuscript Division, Library of Congress (microfilm copies in the Archives Collection, University of Texas Library, Ramsdell Microfilms, Roll 192B). The Civil War portion of these papers bear chiefly on the activities of state troops on the Red River frontier of Texas.

Boyd, David F., Civil War Papers. Department of Archives and Manuscripts, Louisiana State University Library. This large and important collection is most useful for military operations in Louisiana and particularly for the information it provides on the breakup and surrender of the Trans-Mississippi Department. Boyd was, for a time, General Brent's adjutant.

Brent, Joseph L. Collection. Adjutant General's Office Library, Louisiana State Military Department, Jackson Barracks. These materials consist of correspondence and military orders throughout the war years as well as records of Brent's Cavalry Brigade from January to May, 1865.

Brent, Joseph L. Papers. Louisiana Historical Association Collection, Tulane University Library. This important collection contains remarkably complete information on the operations of the ordnance department in Louisiana from 1862 through 1864 and information on military operations in Louisiana generally. As Brent was also involved in the surrender of the Trans-Mississippi Department, there is considerable detailed information on these negotiations as well.

Bryan, Guy M. Papers. Archives Collection, University of Texas Library. Because of his position on Kirby Smith's staff and his heavy involvement in Texas public affairs the papers of Bryan are highly useful for a study of the Trans-Mississippi Department. There is some material on the organization of the Texas Cotton Bureau.

Civil War Papers. Louisiana Historical Association Collection, Tulane University Library. This large collection of correspondence, telegrams, diaries, military orders, maps, and other materials contains many items relating to the Trans-Mississippi Department and its districts as well as items relating to other departments and wartime affairs in general.

Coit Family Papers. Dallas Historical Society. A few of these personal letters refer to Civil War events.

Confederate States Army Papers (B), May 30, 1861-July 26, 1867. Department of Archives and Manuscripts, Louisiana State University Library. This collection contains the Civil War papers of Major William H. Thomas, chief commissary of subsistence of the Trans-Mississippi Department and of Major John W. Reid, chief commissary of subsistence of the Army of the West.

Confidential Letters and Telegrams sent, Department of the Trans Mississippi, 1865, Chap, II, Vol. 71 1/2, Military Departments. Record Group 109, National Archives.

Davis, Jefferson Collection. Louisiana Historical Association Collection, Tulane University Library. This important collection contains many official documents issued by Davis as President of the Confederate States.

General Orders, Department of Texas, October, 1861-November, 1862, Chap. II, Vol. 112, Military Departments. Record Group 109, National Archives.

General Orders, Department of the Trans-Mississippi, 1863-1865, Chap. II, Vol. 74, Military Departments. Record Group 109, National Archives.

Hensley-Beaumont Papers, 1846-1948. Dallas Historical Society. These are mostly personal letters, some relating to Civil War events.

Hindman, Major General T. C. Papers of Various Confederate Notables. Record Group 109, National Archives.

Holmes, T. H., Correspondence of, 1861-1864, Chap. II, Vol. 358. Record Group 109, National Archives.

Inspector General's Office, District of Indian Territory, Chap. II, Vol. 260, Record Group 109, National Archives.

Johnston, Albert Sidney and William Preston Papers, 1803-1900, Mrs. Mason Barret Collection of. Tulane University Library. This very large collection of both official and family papers contains many items on Trans-Mississippi affairs including copies of correspondence between Ben McCulloch, Sterling Price, and Claiborne Fox Jackson.

Letters Received from the War Department in Richmond, Virginia, December, 1862-August, 1864, District of Texas, New Mexico, and Arizona, Trans-Mississippi Department, Military Departments, Chap. II, Vol. 252. Record Group 109, National Archives.

Letters and Telegrams Received and Sent (Incomplete), 1861-1865, Trans-Mississippi Department, Departmental Records. Record Group 109, National Archives.

McCulloch, Ben and Henry Eustace Papers, 1813-1920. Archives Collection, University of Texas Library. Of some interest these papers include correspondence, journals, and memoranda of both McCulloch brothers.

Magruder, Major General J. B., Correspondence, 1861-1865, Papers of Various Confederate Notables. Record Group 109, National Archives.

Moore, John Marks Papers, 1838-1925, Dallas Historical Society. Civil War items in this collection pertain to Moore's position as purchasing agent for the Texas State Military Board.

Moore, Thomas O. Papers, 1832-1877. Department of Archives and Manuscripts, Louisiana State University Library. These papers of one of Louisiana's wartime governors contain valuable information on war conditions in Louisiana and on military affairs during Moore's tenure as governor.

Oldham, William S. Collection, 1843-1865. Archives Collection, University of Texas Library. Among items of interest in this group are the "Memoirs" and the "Oldham Journal from Richmond to the Rio Grande, 1865 Chapter 9."

Reynolds, Thomas C. Papers. Manuscript Division. Library of Congress (microfilm copies in Archives Collection, University of Texas Library, Ramsdell Microfilms, Rolls 145C, 146A). These papers, mostly letters both official and private of the extremely active "Confederate" governor of Missouri, are indispensable sources for a study of the Trans-Mississippi Department.

Smith, Ashbel Papers, 1823-1926. Archives Collection, University of Texas Library. The letters and military order books pertaining to the Civil War in this collection refer particularly to events in the Galveston area where Smith commanded the defenses in the last months of the war.

Smith, Edmund Kirby Papers. Southern Historical Collection, University of North Carolina (microfilm copies in the Archives Collection, University of Texas Library, Ramsdell Microfilms, Rolls 209A and B, 210A). A notation with the microfilm at the University of Texas points out that not all of the papers were filmed but that all of those pertinent to the Trans-Mississippi Department presumably were. Needless to say the papers of the commanding general are highly important to a study of the department.

Special Orders, Maj. Gen. Earl Van Darn's Command, January-May, 1862, Chap. II, Vol. 210, Military Departments. Record Group 109, National Archives.

Special Orders, Trans-Mississippi Department, Lt. Gen. E. K. Smith, 1863-1864-1865, Departmental Records, Record Group 109, National Archives.

Thomas, Dewitt Clinton Sr., "Reminiscences." Archives Collection, University of Texas Library. The "Reminiscences" are in the form of a typescript prepared by James B. Thomas, September 18, 1964. They are interesting but of limited value for general study of the Trans-Mississippi.

Thompson, General M. Jeff Collection. Tulane University Library. An interesting collection of some use in this study regarding the surrender in northern Arkansas.

Wallace, H. A. Papers. Archives Collection, University of Texas Library. Wallace's "Reminiscences of the Last Vestiges of a Lost Cause, Recollections, 1865," a typescript, purports to be a first person account of a meeting between Kirby Smith and General Gordon Granger aboard the USS *San Jacinto*, on June 18, 1865, off Galveston.

Wigfall, Louis T. Family Papers. Archives Collection, University of Texas Library. Of particular interest in this collection is the bound volume of typescripts titled, "Wigfall, Louis T., Letters of Joseph Eggleston Johnston to, 1862-1868."

Newspapers

Daily State Journal. Little Rock. November 2, 22, 1861; January. 25, 31, February 2, 1862.

South-Western. Shreveport. April 1, 1863; June 7, 1865,

State Gazette. Austin. January 12, May 11, 27, June 8, 15, 1861.

Texas State Gazette. Austin. July 27, 29, 1861; April 12, 1862.

Times. New York. March 8, February 27, 1861.

Times and Herald. Fort Smith. June 27, August 30, 1861.

Weekly Telegraph. Houston. November 10, 1863.

Printed Sources

Amann, William Frayne, ed. *Personnel of the Civil War.* 1961; 2 vols. in 1, New York: Thomas Yoseloff, 1968. reprint,

Anderson, Ephraim McD. *Memoirs: Historical and Personal, Including the Campaigns of the First Missouri Confederate Brigade.* St. Louis: Times Printing Co, 1868.

Barr, Alwyn, ed. "Records of the Confederate Military Commission in San Antonio, July 2-October 10, 1862." *Southwestern Historical Quarterly,* LXX (July, 1966), 289-313 (April, 1967), 623-644; LXXI (October, 1967), 247-277, and LXIII (July, 1J69), 83-104.

Barron, S. B. *The Lone Star Defenders: A Chronicle of the Third Texas Cavalry, Ross' Brigade.* New York: Neale Publishing Co., 1908.

[Blessington, J. P.] *The Campaigns of Walker's Texas Division by a Private Soldiers.* New York: Lange, Little & Co., 1875.

Boggs, Gen. William R. *Military Reminiscences of Gen. Wm. R. Boggs, C.S.A.* Edited by William K. Boyd, Durham, N.C.: Seeman Printery, 1913.

Committee of the Regiment. *Military History and Reminiscences of the Thirteenth Regiment of Illinois Volunteer Infantry in the Civil War in the United States, 1861-1865.* Chicago: Woman's Temperance Publishing Association, 1892.

Confederate States Army. *General Orders Head Quarters Trans-Miss, Department from March 6, 1863, to January 1, 1865, in Two Series.* Houston: R. H. Cushing & Co., 1865.

Dorsey, Sarah A. *Recollections of Henry Watkins Allen, Brigadier General Confederate States Army Ex Governor of Louisiana.* New York: M. Doolady, 1866. New Orleans: James A. Gresham, 1666.

Edwards, John N. *Shelby and His Men: or, The War in the West.* Cincinnati: Miami Printing and Publishing Co., 1867.

Ford, John Salmon. *Rip Ford's Texas.* Edited by Stephen B. Oates. Austin: University of Texas Press, 1963.

Freeman, Douglas Southall, ed. *Lee's Dispatches, Unpublished Letters of General Robert E. Lee, C.S.A. to Jefferson Davis and the War Department of the Confederate States of America, 1862-1865: From the Private Collection of Wymberley Jones de Renne of Wormsloe, Georgia*, 1915; reprint with additional dispatches and Foreword by Grady McWhiney, New York: G. P. Putnam's Sons, 1957.

Fremantle, Arthur J. L. *Three Months in the Southern States.* April June, 1963. New York: John Bradburn, 1864.

Gammage, Washington Lafayette. *The Camp, The Bivouac and The Battle Field: Being a History of the Fourth Arkansas Regiment from its First Organization Down to the Present Date.* Selma: Cooper and Kimball, Mississippian Book and Job Office, 1864. Reprint, Little Rock: Arkansas Southern Press, 1958.

Gorgas, Josiah. *The Civil War Diary of General Josiah Gorgas.* Edited by Frank E. Vandiver. University, Ala.: University of Alabama Press, 1947.

Heartsill, William W. *Fourteen Hundred and 91. Days in the Confederate Army: A Journal Kept by W. W. Heartsill for Four Years, One Month and One Day or Camp Life Day by Day of the W. P. Lone Rangers from April 19, 1861 to May 20, 1865.* 1876; reprint edited by Bell Irvin Wiley, Jackson, Tenn.: McCowat-Mercer Press, 1954.

Hindman, Thomas C. *Report of Maior General Hindman of his Operations in the Trans-Mississippi District.* Richmond: R. M. Smith, Public Printer, 1864.

Johnston, Joseph E. *Narrative of Military Operations Directed During the Late War Between the States.* New York: D. Appleton and Company, 1874.

Kean, Robert Garlick Hill. *Inside the Confederate Government: The Diary of Robert Garlick Hill Kean, Head of the Bureau of War.* Edited by Edward Younger. New York: Oxford University Press, 1957.

Knox, Thomas W. *Camp-Fire and Cotton-Field: Southern Adventures in Time of War. Life with the Union Armies and Residence on a Louisiana Plantation.* New York: Blelock and Co., 1865.

Lathrop, David. *The History of the Fifty Ninth Regiment. Illinois Volunteers.* Indianapolis: Hall and Hutchinson, 1865.

Lubbock, Francis Richard. *Six Decades in Texas or Memoirs of Francis Richard Lubbock, Governor of Texas in War-Time, 1861-1863: A Personal Experience in Business, War and Politics.* Edited by C. W. Raines. Austin: Ben C. Jones & Co., 1900.

Official Records of the Union and Confederate Navies in the War of the Rebellion. 30 vols. Washington, D.C.: Government Printing Office, 1894-1927.

Poche, Felix Pierre. *A Louisiana Confederate. Diary of Felix Pierre Poche.* Edited by Edwin c, Bearss. Translated by Eugenie Watson Somdal. Natchitoches: Louisiana Studies Institute, Northwestern State University of Louisiana, 1972,

Ramsdell, Charles W. "The Last Hope of The Confederacy – John Tyler to the Governor and Authorities of Texas," *Quarterly of the Texas State Historical Association,* XIV (July, 1910), 129-145,

Richardson, James D., ed. *A Compilation of the Messages and Papers of the Confederacy; Including the Diplomatic Correspondence, 1861-1865.* 2 vols. Nashville: United States Publishing Co.

———, ed. *The Messages and Papers of Jefferson Davis and the Confederacy Including Diplomatic Correspondence, 1861-1865.* 1905; 2 vols. Reprint with an Introduction by Allan Nevins, n.p.: Chelsea House, 1966.

Taylor, Richard. *Destruction and Reconstruction, Personal Experiences of the Late War.* 1879; edited by Richard B. Harwell. New York: Longmans, Green, and Co., 1955.

Watson, William. *Life in the Confederate Army. Being the Observations and Experiences of an Alien in the South during the American Civil War.* New York: Scribner & Welford, 1888.

War of the Rebellion: A Compilation of the Official Records of the Union and Confederate Armies. 70 vols. in 128. Washington, D.C. Government Printing Office, 1880-1901.

Wilkie, Francis B. *Pen and Powder.* Boston: Ticknor & Co., 1888.

Woodruff, William Edward. *With the Light Guns in '61-'65: Reminiscences of Eleven Arkansas, Missouri, and Texas Light Batteries in the Civil War.* Little Rock: Central Printing Co., 1903.

Secondary Books

Bragg, Jefferson Davis. *Louisiana in the Confederacy.* Baton Rouge: Louisiana State University Press, 1941.

Britton, Wiley. *The Civil War on the Border.* 2 vols. New York: G. P. Putnam's Sons, 1890-1899.

Castel, Albert. A Frontier State at War: Kansas, 1861-1865. Ithaca: Cornell University Press for the American Historical Association, 1958.

————. *General Sterling Price and the Civil War in the West.* Baton Rouge: Louisiana State University Press, 1968.

Cravens, John Nathan. *James Harper Starr, Financier of the Republic of Texas.* Austin: Daughters of the Republic of Texas, 1950.

Dufour, Charles L. *Nine Men in Gray.* Garden City, N.Y.: Doubleday & Co., 1963.

Freeman, Douglas Southall. *Lee's Lieutenants: A Study in Command.* 3 vols. New York: Charles Scribner's Sons, 1942-1945.

Goff, Richard D. *Confederate Supply.* Durham: Duke University Press, 1969.

Hall, Martin Hardwick. *Sibley's New Mexico Campaign.* Austin: University of Texas Press, 1960.

Harrell, John M. "Arkansas." Vol. X of *Confederate Military History.* Edited by Clement A. Evans. 12 vols. Atlanta: Confederate Publishing Company, 1899.

Hartje, Robert G. *Van Dorn: The Life and Times of a Confederate General.* Nashville: Vanderbilt University Press, 1967.

Hughes, Nathaniel Cheairs, Jr. *General William J. Hardee, Old Reliable.* Baton Rouge: Louisiana State University Press, 1965.

Johnson, Allen, Dumas Malone, Harris E. Starr, Robert Livington Schuyler, and Edward Topping Jones. *Dictionary of American Biography.* 22 vols. in 11. New York: Charles Scribner's Sons, 1957-1958.

Johnson, Ludwell H. *Red River Campaign: Politics and Cotton in the Civil War.* Baltimore: Johns Hopkins Press, 1958.

Jones, Archer. *Confederate Strategy from Shiloh to Vicksburg.* Baton Rouge: Louisiana State University Press, 1961.

Kerby, Robert L. *Kirby Smith's Confederacy: The Trans-Mississippi South. 1863-1865.* New York: Columbia University Press, 1972.

McKim, Randolph H. *The Numerical Strength of the Confederate Army: An Examination of the Argument of the Hon. Charles Francis Adams and Others.* New York: Neale Publishing Company, 1912.

Nichols, James L. *The Confederate Quartermaster in the Trans Mississippi.* Austin: University of Texas Press, 1964,

Oates, Stephen B. *Confederate Cavalry West of the River.* Austin: University of Texas Press, 1961.

O'Flaherty, Daniel. *General Jo Shelby, Undefeated Rebel.* Chapel Hill: University of North Carolina Press, 1954.

Owsley, Frank Lawrence. *King Cotton Diplomacy: Foreign Relations of the Confederate States of America.* Chicago: University of Chicago Press, 1931.

Parks, Joseph Howard. *General Edmund Kirby Smith, C.S.A.* Baton Rouge: Louisiana State University Press, 1954.

Parrish, William E. *Turbulent Partnership: Missouri and the Union, 1861-1865.* Columbia: University of Missouri Press, 1963,

Robinson, William M., Jr. *Justice in Grey: A History of the Judicial System of the Confederate States of America.* Cambridge, Mass. Harvard University Press, 1941.

Rose, Victor M. *The Life and Services of Gen. Ben McCulloch.* Philadelphia: Pictorial Bureau of the Press, 1888.

Shalhope, Robert E. *Sterling Price, Portrait of a Southerner.* Columbia: University of Missouri Press, 1971.

Speer, Williams., ed. *The Encyclopedia of the New West.* 2 vols. Marshall, Tex.: United States Biographical Publishing Company, 1881.

Thomas, David Y. *Arkansas in War and Reconstruction, 1861-1874.* Little Rock: Arkansas Division, United Daughters of the Confederacy, 1926.

Williams, Kenneth P. *Lincoln Finds a General: A Military Study of the Civil War.* 5 vols. New York: Macmillan Co., 1949-1959.

Hinters, John D. *The Civil War in Louisiana.* Baton Rouge: Louisiana State University Press, 1963.

Unpublished Studies

Brown, Walter Lee. "Albert Pike, 1809-1891." Unpublished Ph.D. dissertation, University of Texas, 1955. // Published as *A Life of Albert Pike.* University of Arkansas Press, 1997.

Lambie, Agnes Louise. "Confederate Control of Cotton in the Trans Mississippi Department." Unpublished M.A. thesis, University of Texas, 1915.

Mitchell, Leon, Jr. "Prisoners of War in the Confederate Trans Mississippi." Unpublished Ph.D. dissertation, University of Texas, 1961.

Morrow, Norman Potter. "Price' s Missouri Expedition, 1864." Unpublished M.A. thesis, University of Texas, 1949.

Muir, Andrew Forest. "The Thirty-Second Parallel Railroad in Texas to 1872." Unpublished Ph.D. dissertation, University of Texas, 1949.

Sholars, Fannie Baker. "Life and Services of Guy M. Bryan." Unpublished M.A. thesis, University of Texas, 1930.

Articles

Barr, Alwyn. "Texas Coastal Defense, 1861-1865." *Southwestern Historical Quarterly*, XLV (July, 1961), 1-31.

Dale, Edward Everett. "The Cherokees in the Confederacy." *Journal of Southern History*, XIII (May, 1947), 159-185.

Day, James M. "Leon Smith: Confederate Mariner." *East Texas Historical Journal*, III (March, 1965), 34 39.

Ellis, L. Tuffly. "Maritime Commerce on the Far Western Gulf, 1861-1865." *Southwestern Historical Quarterly*, LXXVII (October, 1973), 167-226.

Fitzhugh, Lester N. "Saluria, Fort Esperanza and Military Operations on the Texas Coast, 1861-1864." *Southwestern Historical Quarterly*, LXI (July, 1957), 66-100.

Geise, William R. "Missouri's Confederate Capital in Marshall, Texas." *Southwestern Historical Quarterly*, LXVI (October, 1962), 193-207.

Holladay, Florence Elizabeth. "The Powers of the Commander of the Confederate Trans-Mississippi Department, 1863-1865." *Southwestern Historical Quarterly*, XXI (January, 1918), 279-298 (April, 1918), 333-359.

Huff, Leo E. "The Last Duel in Arkansas: The Marmaduke-Walker Duel." *Arkansas Historical Quarterly*, XXII (Spring, 1964), 36-49.

————. "The Military Board in Confederate Arkansas." *Arkansas Historical Quarterly*, XXVI (Spring, 1967), 75-95.

Keith, K. D. "Military Operations, Sabine Pass, 1861-63." *Burke's Texas Almanac and Immigrant's Handbook for 1883, with Which Is Incorporated Hanford's Texas State Register*. Houston: J. Burke, 1883. Reprinted in "Program of the Texas State Historical Assn., Sixty-Seventh Annual Meeting." Austin, Tex., Apr. 26-27, 1963.

Lathrop, Barnes F. "The Lafourche District in 1862: Invasion." *Louisiana History*, II (Spring, 1961), 175-201.

Scheiber, Harry N. "The Pay of Troops and Confederate Morale in the Trans-Mississippi West." *Arkansas Historical Quarterly*, XVIII (Winter, 1959), 350-365.

Shirk, George H. "Indian Territory Command in the Civil War." *Chronicles of Oklahoma*, XLV (Winter, 1967-1968), 464-471.

Tyler, Ronnie C. "Cotton on the Border, 1861-1865." *Southwestern Historical Quarterly*, LXXII (April, 1970), 456-477.

Editor's Supplemental Bibliography

Primary Sources

Peterson, Cyrus A. *Pilot Knob: Thermopylae of the West.* Reprint of 1914 Edition. Lexington, entucky: Forgotten Books, 2012.

Pitcock, Cynthia D. and Bill J. Gurley, eds. *I Acted From Principle: The Civil War Diary of Dr. William M. McPheeters, Confederate Surgeon in the Trans-Mississippi.* Fayetteville: University of North Carolina Press, 2002.

Reynolds, Thomas C. *General Sterling Price and the Confederacy.* Columbia: Missouri State Historical Society, 2009.

Sibley, Henry Hopkins. *The Civil War in Texas and New Mexico: The Lost Letterbook of Brigadier General Henry Hopkins Sibley.* Jerry Thompson and John P. Wilson, eds. El Paso: Texas Western Press, 2001.

Walker, John G. "The War of Secession West of the Mississippi River During the Years 1863-4 & 5." Mss. Myron Gwinner Collection, United States Army History Institute, Carlisle Barracks, Pennsylvania.

Wright, John C. *Memoirs of Colonel John C. Wright.* Pine Bluff, Arkansas: Rare Book Publishers, 1982.

Secondary Sources

Arceneaux, William. *Acadian General Alfred Mouton and the Civil War.* Lafayette: University of Louisiana Lafayette Press, 1981.

Bailey, Anne J. "The Abandoned Western Theater: Confederate National Policy Toward the Trans-Mississippi Region." *Journal of Confederate History,* V (1990), 35-54.

Bailey, Anne J. and Daniel E. Southerland, eds. *Civil War Arkansas: Beyond Battles and Leaders.* Fayetteville: University of Arkansas Press, 2000.

Bearss, Edwin C. *Steele's Retreat from Camden and the Battle of Jenkin's Ferry.* Little Rock: Pioneer Press, 1961.

———. *The Battle of Wilson's Creek.* Springfield: Wilson's Creek National Battlefield Foundation, 1992.

Brooksher, William Riley. *Bloody Hill: The Civil War Battle of Wilson's Creek.* Gaithersburg, Maryland: Potomac Books, 1999.

———. *War Along the Bayous: The Red River Campaign in Louisiana.* Washington, DC: Brassey's, 1998.

Brown, Walter L. *A Life of Albert Pike.* Fayetteville: University of Arkansas Press, 1997.

Carter, Arthur B. *The Tarnished Cavalier: Major General Earl Van Dorn, CSA.* Knoxville: University of Tennessee Press, 1999.

Chatelain, Neil P. *Defending the Arteries of Rebellion: Confederate Naval Operations in the Mississippi River Valley, 1861–1865.* El Dorado Hills, California: Savas-Beatie Publishing Co., 2020.

Casdorph, Paul D. *Prince John Magruder: His Life and Campaigns.* Hoboken, New Jersey: Wiley & Sons Publishing, 1996.

Christ, Mark K. *Civil War Arkansas, 1863: The Battle for a State.* Norman: University of Oklahoma Press, 2010.

———. *Rugged and Sublime: The Civil War in Arkansas.* Fayetteville: University of Arkansas Press, 1994.

Crowe, Clint. *Caught in the Maelstrom: The Indian Nations in the Civil War, 1861-1865.* El Dorado Hills, California: Savas-Beatie Publishing Co., 2019.

Cutrer, Thomas W. *Ben McCulloch and the Frontier Military Tradition.* Chapel Hill: University of North Carolina Press, 1993.

———. *Theater of a Separate War: The Civil War West of the Mississippi River, 1861-1865.* Chapel Hill: University of North Carolina Press, 2017.

Eicher, John H. and David J. Eicher. *Civil War High Commands.* Redwood City, California: Stanford University Press, 2001.

Flaherty, Daniel O. *General Jo Shelby: Undefeated Rebel.* Chapel Hill: University of North Carolina Press, 1954.

Forsyth, Michael J. *The Camden Expedition of 1864 and the Opportunity Lost by the Confederacy to Change the Civil War.* Jefferson, North Carolina: McFarland & Co., Publishers, 2003.

———. *The Great Missouri Raid: The Last Confederate Invasion of the North.* Jefferson, North Carolina: McFarland & Co., Publishers, 2015.

———. *The Red River Campaign of 1864 and the Loss of the Civil War by the Confederacy.* Jefferson, North Carolina: McFarland & Co., Publishers, 2002.

———. "The Forgotten Trans-Mississippi Theater and Confederate Strategy," in *Southern Strategies: Why the Confederacy Failed.* Christian B. Keller, ed. Lawrence: University of Kansas Press, 2021.

Gerteis, Louis S. *The Civil War in Missouri: A Military History.* Columbia: University of Missouri Press, 2016.

Grear, Charles D. ed. *The Fate of Texas: The Civil War and the Lone Star State.* Fayetteville: University of Arkansas Press, 2008.

Hewitt, Lawrence Lee and Thomas E. Schott, eds. *Confederate Generals in the Trans-Mississippi.* Knoxville: University of Tennessee Press, 2019.

Hildermann, Walter C. *Theophilus Hunter Holmes: A North Carolina General in the Civil War.* Jefferson, North Carolina: McFarland & Co., Publishers, 2013.

Horn, Huston. *Leonidas Polk: Warrior Bishop of the Confederacy.* Lawrence: University Press of Kansas, 2019.

Hughes, Jr. *Nathaniel C. The Life and Wars of Gideon J. Pillow.* Knoxville: University of Tennessee Press, 2011.

———. *General William J. Hardee: Old Reliable.* Baton Rouge: Louisiana State University Press, 1992.

Joiner, Gary Dillard. *One Damn Blunder from Beginning to End: The Red River Campaign of 1864.* Wilmington, Delaware: Scholarly Resources, 2003.

Lause, Mark A. *Price's Lost Campaign: The 1864 Invasion of Missouri.* Columbia: University of Missouri Press, 2011.

Mackey, Robert R. *The Uncivil War: Irregular Warfare in the Upper South, 1861-1865.* Norman: University of Oklahoma Press, 2004.

Monaghan, Jay. *Civil War on the Western Border, 1854-1865.* Lincoln: University of Nebraska Press, 1955.

Monnett, Howard N. *Action Before Westport, 1864.* Boulder: University of Colorado Press, 1964.

Mueller, Doris Land. *M. Jeff Thompson: Missouri's Swamp Fox of the Confederacy.* Columbia: University of Missouri Press, 2007.

Oates, Stephen B. *Confederate Cavalry West of the River.* Austin: University of Texas Press, 1961.

Neal, Dianne and Thomas W. Kremm. *The Lion of the South: General Thomas C. Hindman.* Macon, Georgia: Mercer University Press, 1997.

Parrish, T. Michael. *Richard Taylor: Soldier Prince of Dixie.* Chapel Hill: University of North Carolina Press, 1992.

Phillips, Christopher. *Missouri's Confederate: Claiborne Fox Jackson and the Creation of Southern Identity in the Border West.* Columbia: University of Missouri Press, 2000.

Prushankin, Jeffery S. *A Crisis in Confederate Command: Edmund Kirby Smith, Richard Taylor, and the Army of the Trans-Mississippi.* Baton Rouge: Louisiana State University Press, 2005.

Savas, Theodore P., David A. Woodbury, and Gary D. Joiner, eds. *The Red River Campaign: Union and Confederate Leadership in the War in Louisiana.* Shreveport: Parabellum Press, 2003.

Settles, Thomas. *John Bankhead Magruder: A Military Reappraisal.* Baton Rouge: Louisiana State University Press, 2009.

Shea, William L. *Fields of Blood: The Prairie Grove Campaign.* Chapel Hill: University of North Carolina Press, 2013.

——— and Earl J. Hess. *Pea Ridge: Civil War Campaign in the West.* Chapel Hill: University of North Carolina Press, 1992.

Sinisi, Kyle S. *The Last Hurrah: Sterling Price's Missouri Expedition of 1864.* Lanham, Maryland: Rowman & Littlefield, 2015.

Thompson, Jerry. *Confederate General of the West: Henry Hopkins Sibley.* College Station: Texas A&M Press, 1996.

Westport Historical Society, ed. *The Battle of Westport, October 21-23, 1864.* Kansas City: Westport Historical Society, 1996.

Woodworth, Steven E. *Jefferson Davis and His Generals: The Failure of Confederate Command in the West.* Lawrence: University Press of Kansas, 1990.

Wooster, Ralph A. *Civil War Texas.* College Station: Texas A&M University Press, 1999.

———, and Robert Wooster, eds. *Lone Start Blue and Gray: Essays on Texas in the Civil War.* Austin: Texas State Historical Association, 2015.

Index

Savas Beatie is pleased to include this brief excerpt from our recent title *Thirteen Months in Dixie,* one of the most remarkable memoirs to come out of the Trans-Mississippi Theater.

We hope you enjoy it.

THIRTEEN MONTHS
IN
DIXIE,
OR, THE
ADVENTURES OF
A FEDERAL PRISONER
IN
TEXAS

William Francis Oscar Federhen

Jeaninne Surette Honstein and
Steven A. Knowlton, editors

Savas Beatie
California

W. F. OSCAR FEDERHEN

Postwar portrait from a composite photograph with portraits of 116
members of the John A. Logan Post No. 127 of the Grand Army of the
Republic in Salina, Kansas, c. 1911.

*Smoky Hill Museum Object Identification Number 1946.12.1. Donated by
Cora Walker Shelton to the Smoky Hill Museum, Salina, Kansas.*

INTRODUCTION

IT WAS in 2015 when my father told me he had a Civil War manuscript. This memoir was passed to him through his adoptive parent he affectionately called "Aunty." The manuscript belonged to Aunty's father, William Francis Oscar Federhen, a Civil War prisoner who wrote about his remarkable experiences during the conflict.

When Aunty passed in 1951, my father found a tin box with two manuscripts inside. They were a common type of journal that people used in the 1800s. My father took the box home and forgot about it until 2015 when he passed the books to me.

I found the story almost fantastical, and it certainly grabbed my full attention. I dove deep into the pages trying to validate as much as I could. I tried to map his escape routes and follow his descriptions. I often found his story making historical sense as he

Binding of Federhen's
revised manuscript.

Jeaninne Surette Honstein

described his capture from along the Red River, his life as a prisoner, and his escapes from his captors. The research led me down many new paths and opened my eyes to a part of the Civil War completely new to me.

At one point I asked my father if he remembered Oscar. His only memory—a very distant one—is of an old man in the side room of their apartment. He remembers seeing medicine bottles and something about his feet being of certain concern; the aging veteran lay in a bed with a sheet tented over his feet. My father turned five in January of 1933, the same year Oscar passed away.

With the manuscripts in my possession, I did as much research as I could. I am not a seasoned Civil War researcher and knew I needed help validating much of what Oscar had written. I reached out to Anne Jarvis, Princeton University Librarian, who connected me with Steven A. Knowlton, Librarian for History and African American Studies at the same institution. Steve proved an excellent partner on this project. Once he had the manuscript in hand, he jumped right in and validated more details than I believed possible.

Throughout this project I kept thinking about how connected we are to the past. I find it particularly amazing that, here I am, sitting with my father who personally knew someone who fought in the Civil War. His recollection as a young child of having to be quiet when the old man was sleeping gives me chills, yet at the same time enlightens me to realize the war was really not that long ago, and how necessary it is to remember this.

Jeaninne Surette Honstein

EDITORS' PREFACE

THE TEXT that follows was transcribed from a manuscript prepared by W. F. Oscar Federhen, a Union soldier in the Civil War who served in 1864 and 1865.

Federhen probably wrote his first draft after 1869 because the notebook in which he wrote his recollections was purchased from George B. Brown and Co., Stationers, of 94 State Street in Boston. According to existing city directories,

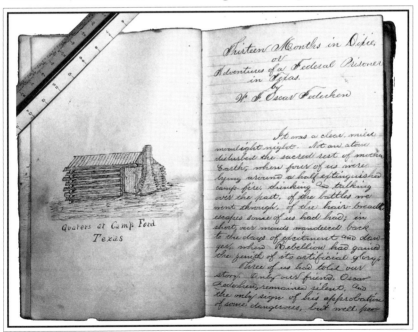

A spread from Federhen's first draft depicting one of his original drawings.

Jeaninne Surette Honstein

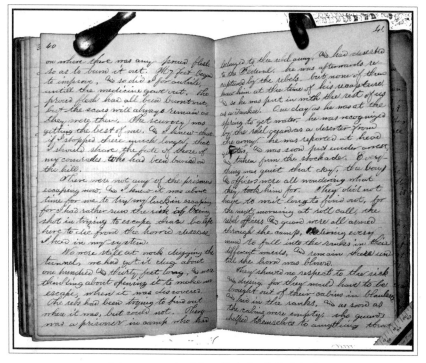

A two-page spread from Federhen's first draft.

Jeaninne Surette Honstein

that business was located at that address between 1869 and 1872.

There is some evidence that the primary composition of the manuscript probably occurred around 1877. In his initial first-draft version of the manuscript, Federhen ends his narrative during his second imprisonment in Bonham, Texas, and then proceeds, as he puts it, to "coppy from a Kansas newspaper the Sack of Lawrence, by the noted Guerilla Quantral, written by Maj. John Edwards of Missouri, an Ex Confederate." As it turns out, an article on that very

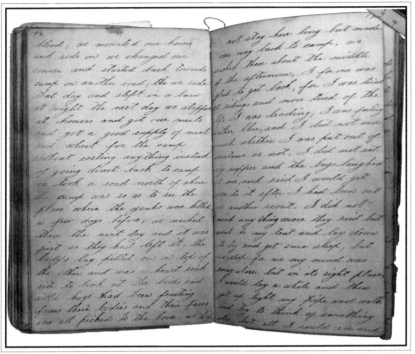

A two-page spread from Federhen's revised manuscript.

Jeaninne Surette Honstein

topic was published in the *Saline County Journal* of Salina, Kansas, on March 8, 1877.[1]

At a later unknown date Federhen made a fair copy that also revised his earlier draft. The transcription you are about to read was made from the second version of his text. The revisions consist of rephrasing sentences and paragraphs. There were no important stories added or removed up

---

1 Federhen may have seen the article "The Sack of Lawrence from Its Inception to Its Ghastly Culmination," published in the *Saline County Journal* (Salina, Kansas) on March 8, 1877. According to the paper, the story was originally filed by the *Chicago Times*' St. Louis correspondent.

through the point at which the first draft terminated. The conclusion of the narrative appears only in the second draft.

Both manuscripts were passed down through Federhan's dependents until they were held by Oscar's adopted grandson, William Federhen Surette. William passed them to his daughter, Jeaninne Surette Honstein of Princeton, New Jersey. Jeaninne transcribed the revised manuscript, and Steven A. Knowlton annotated the document in 2017 and 2018. The spelling, punctuation, and grammar of the manuscript have been preserved. Chapter titles were added by the editors.

Convoluted punctuation and grammar notwithstanding, Federhen's narrative is a compelling tale. His keen eye for detail is novelistic in its flair, and his ability to convey desperation and danger in just a few words would have made him a successful writer of dime novels. There is a powerful flow to the story such that a reader cannot help but worry about and cheer for Federhen during his many escapades. His account of the last months of the Civil War carry with it a vividness that most non-fiction accounts rarely aspire to achieve.

While many key elements and observations Federhen recorded can be confirmed by the historical record, others are more suspect. In at least one instance, Federhen claims to have encountered historical figures who could not have been in the place he described at the time he claims to have been there. Notorious Confederate guerrilla leader William T. "Bloody Bill" Anderson, for example, was dead by the time Federhen claims he made his way into Indian Territory, and William Quantrill's Raiders had dispersed into Missouri, Kentucky, and Tennessee by the time Federhen writes about riding with them.

Similar problems arise trying to corroborate Federhen's stories of escape from various Confederate installations, but that is unsurprising given the sparse nature of Southern record keeping during the last year of the war, and especially in that part of the Trans-Mississippi Theater. Some of Federhen's escapes seem fanciful, but they correspond with the accounts of other escapees such Aaron Sutton and S. A. Swiggett.[2]

His stories of robbery, murder, and mayhem were not uncommon in that region, especially during the ending months of the Civil War when irregulars, guerillas, and outright criminals roamed the prairies from Missouri all the way south to the Rio Grande. We know with certainty that he was captured in May of 1864 and returned as a prisoner of war about a year later. He spent those eventful months doing *something, somewhere,* and his version of what he did and where is inside these pages.

Readers will have to judge for themselves the reliability of Federhen's account; we have faith few will deny that it is a gripping tale and one you won't soon forget.

---

2 See, for example, David G. MacLean, ed., *Prisoner of the Rebels in Texas: The Civil War Narrative of Aaron T. Sutton* (Decatur, IN: Americana Books, 1978), and S. A. Swiggett, *The Bright Side of Prison Life* (Baltimore: Fleet, McGinley, & Co., 1897).

About the Author

WILLIAM ROYSTON GEISE'S journey to becoming the author of a published book was as fitful as it is interesting. The St. Louis native graduated from the Missouri Military Academy in 1936 and was in his second year at the University of Texas at Austin when the Japanese bombed Pearl Harbor. Geise joined what would become the Air Force and served during World War II little realizing it would be his career for 22 years before his retirement as a lieutenant colonel in 1961. He returned to school and earned a bachelor's degree in English from the University of Arizona, then circled back to Austin to earn his master's in English and his Ph.D. in American History in 1974. Undergraduates received the benefit of his experiences when he taught history courses at San Antonio College for 15 years.

Geise, an ardent sailor and chess player, published a number of articles in a variety of periodicals, including the *Military History of Texas and the Southwest* and *The Southwestern Historical Quarterly* before passing away in 1993. *The Confederate Military Forces in the Trans-Mississippi West, 1861-1865: A Study in Command* was originally written and presented as his dissertation.

About the Editor

MICHAEL J. FORSYTH is a retired U.S. Army field artillery colonel and currently an assistant professor in the Department of Joint, Interagency, and Multinational Operations at the U.S. Army Command and General Staff College. He commanded at every level through brigade and served as chief of staff of Alaskan Command and Alaska NORAD Region. He is a veteran of Operation DESERT STORM, served three tours in Afghanistan, and is a Ph.D. candidate at the Royal Military College of Canada completing his doctoral dissertation.

He is the author of *The Camden Expedition of 1864 and the Opportunity Lost by the Confederacy to Change the Civil War* (2007), *The Great Missouri Raid: Sterling Price and the Last Major Confederate Campaign in Northern Territory* (2015), and *A Year in Command in Afghanistan: Journal of a United States Army Battalion Commander, 2009-2010* (2016). He has also written for a wide variety of scholarly publications.